Embracing Life

Toward a Psychology of Interdependence

David "Lucky" Goff, PhD

ICRL Press

Princeton, New Jersey

Embracing Life: Toward a Psychology of Interdependence
Copyright © 2018 by David Goff, Ph.D.
ISBN: 978-1-936033-31-7

This is a revised edition of a book originally published by Mill City Press, Inc, in 2013.

Cover Design by Mary Ross
Book Design: Smythtype Design

TABLE OF CONTENTS

Interdependence is, and ought to be,
as much the ideal of man as self-sufficiency.
Man is a social being.

—GANDHI

INTRODUCTION

At the heart of existence there is Mystery, compelling and deeply mystifying. It is the mystery of Life. It informs our lives, constantly surging through each of us, through our lived experiences, through much of the hardship we experience, and through opportunities we barely recognize. This book is intended to offer a look at Mystery, a look that does not try to solve its perplexing qualities, but instead offers a way to relate to it that informs our lives.

In essence, this is a book about relationship, about how Mystery has employed relationship from the beginning of time to give us life, to provoke our growth, and to ultimately awaken us. We are a product of Mystery. Our lives are played out according to it, and we find ourselves involved in a dance, a love-making, an eternal embrace. We, the human species with our complex consciousness, have co-arisen, we have been roused into existence by Mystery, for Mystery's purposes.

This story starts a long time ago, well before I was tripped up and stumbled toward seeing a new way of making sense of my personal confusion and heartache. I was moved by my own condition. Being an idealist and environmentalist, I was also moved by a desire for change on a larger scale. So, inadvertently at first, and consciously later on, I looked for a connection between my personal feelings of hope, anxiety, and fear, with what is going on in the world, and even more importantly, to the evolutionary process itself.

Little did I know that I was looking at the between, the place where things connect. Here, in the space between, I would begin to see patterns, patterns that prevailed at multiple levels, patterns that wove me into the fabric of the world and thereby altered my perception of what it means to be human. The between endowed me with new awareness, awareness I hope to convey in the following pages, awareness that I hope will alter our psychological story forever.

This is then a story about the between, about how things connect. A story about how the things that go on within me, like my anxieties, dreams and desires, connect me with not only what is going on in my relationships and family, the primary focus of much of today's psychology, but also with my community, and with the more-than-human community (which includes the Cosmos) of which I am part. But I get ahead of myself—I want to tell the story of how the between discloses itself, first in nature, then later in human social systems and development.

This way, the way of the between, it seems to me, offers human-kind a key, a more hopeful, connected, and ennobling way of perceiving the human dilemma. It suggests not only a different way of making sense of what all of us are confronted by, but offers a set of maps, which we as a species and as individuals seeking to be as healthy-minded as possible, could employ to better align our lives with the Cosmos.

How can anything new emerge after all this time? The truth is that this orientation isn't truly new. The notion that our fates are inextricably interwoven with that of the Universe, that what happens between us, between our kind and nature, affects everything, has been posited by various spiritual and indigenous traditions for millennia. What is new, is that we now have access to scientific evidence that transforms this notion from being an intuitive spiritual belief, to a palpable perception, to a very real, very meaningful possibility.

So, a portion of this story addresses some of the light that has been shown upon the human dilemma by different scientific perspectives. (Chapters 1 thru 3). I am a psychologist, not a scientist, so perhaps the meaning I extract from these scientific inquiries is incomplete or naïve. I leave it up to those who have a true scientific bent to make this story more accurate. In the meantime, a non-scientific reader will find I have made an effort to describe the things about evolution, the life sciences, and systems theory in a way that is accessible.

I want to share this story with you, my inquiry into the depths of the between, because it is a piece of our story, an unfolding new chapter in the story of humankind's quest to find a way to live within the creative processes of Creation. This story is timely, not only because it can reduce unnecessary suffering, but also because it can make the necessary pain of being human more productive and ennobling. This story unlocks the map room where some possible futures await.

We, as a species, are at an evolutionary crossroads. The time is here, when we need to settle ourselves down and decide we are willing to do what it takes to be around for a while. Our long adolescence needs to end. It is time for us to have a grown-up story of our own psychological and spiritual relationship with the unfolding of Creation. The story we have, at least the psychological story, is tragically incomplete.

We cannot actualize our potential as individuals, with the current story. We cannot even see our social potential, much less begin to actualize it, within the current story. What resides in the between, what connects us, must now become conscious, must now inform us. A new story, a new psychology based on our strengths, based on the strengths of Life itself, a psychology of interdependence, is now necessary. This is the beginning of unfolding that story.

Locating Myself

I awoke this morning in my studio apartment, a single room in a remodeled two-car garage. The place I rent is located in what seems to me to be the middle of a park, but in actual fact is the back of a three-acre parcel in which there is a main house, a one-bedroom cottage, and my studio apartment disguised as a two-car garage. My industrious landlord takes care of this parcel of land. He has planted an abundance of trees and maintains this place like it is his little piece of Shangri-La. I am very lucky to live in the quiet and peace of this place.

I live in the most desirable area of a formerly rural county rapidly becoming a bedroom community, an adjunct to the expanding metropolitan area of the Greater Bay Area. The countryside is reminiscent of the most beautiful parts of rural Italy. It is dotted with apple orchards and vineyards between redwood-strewn hillsides sometimes covered by fog. This stunning landscape has recently become festooned with McMansions. The city is transforming the countryside into a suburb of itself.

I tell you this little story to let you know that despite my favorable location, my life is subject to the same cultural forces that define this age: the larger processes of modernization, which manifest in this county as increased population, traffic, escalating home prices, urbanization and general busyness. As the years have passed from the mid-sixties when I arrived, this county shows all the signs of what is perhaps more advanced in other locales, that is, the rapid fragmentation of community and a lifestyle tied to the natural cycles of the place.

From this place I want to tell you how I came to appreciate what lies mysteriously and accessibly in the heart of the between. To do that, I am going to start by telling a little bit of my personal story. It is the story of my pursuit of freedom, of a journey in consciousness, of a long climb out of a deep valley of culturally-inspired despair, to a landscape of connection and meaning.

My Ongoing Quest for Community and a Sense of Hope

This story is not about the cultural and historical forces that have caused the experience of fragmentation, dislocation, and anxiety that have come to dominate our age; that story may be better told by other more qualified observers of culture than I. No, this story takes place in the context of a fragmenting society, during an historical epoch that is dominated by a scientific paradigm that views life and all living things as mechanisms, soulless machines. My life, whether I knew it or not (and at first, I didn't), was being shaped by forces so much greater and more impersonal than I could have imagined.

All I knew in those early days was that I didn't really feel any sense of belonging and that I had an agitated, restless, inchoate longing for a place for myself in this world. I didn't know then what I know now, that the world and I could become more identified with each other. I only knew that my life seemed to be haunted by a feeling of brokenness. I felt terribly hopeless and inadequate. I was afraid that my limitations would, if they became visible, reveal me as the inadequate person I believed myself to be. I spent most of my time hiding in relationships and jobs that didn't ask very much of me.

I didn't know at the time that my restlessness, my tendency toward boredom, and my curiosity were all indicators of intelligence. I didn't think I was very smart. I believed my grades in high school and eight listless undirected years as an undergraduate all bespoke a man of mediocre capacity. I stayed in college and referred to it as my never-never land, because the world of adulthood was so unappealing to me. At the time my refusal to join the ranks of those who were gainfully employed and on track for career, families, and owning homes, was only attributable to the shortcomings I was sure I embodied.

Now, I can see that my ambivalence was based on a kind of wisdom. I was reticent to give my life to a life-process that would ensure my bad feelings about myself. Instead of that hard-won awareness, however, I had a terrible feeling of inferiority. I had no prospects and for a long-time my life would be defined by a series of low-wage, boring, jobs.

Having grown up a military brat, I avoided service in the Vietnam War; not because I had any kind of political awareness, but because I had already spent my childhood in the military. I had no illusions about military service. When some of my friends and classmates started coming back from the war in bad shape, I developed survivor guilt. It was clear to me that I could have been any of them, and I cared about them, so I chose to become involved with these men.

And so it was that I first inadvertently experienced community. Community came to me because the only surcease combat veterans from Vietnam could find was in sharing their painful and confusing experiences with each other. The aid (and nurturing) these combat-hardened men brought to each other gave me my first hint of hope that I could belong.

What I sensed, though not yet consciously, was that I felt whole when I was with these other broken and uncertain men. I felt something about my life, about all human lives, that gave me hope, which gave me a sense that my life could make sense, that I could be related to the world I found myself within. And I wanted more of this feeling, this connection. This drove me into the men's movement where I found that when a group of men sat down together, and opened up with each other, it aroused tremendous feelings of caring, nurturing, and a sometimes-fierce kindness. I came to think of this as a men's community and came to rely on it as a kind of compass, a reference point from which I could view the conventions of the world, and know whether they made me excited about life, or whether they made me dread my very existence.

Having discovered community, I didn't realize that I had come across anything unusual. It wasn't until later, when my first marriage unraveled and I went off to graduate school that I began to see how rare my experience had been, and just how precious community really was. During my years in graduate school, I learned many things, most notably how to be a therapist and the value of the spiritual dimension in a well-integrated life. But my most important learning came from outside my school experience. I learned that community is not just a place where people meet, but a way of meeting that brings people, through experience, to a new way of perceiving themselves, each other, and the world in which they live. This fascinated me, and has delivered me to another way of seeing this world

In Search of a Psychology of Interdependence

As a graduate student and later as a psychotherapist, I felt like a pariah in my field. Why? Because where others, including many of my teachers, saw pathology, I saw the need for initiation. Where others were labeling the symptoms they saw in terms of the diagnostic manuals, with names like Affective or Personality Disorder, I was seeing people coping and mostly overwhelmed by circumstances internal and external that were beyond their control. My colleagues were busy finding more sophisticated ways of diagnosing and treating the problems of the individuals they saw. All during this time, I was worried about myself, and my practice. The isolation that was causing all my clients to have distorted reactions to themselves and to others, haunted me, but I didn't know what to do about it.

I worked mostly with men then. Because I spoke to men in terms of initiation, I seemed to have much more success drawing them into therapy and helping them find better ways of being in the world, and in their relationships. At that time, men were said to be largely therapy-phobic. It seemed to me, that instead of being phobic men, they were less interested in being diagnosed and treated like they had psychological problems, and more interested in finding meaningful ways of becoming the men they wanted to be.

I was at a loss for a way to articulate what seemed to me to be a yawning schism between the world I saw and the world of psychotherapy I was being prepared for. I went along with what I would later come to see as the mainstream, conventional approach to psychology, because I wanted to practice. I needed to demonstrate that I understood the basic assumptions and could competently employ the prevalent modalities of the field, but I wasn't firmly in the fold. Without really knowing it, I was already chafing at what I considered a limited, and limiting, way of perceiving reality.

Unbeknownst to myself, I was looking for a better way of explaining the pain I was seeing and experiencing. It was during this time that I experienced my first community-building workshop. A group of about 50 people got together for a weekend with the intention of creating an experience of community. The workshop wasn't perfect, but it was compelling. What was most powerful for me was that many people shared a kind of vulnerable encounter with a large and complex reality that was both overwhelming, and freeing.

I was impressed by what had happened, despite people's differences. I was impressed by what I considered to be a shared experience of what we had in common, our humanity. I observed that we had entered, through our differences, a kind of shared altered state, a state where tremendous feelings of unity, compassion, and learning took place. This was an experience of community that I had never had before. I was fascinated. I wanted to know more about this form of community, for my sake and for the sake of the many people, like me, who were suffering because they lived in what they perceived as a fragmented world of isolation and meaninglessness.

Little did I know that this marked the beginning of a turn for me, a turn that would take 20 more years to unfold, a turn that would be away from the mainstream to the non-pathologizing fringe, where I tried to put together an alternative way of explaining and responding to the forms of pain I experienced in my own life, and in the lives of those who, in their confusion and heartache, came to me for help. I was, still without knowing it, on a quest for a psychological orientation that confirmed our connection to the larger processes of life, a psychology of interdependence.

The Web of Life

Amazingly, I started my post-undergraduate career in the state parks. It was my ambition at the time to become a naturalist. I wanted to spend my days out in Nature learning about its magnificent ways. I also felt that I would enjoy introducing and explaining nature to people who were not aware of her fascinating creativity and awesome abundance. Now, over 30 years later, I am delighted to find that my naturalist sensibilities shed light on how we humans, and what goes on within and between us, is a manifestation of Nature herself. Let me explain.

The web of life began to create itself several billion years ago. In the process it developed some tendencies, which we have slowly come to recognize through scientific investigation. These tendencies, evolution towards complexity, building upon what has come before and resilience, to name just a few, have been gifted to us as part of this web. The story of the between cannot be told, cannot even be perceived, without recognizing the role that Life itself has played in shaping our humanity, our possibilities. Chapter 1 describes the processes of the Universe. Chapter 2 details the nature of evolution and how these dynamics shape and potentiate the human experience.

There is a revolution going on in the Life Sciences that is bringing forward a whole new story of human origins, of the origins of Life. This new story, founded upon new science, reveals to us a whole new range of possibilities. Science is recognizing that humanity is an extension of Life. (We are organisms, not machines.) It is becoming evident that we have inherited all of the qualities of evolution, including its strength, resilience, and creativity.

These changes in perception alter the way we can see each other, ourselves, and what is possible between us. They provide the foundation for a new way of being with and responding to our pain. They also show us how our pain is often connected to the larger processes of Life itself, to processes which, if we recognize them, reveal new ways of making our pain meaningful, as well as making visible new qualities of support that are available to us. When we become cognizant of the pattern that connects us to one to another, to the social systems we are a part of, to the larger processes of Life on the planet, and even to evolution itself, then a whole new way of making our travails meaningful becomes evident, and a whole new way of responding to them becomes available.

The Pattern that Connects

What is this pattern that connects us in such a big way?

It is holism (see Chapter 4). Holism is a way of looking at things that only came into play with the advent of holography in the late 60s. Arthur Koestler, a science writer, coined the term, to describe (for the first time) a pattern he perceived that connected all things. Holism referred to his perception, later most famously elaborated on by philosopher Ken Wilber, that all things are embedded in larger things. In fact, everything seems to have a dual nature. Not only is everything embedded, in other words, connected to things larger and smaller than itself, but everything has an integrity, a wholeness of its own.

The science of holism posits that all living things are holons. A holon is an entity that is simultaneously whole in itself AND a part of some other whole. For example, the whole atom is a part of a whole molecule, and a whole molecule is a part of a whole cell, and the whole cell is a part of a whole organism, and so on. Each of these entities is neither a whole nor a part, but a whole/part, a holon. From this viewpoint, all living things and life processes, including human beings, are not merely wholes unto themselves but parts of something else; there is no whole that is not simultaneously a part of some other whole.

Since every holon is a whole/part, it has two "tendencies," or "drives"—it has to maintain both its wholeness and its partness. So one characteristic of all holons, no matter what domain they exist in, is that they have to maintain their own wholeness, their own identity and autonomy. This drive to maintain their own identity and wholeness is described by life scientists as an organism's ability to retain its own agency. Agency is a holon's capacity to maintain its own wholeness in the face of environmental pressures that would otherwise absorb or obliterate it. As we shall see, we human beings, as holons, are constantly involved in the process of discovering, establishing, losing and re-establishing our capacity for agency, or autonomy.

This trait, the pursuit of autonomy, of agency, has been the primary focus of traditional Western psychology. In our individualistic American society, we have focused almost all of our energy on only one part of our dual nature, associating freedom and wholeness with being separate, and apart from, the relationships, social systems, and environment upon which we depend. This has created a distortion that undermines our relationships, community, and our species' chances for survival. We are more than separate entities and we need a psychological orientation that reflects this.

Since a holon is also a part of some other system, it is not enough that it simply preserves its agency; it must also maintain a capacity to fit into its environment. So a holon, be it a molecule, animal, or human, must also maintain what life scientists refer to as, its capacity for communion, the ability to fit in and belong as a part of a larger system. For a holon to survive it must maintain this partness in the face of environmental pressures (including cultural) that would try to separate it out from a larger whole and thus destroy it. We shall see in Chapter 4 that, as holons, we are constantly struggling to discover and maintain a vital sense of connection with the larger social processes in which our lives are immersed, or paying the price (in distorted lives) of not doing so.

These twin drives, the urge to merge into a larger whole and the desire to maintain a sense of autonomy and distinctness, underlie the human experience. They create a dynamic tension that shapes our evolution as individuals and as participants in the social systems in which we are immersed. They form the plight of the human holon, that our nature is fundamentally dialectical. As whole/parts our lives are forever being lived out in a dynamic tension between our desires for communion and for autonomy. And it is this "between," the plight of the human holon, that is a concern of a psychology of interdependence. It is this between, this dynamic holonic tension that reveals a whole new vista of human personal and social potential.

Holism and the Life of Natural Systems

Holism makes it clear that everything in life is embedded. Everything is connected, comprised of lesser components while at the same time a part of something bigger. At every level an organism, such as a human being, is dependent for its well-being and health upon the health and well-being of the part/ wholes that make it up, and the part/wholes that it helps make up. In fact, there is an interdependent relationship between all of these levels and the well-being of any of them is dependent upon the well-being of all of them.

What all of this connection reveals is just how important it is that all organisms fit into their place in the scheme of things. I think this viewpoint transforms the evolutionary imperative from "survival of the fittest" to "survival of that which fits best." This raises the specter that all of life is comprised of living systems, networks or communities, if you will, that rely upon each other, that constellate each other, to serve the dance of life. We will see in Chapters 2 and 3 that life seems to rely on all of these system levels, all of these living systems, for its diverse profusion and its integrated wholeness.

We, too, participate in this dance. We are an interdependent part of it. In order to fulfill our potential, to be truly healthy, well-adjusted and free, we have to fulfill the evolutionary imperative of our twin holonic desires. We must become whole unto ourselves, not by severing connections, but through connection. We must also succeed in becoming part of something larger, not by sacrificing our wholeness and autonomy, but by actualizing them in the context of relationship with this something larger. Doing this not only ensures our well-being, but the well-being of the system-levels, the whole/parts that make us up and the whole/parts to which we contribute.

We fear becoming parts because we do not have models or guides that recognize and value the healing and wholing power of relationships. The civility we depend upon to viably address the larger problems we face as neighborhoods, civic communities, tribes, and nation-states is also undermined by this same distorting over-reliance upon autonomy and separation from others. We are essentially disabled by an inadequate story, a half-truth, which undermines our confidence, and leaves us feeling hopeless.

The misplaced emphasis upon pseudo-wholeness costs individuals and society alike. Besides the rising tide of hopelessness, there is the ever-increasing toll on marriages, families, communities, civic comity, and confidence in ourselves as a species. All of this is the result of a fundamental misperception made a long time ago. Perhaps we are now ready for a new story. One that considers the pattern that connects us to one another, to the social systems we rely upon, to our environment, cultural and natural, and to the larger processes of evolution itself.

Such a story would place an equal emphasis upon both aspects of our holonic nature. If this were to happen, we would begin to value much more our social nature and begin to realize that we haven't gone far enough towards really actualizing our human potential. We have yet to begin to actualize our social potential. The limits placed upon our social potential by an inadequate story also place a restriction, paradoxically, upon how fully developed an individual can become.

A new, more accurate story, would increase recognition of the significant role played by our social contexts. One could argue that traditional psychology has placed an emphasis upon primary relationships and families. This is accurate. But, with few exceptions, traditional approaches have looked at these contexts with primary consideration being placed upon their impact upon the individuals involved.

Only in recent years have systemic approaches evolved that equally emphasize the wellbeing of the system, the primary dyad, and the family. And even more recently, developmental psychologists (see Chapter 6) have begun to see that social contexts play an essential role in human development. Now it is imperative that we see these social systems as having intrinsic value, as essential whole/parts, which have an integrity and value of their own. In addition to being important for the development of individuals, these social contexts bind us together and provide us access to meaning and the collective ways of knowing that are so notably missing today.

Crucibles of Development

When I was in graduate school I learned that I needed a theoretical orientation, preferably one that addressed family systems, to help me pass the exams for licensure. I didn't have a particular orientation and I was advised that I couldn't expect to pass the oral part of the test without demonstrating that I had an orientation, and that I used it consistently, to evaluate what my clients presented and to provide justifiable treatment. This turned out to be fortuitous for me.

I chose differentiation theory because it seemed the easiest to learn, had the fewest treatment options, and could be used both with individuals and families. It was a choice based not on any particular affiliation with this theoretical orientation, but the simple necessity that licensure required it. I only learned later how lucky I was to have made this choice.

Differentiation theory was first developed and applied by a man named Murray Bowen (see Chapter 5). He knew that the term differentiation had first been used by biologists, studying the way cells behaved. They used the term to describe how an individual cell distinguished itself from a mass of cells, and how that cell went on and became functional in a way different from the mass of cells it originated within. Bowen made the leap from this biological feat, accomplished at the cellular level, to the individual human struggling for identity and functionality within the family. He developed a whole way of viewing what went on within the family based upon a biological process.

I didn't realize the significance of this move until much later. At the time I merely contented myself with learning what I needed to know to demonstrate basic competency. But differentiation theory was going to deliver me to a totally different way of seeing, one that soon led me to see that not only was there a pattern that connects us, but that pattern was dynamic, designed by Nature, and could, if we cooperated with it, reveal a whole new notion of the psychological project.

The story of the evolution, of Murray Bowen's differentiation theory (Chapter 5), is also a story about a gradual recognition of how human development hinges upon key social contexts (social crucibles) that can impede and propel us along an arc of development. It is the story of how a system of psychological thinking grew in unexpected ways, and soon revealed the active dimension of the pattern that connects, revealing how Life, the evolutionary process, is engaged in all our psychological and social lives.

What I most want to convey is that everything changes when we see that the dilemmas many of us face are brought about by natural processes surging through our lives, and that Nature also simultaneously endows us with the strength, creativity, and resilience needed to make these dynamics growthful. Life underlies much of what ails us. And Life provides us a way through what ails us, which can open us to a whole new way of experiencing life (see Chapter 8). I have found that differentiation dilemmas are inevitable, exacting, and lead us to grow in ways that support our personal development and that can assist our species in the effort to evolve consciously.

Resilience, Creativity, and Durability

To me, what is most exciting about this change in perception is the realization that it is Life that provides the impetus for my growth and development. Life provides what I need to accomplish the transformations in my consciousness that Life demands. This support is built-in. It exists in the dilemmas themselves. It exists in the struggle to find a way to come to grips with these dilemmas. And, it manifests in the variety of ways that typical, everyday dilemmas get solved innovatively.

I am continually awed by the elegance of the whole. Yes, it seems that Life asks much of humankind, but it also provides much of what we need to meet the questions that it asks us. This is most evident when we view the progress of evolution and the adaptability of living systems. By looking at the larger picture of evolution we can see the same processes being played out in the details of an individual's struggle, the life-cycle of a relationship, or the dynamic tensions in a community. The story of this nascent psychological approach, a psychology of interdependence (Chapters 7, 8 and 9), is a story that incorporates the elegance, creativity, resilience and strength of the unfolding Universe with the unfolding of the human experiment. And, it is a story that has had a lot of personal relevance to me.

October 6, 2003

My life changed radically on October 6, 2003. I had a hemorrhagic stroke, a brain aneurism. I don't think I ever recovered. The life I knew became this unprecedented, ongoing surprise that has led me to the precipice and holds me there. I subsequently learned that the hemorrhage was accompanied by a very rare brain disorder, so rare that only one in every 200,000 people who had the kind of stroke I did contract it. I found myself alone, brain-damaged and experiencing terrible losses.

This was the most difficult era of my life (thus far), a time that changed everything. In some strange combination of paradox, irony, persistence and luck, I survived, and I became something different. David didn't totally die, but he became significantly diminished, and Lucky was born. Thus began the most arduous part of my journey, from which this book came into being. I was to spend three years in the underworld, more dead than alive, having no future, believing, as I do now, that I could die at any moment. And, I was to be transformed.

With the birth of Lucky came the realization that I had been shoved into a new awareness. That awareness permeates this book. It didn't start out full-blown, however. I had done a lot of the research earlier while teaching, my work with clients had shifted over the years, and I had actually started writing some scholarly articles to try to convey some understanding of what I was beginning to see emerging. But it was the proximity of death, the limitations I had to embrace and adapt to, and the overwhelming uncertainty that sharpened my focus, and made me realize that I would regret it if I didn't give words to what I could see, if only dimly.

As I write now I am a wheel-chair bound person who has no balance, tremors on the left side of my body, a patch over one eye, and I can type with only my right hand. I am a disabled person, and

I am so much more than that. So much has been taken away from me, and so much remains. I have come to know that everything passes very quickly, that relationship is precious, and that Life is fragile and strong, vulnerable and persistent. I am Lucky, to have survived, to have so much left to turn to, and most of all, to know what I now know.

For a long time, I felt a kind of ethical dilemma that undermined me, and my work with others. I wondered how I could be effective, how I could assist anyone with really changing their life if I had failed to change my own. I knew that the changes I now embodied had not happened because of my efforts, but because I had had a stroke. I remember the fateful day I was lamenting this fact to my men's group, when I suddenly was seized by the realization that although I hadn't changed me, Life had!

I had already come to accept that my life was no longer my own. Now I knew deeply that what had been my life, was now Life's. From such a place I could begin to see how I had kept myself separate all these years because of my own insistence that it was I who was the central actor in my life, when in fact what I had thought of as my life was a life that belonged to Life all along. This realization calmed me and provided the perspective that ultimately freed me from the oppressiveness of my own striving. Life was the deliverer, not me.

Now what remains is to live accordingly, and to discover the wonders of the world that have always existed beyond my insistent perception. Because I lived constantly with the specter of death, I realized that I didn't want to go to my grave without giving away the keys to the map room that I had found. What map room? That's what this book is all about. The map room is always around, but it is imperceptible to most of us. And inside there are maps, maps to possible futures, to a New World, to a way to not just survive, but to thrive.

Maybe one has to be similarly lucky to gain access, but I don't think so. I think these maps exist to be found, that these possible futures, and the New World that comes with them, are just on the other side of the questions Life asks us. Yes, I certainly know that Life can ask us hard questions, can give us seemingly impossible choices, can bring us to our knees, but now I also know, that Life also provides what is needed to rise to the occasion.

So, that is the spirit behind this writing. I want you to have a chance to know that there is a world beyond ours, a world completely contiguous with ours. It isn't waiting to be born. It is here, causing us lots of disruptions and strange failures. We have the ability to respond, to know it as our homeland, but there is a price for admission, there always is. Life will deliver, but we must give ourselves whole-heartedly to the process of living on Life's terms rather than our own.

Interdependence as Interpenetration

I am referring here to the fact that Life seems to be a partner, a co-conspirator, perpetually offering us opportunities to participate in the process of evolution. Alongside these opportunities Life offers the means. These means aren't always obvious, they often exist enfolded in the very dilemmas with which Life confronts us.

This is the underlying premise of a psychology of interdependence; Life has a need for us, just as we have a need for Life.

In fact, it seems that the story of human development is, in the final analysis, a story of the co-arising of Life and consciousness. The apex of human development seems to be enlightenment, the seamless, unboundaried oneness with all being. This represents the absolute interpenetration of self and Life, an interpenetration that paradoxically produces a totally idiosyncratic individual and the full embodiment of Life, a union with all things.

This co-arising relationship, between the self and Life, this inter-dependent dance, is what actually determines wellbeing, not just for the individual but for every level of human engagement. This is a more holistic basis for the psychological project. We are desperately in need of a whole new way of seeing ourselves, a way that ennobles our effort to become ourselves, that focuses equal attention upon our relationships and social systems, and that is concerned with our species' relationship with the Cosmos, with the processes of evolution itself.

The reliance upon a one-sided psychology that mistakenly placed individuality at the apex of psychological achievement, has delivered us to an age of narcissism, divorce, civic distrust and environmental destruction. It is time for a more holistic approach, an approach that values our social potential as much as our individual potential, an approach that recognizes the embeddedness that allows us to thrive, that strives to align our endeavors with the things that support Life and evolution.

It is time to consider what the big picture tells us about wellbeing. Instead of settling for the individualistic, atomized, mechanized, "survival of the fittest" picture that dominated the 20th century, we need a contemporary orientation that takes into consideration the rapidly increasing evidence that we are more than just individuals, we are extensions of the evolutionary process, participating in a living Universe busily creating itself.

Here, then, we pick up on a story that has been unfolding with the gradual evolution of our consciousness. This is not the beginning of that story. Nor is it the totality of that story. Rather, it is merely a reflection of that larger story, which is coming forward, though this, my life. I tell it knowing the story is so much bigger, so much richer, so much more nuanced than I can tell, than I can even perceive. I call attention to this story because it is my key to the map room, to a possible future, to the between, to the Great Mystery that lies at the heart of everything.

I talk to my inner lover, and I say, why such rush?

We sense that there is some sort of spirit that
loves birds and animals and the ants—
perhaps the same one
who gave a radiance to you in
your mother's womb.

Is it logical you would be walking around
entirely orphaned now?

The truth is you turned away yourself,
and decided to walk into the dark alone.

Now you are tangled up in others,
and have forgotten
what you once knew,
and that is why
everything you do
has some weird failure in it.

— KABIR (TRANS. BY ROBERT BLY)

SECTION I
OUR NATURAL INHERITANCE

As I recollect the Unity of Life,
Life recollects me in my original wholeness.
PARKER PALMER

Section I

🌿

Our Natural Inheritance — Evolution's Gifts

No departure from the psychology of the past is possible without re-orienting to the present. In this case, that means looking at the world, the Cosmos we inhabit. Traditional psychology was built upon the science of its time. Freud introduced the concepts of the personal unconscious and talk therapy about a hundred years ago. During the Victorian Age, science taught that all things could be reduced, via physics, to their tiniest components, the atoms, and explained by the interactions of these separate bits of matter.

There have been many scientific advances since that time, our senses have been extended by scientific instruments that no one even dreamed of then; we have gained enormous perspective, stretching our view incredibly in both the micro and macro directions. New ideas have emerged, provoking new thoughts about everything from the origin of the Universe to the Alice in Wonderland quantum realm. In reality, humankind does not inhabit the same world that Freud woke up to.

The world, and our outlook upon it, have profoundly changed. In this new context we need to re-conceive our most basic assumptions. Like many of the developments of the past century, the conventional wisdom of the past is still useful; but our times call for a newer, more complex picture—one that takes the past in, includes it, but doesn't hesitate to add the current perspective. Now we are in need of a more cosmological picture. We are products of more than just our family-of-origin. We are products of a 13 billion year-process of evolution. And, as will be shown, there is every reason to believe that evolution has prepared us for the complexities associated with our existence.

In the following chapters we will look at the evolutionary process. First, we will examine the attributes of our cosmological home. We will consider the universe in the same way we look at our parents, to see what of itself it has bestowed upon us to help us survive and thrive. In the process we will also begin to consider our place as lineage bearers, as carriers of the process of creation, as unfolders of the evolutionary process.

Similarly, we will look at the powers that have been bestowed upon us as living beings. We no longer live in the Age of the Mechanism as Freud did. Our age looks to the living organism for hints about our possibilities. Thus, we will consider living systems, the form that evolution took to create the complexity of consciousness and behavior that is us. In the process we will begin to see how Life has bestowed upon us powers of strength, resilience and creativity that can aid us in our encounters with the challenges native to our existence.

All along we will see how life has taken advantage of the potential inherent in sociability, in the properties that emerged as organisms moved together and collaborated to create totally new possibilities. Synergy, the stimulant that provokes emergence of the totally new, has come to be seen as one of the hallmarks of the evolutionary process. Synergy is a social element, one of the primal processes that gave us life and that characterizes our social capacity. We need to recognize the preeminent role that synergy has played in our evolution as social and cultural organisms, so that we have a more realistic appreciation of the social potential inherent in our species, a potential that is currently undervalued.

❦

CHAPTER 1

🌿

The Universe

The horizons toward which we can soar are within us, anxious to break free, to emerge from our imaginings, then to beckon us forward into fresh realities. We have a mission to create, for we are evolution incarnate. We are her awareness, her frontal lobes and fingertips. We are second-generation star stuff come alive. We are neurons of this planet's interspecies mind.
—HOWARD BLOOM, *The Global Brain*

To understand the potency, the mystery, and the reliability of the between is a big task. Full comprehension is elusive. Knowing the facts, having a cognitive picture isn't enough. One must experience it for oneself. So the picture I'm going to paint here, of the between, of the Universe, is a partial one. You have to make it your own. This story, the importance of the potential that lies just beyond what I can describe, is yours to complete. You don't have to work at it or change yourself. It is already there within you, and between you and everyone you encounter. All you need do is open yourself up and experience what I point toward. If you do so, you will feel like you are coming home, there will be a feeling of familiarity, a kind of déjà vu experience, where you recognize what you have known all along.

For in truth, you will be coming home. Home, in this case, is the vastness of the whole Cosmos. One thing that makes this story so compelling is the fact that no matter where you are, you are still at home. The Universe is a big place. The biggest, most extensive place we have ever known. Amazingly, it is where we have been given life, the place where all our dramas, discoveries, and dreams take place. The Universe is many things to us. It is our home, our stage, and our

Teacher. Without it, we have no life, no place to unfold, and no sense that our existence has a purpose and a meaning.

This then is an incomplete story. You must complete it on your own. This is your real, your only, homework. It is a tough task. Familiarize yourself with your home, your birthplace, business, hideaway, favorite vacation spot, crumbling tenement, school, or parkland. The Universe is all of these places. They, like you, are all products, not of humanity, but of the Universe. To know the full story, you must get it in your body. But, don't worry! Your body already gets it. (See: The Biology of The Human Being in Chapter 2.) To complete this story, the story of how each of us is an extension of the Universe, all you need do is remember, as your body does, where you came from, and where you always remain.

Evolution: Our True Parent

If the Universe is our home, then evolution is the Universe's life, and our life too. Despite being perceived by science to be dead, the Universe has evolved. Stars, galaxies, and elemental molecules are born, age, change and die in the Universe we know. The Universe itself has changed and grown over its 13-some billon years of existence. And, of course, the Universe has played a major role in the appearance of life, and the arrival of complex consciousness on the scene.

During all of those eons the Universe seemed to have been discovering and utilizing powers that eventually brought us into being. Evolution is the name science has given this process. Our modern-day penchant for analysis, breaking things down and apart, has led us to forget that evolution and the Universe are inextricably woven together. The truth is that it has been the Universe, some cosmological imperative, which has driven evolution, which has delivered us to this moment.

It is fair then to consider evolution our true parent. Doing so places another level of depth behind our families-of-origin, a more primary one that we ought to consider in our pursuit of psychological adjustment and emotional well- being. Ultimately, whether we were parented well or poorly by our biological parents, we are still the inheritors of a cosmological legacy that is woven into every fiber of our being. We are the offspring of the most colossal thing we can imagine. And we are still discovering the true magnificence of the legacy of which we are a part. For all intents and purposes, Howard Bloom is right: we are cosmological beings, evolution incarnate. As such, we are privy to all the powers of the being that spawned us.

Universal Powers

The Universe is a powerful place. Evolution, and the profusion of life forms that characterize it, are all extensions of this power. We will now devote a little time to remembering some of the powers of the Universe, and in the process, recalling our own potential. The Universe demonstrates many powers that reveal something of its creativity, strength, persistence, and resilience. The Universe acts in our lives, beneath our awareness. I'll refer to this dimension of the human unconscious as our cosmological unconscious, borrowing from Brian Swimm.

The Universe has many dynamic attributes. Naming the few below in no way infers that these are all of the Universe's powers, or that these are the most important powers the Universe demonstrates. As a species we are still early in the process of discovering the full extent of our endowment. The powers I intend to discuss merely point the way for a deeper look at what we have been bequeathed. For the sake of this discussion we will look at the Universe's tendencies towards

- Seamlessness,
- Ceaselessness,
- Fullness/Emptiness,
- Emergence,
- Embrace,
- Synergy.

Seamlessness

The Universe is, quite literally, everywhere. It has no boundaries that we have discovered. Everything is composed of the Universe. Our bodies are composed of molecules that originated in the core of distant stars. The stars themselves were born in galaxies of spinning elements disseminated by the "big bang," our current conception of how the Universe began. Everywhere we go, everything we see, from the tiniest element passing instantly in the cloud chamber to huge stellar objects light years away, confronts us with the presence of an as yet unknown Universe. It is ubiquitous, stretching from the vastness of outer space to the infinitesimally small, and similarly vast quantum spaces between the orbiting electrons and the nuclei of the smallest atoms.

This seamlessness reveals our real source. It conveys what we truly are. We are attributes of the Universe, extensions of a process that began long ago, towards an end we know not. Science, to its credit, has both broken this seamlessness into parts for analysis' sake, and has revealed the wholeness of that which has unfolded us. Thus, what we have come to know as a vast emptiness, devoid of evidence of life, is at the same time revealed to be the source of all life. From the earliest moments imaginable to the present, the Universe has been the playing field, the stage, where the dance of existence has unfolded. All histories, like rivers, merge back into one ocean, one continuum, one unending source.

Ceaselessness

There is no ending to the Universe in time or space. The process of evolution seems to have started at the instant when Creation began. The Universe has demonstrated a ceaseless drive for the products of evolution through the transformations that have been taking place: transformations of matter, of processes, of inner and outer space, of the huge and of the infinitesimally small. The restlessness of the Universe reveals a striving that seems to have a direction. We are a product of that striving, and we have a place as part of a long trajectory. We don't know where everything is headed, but we can conjecture from what has unfolded in the past. The Universe seems to want an organism that is capable of participating consciously in the Universe's self-organizing efforts. Thus, it has endowed us with consciousness, creativity, and the same restless drive.

Fullness/Emptiness

The between, or what connects us, is distributed evenly throughout the Universe. We know of it, but we don't yet know much about it. This mysterious something that connects us defies description yet lends itself to scientific scrutiny. Science calls it the space-time continuum, but I refer to it as the between. We emerged from this between, and our very survival, the sustainability of this particular experiment in complex consciousness may well depend, upon our paying attention to, and cooperating with, the bubbling creativity of the Universe.

Cosmologists have been amazed at the paradoxical emptiness and fullness of the Universe. This paradoxical richness extends seamlessly from vast interstellar spaces to the equally vast spaces that exist within the atom. In each case, the space seems empty, but on closer inspection it froths with energy and quantum events. The Earth, like all those familiar seemingly solid objects around us, is a cloud more full of empty space than anything we recognize as matter. Actually, more full of energy and quantum potential than we've ever imagined.

This fullness exists mostly as pure potential that we are just now learning to recognize and even to utilize. It is said that one square yard of the so-called vacuum of space contains more energy than humankind has yet used. Naturally, some scientists are endeavoring to find ways of tapping this vast energy potential for humankind's use. The Space Energy and Zero Space Energy projects are currently working to bring this energy on line to provide the world with a cheap and sustainable energy source, as well as to slow down global warming.

It is this pure potential, quantum possibility, that binds everything together, that fills up the emptiness. This is what exists at every level of the between, waiting to be released into form. In other words, at every level of Universal existence, including ourselves, space is both empty and full.

We exist with vast reaches of emptiness separating us, and with huge amounts of pure potential joining us

Emergence

One of the significant qualities that the Universe has demonstrated is emergence. It has shown a marvelous capacity to produce brand new things just when they are needed. And where do these innovations come from? Mysteriously, from the between. They are born, or emerge, from the interactions of cosmic events, atoms colliding, cells cooperating, and people relating with each other (see Chapter 3, on synergy).

Science, particularly systems thinking, refers to this capacity as the generation of emergent properties. These emergent properties are new things or processes that appear as a result of an interaction. Utterly new and innovative developments appear and solve old and enduring problems. From nothing but fervent interaction there appears a pattern that announces the presence of something entirely new. This pattern may or may not be recognized, but it emerges anyway. Amazingly, the new is a product of the old and includes the characteristics of the interacting parties, but integrates these qualities into a larger whole, a broader, more functional pattern.

As far as we can tell these emergent properties arise through the interaction of apparently separate entities and something that exists between them. What this is we don't know. We can see, however, that this tendency exists, that we have benefited from it in the past, that we probably exist because of it, and that we can utilize it for further benefit if we can learn to interact in ways that optimize this possibility. Scientists have recently begun to speculate that the potential inherent in the quantum realm is somehow stirred into form through interactions, but the exact mechanism, or chemistry, still evades us.

Emergence, the appearance of timely new capabilities, allows the Universe to evolve further along a trajectory that seems to increase the probability of life. We, as extensions of the Universe, participate in this mysterious dance. The between, with all of its latent potential, connects us. All we need do to activate the power of emergence, to discover our social potential, is improve the quality of our interactions.

Embrace

I call this universal power embrace because I want to convey the essential, enduring involvement that has been occurring since the beginning of time. Life (our lives) has not come about because of random processes that happened to take place under fortuitous circumstances. No, it seems like the Universe intended all along, and actively participated in, evolving a living organism with complex consciousness, such as ourselves.

Recent science has revealed many enigmatic facts about the Universe that suggest this possibility. One of the most compelling has been the constant rate that the Universe is expanding. It happens that it is expanding at just the rate that makes life possible. If the Universe expanded faster, then everything from the galaxies, which are where stars are born, to the heavy atoms, which are building-blocks of life, would have flown apart. If the rate of expansion were slightly slower, then it all would have collapsed into a dense singularity from which nothing distinct could emerge. For some strange reason, unaccountable to mainstream science, right from the beginning the Universe hit upon just the right rate of expansion for life.

Is this an accident? If so, then it seems that the Universe is in constant peril, and the odds of it persisting for 13.7 billion years, as it has, seem incredibly unlikely. I am inclined to believe that my existence and the universal conditions that make my life possible are not the result of randomness, but rather the result of the Universe embracing the potential for life. I think the Universe did intend, if not me, mankind. I am inclined to believe, and the newly emerging scientific perspective seems at least to suggest, that the Universe has moved as it has to preserve and actualize the possibility that it could become conscious. We, you and I, are products of that movement, manifestations of the Universe's development, and its embrace of the possibility of life.

Synergy

The arrival of life on the universal stage was not an accident. We don't know the whole story yet, but we know that life emerged through an erotic process we now call synergy. We will take a deeper look at synergy and the role synergy has played in evolution in Chapter 3. But for now, it is important to stress that synergy is a universal power that reveals the highly social nature of the Universe.

It is only in the last few decades that humankind, and science in particular, even had a word to describe the fact that two or more discreetly different entities or processes could get together, interact, and create something new that is actually more than the sum of the parts involved. Evolution has known, and used, this mechanism for a long time. It started from the beginning, when after the big bang elemental particles and energies began to combine and create synergetic relationships that first populated the space-time continuum with the basic atoms and elements that became the building blocks of the Universe as we know it.

Synergy, then, is a quality of relationship. It differs from emergence, which is a product of relationship, the something new that comes about because of the synergetic quality of interaction that is taking place. When a relationship achieves a degree of collaboration that is capable of generating something qualitatively different and new, synergy is occurring. Synergy arouses potential, while emergence manifests that same potential in a form or pattern. The Universe has employed synergy over and over to evoke emergence, to solve problems and overcome obstacles, to forward the process of evolution. As a power of the Universe, synergy is a part of our birthright, an inheritance that we have yet to make a concerted effort to truly utilize. Synergy reveals a pathway toward emergence, a way to tap the social potential that lies between us.

Our Endowment

We are more than just human. Humanity has been endowed with the ceaseless, seamless, synergetic powers of the Universe. We know how to tap into the incredible creativity inherent in the pure potential of the Universe. Yet, we have thus far failed to realize the creative potential we have been endowed with because we have chosen to emphasize and express only the individualistic portion of our nature. This choice was perhaps natural. Maybe it was necessary for us, as a young species and as an experiment in self-consciousness, to go through an adolescent phase, to seemingly distinguish ourselves through emphasizing our separate uniqueness. Or maybe the Universe desires diversity as much as it does unity. But, whatever the case, we have come to a time where it is necessary and possible to reorient ourselves, to balance our twin natures as beings capable of heroic individualism and creative union.

If we are going to actualize the potential with which we have been endowed as living extensions of the Universe, it will help us to know that we have not been merely abandoned here. We are the recipients and agents, of a 13.7-billion-year-long process. We are expressions of a universal dynamic. We are embodiments of the Universe's urge to merge and its will to create as many options as possible. The life force that beats our hearts is an expression of the restlessness and ongoing desire of creation, of a living Universe.

We may have wandered away from Nature. Or, we might have gone upon a necessary developmental path, which ultimately contributes to the whole. But, whatever the case may be, the Universe, like a good parent, continues to endow us with the strength, creativity and resilience we need to re-balance ourselves, to fit ourselves into what is unfolding. As we shall see, Nature has never wandered away from us. We have been given what we need, now is the time to claim it, to re-discover our birthright, to foment harmony for our own sakes. How? By relying more consciously upon the qualities we have been endowed with: strength, creativity, and resilience.

Strength

The ceaselessness of the Universe is an expression of its strength. We are party to that strength. It permeates our cells, drives our inquisitiveness, beats our hearts, infuses our love lives with meaning, and finds its ultimate expression in our will to live. The strength of the Universe, through its evolutionary zeal, made our ancestors stand erect and developed the backbone to make that a permanent advantage. This strength is everywhere where life thrives. It is within each one of us.

But more importantly, this strength lies within the matrix of relationships that support us, and which we support, becoming most palpable in the larger organisms of which we are a part. These organisms, which we call social systems, like intimate relationships, families, communities, and other types of organizations like nation-states, all confer upon us a kind of strength. Beyond the strength in numbers that participation in larger organisms imparts, there is the strength and durability, or sustainability, which comes with alignment. The more closely aligned an organism is with its environment, with its neighbors, associates, and loved ones, the stronger that organism is. In essence, the more closely aligned we are with the powers of the Universe, the greater the pool of strength in which we participate.

Humans have always partaken of the strength of the Universe. We know the power of numbers very well. It can be said that we live in a time of great massification. Corporations, states, empires and ideologies all project great strength through moving masses of people to align with their endeavors. But the strength of numbers heretofore has only mimicked the strength available when an endeavor aligns with evolution. As a species, we have yet to discover our real potential because we have not as yet aligned ourselves or our important relationships with the life force of the Universe.

Creativity

All one needs do to glimpse the real creativity of the Universe is to look at some of the images captured by the Hubble telescope. Gazing deeply into the Universe, Hubble rather miraculously looks as deeply into the past. As it looks farther into space to the most distant objects, Hubble reveals the history of creation. Light traveling for all of eternity shows us some of the permutations the Universe has gone through since its beginning. What we see are great protogalaxies and clouds of energy that form themselves into galaxies, stars and planets. With Hubble, we are able to see and to know the powerful and persistent process of creation that has been going on since nothing became everything.

This, too, is part of the legacy, the endowment with which the Universe has infused us. Because it serves the unfoldment of creation, the Universe has evolved us and endowed us with the imagination and the means to further its purposes. What are the purposes of the Universe? We don't know. And even if we did, we probably couldn't agree. But agreeing or not, we are participants and recipients of a creative capacity heretofore never seen anywhere else but in Nature itself. We are the products and the carriers of that creativity. We have also been given the means to perceive it. We are party to, a part of, the ongoing process of creation. Creativity begat us, endowed us, and now invites us to join in the process of creation.

This effulgence, this profusion of means, is the backdrop of human existence. It suffuses us with hope, offering visions of the possible. We have the sense, as a species, that we can, given enough time, actualize our dreams. And as time has passed we have seen our own capacity to create soar. The time from Daedelus' mythical flight to man's first actual flight was three thousand years. The time from JFK's vision of a man walking on the moon until actualization was only ten years. We have achieved such a degree of technical prowess that it now threatens us.

Our social creativity has not kept pace. Yet, we are equally endowed to be socially creative. But our emphasis upon individualism has blinded us and has led us to ignore our social potential, our capacity to align ourselves with each other and the Universe. On some level we know this unbalanced choice is not sustainable, and this knowledge is a part of the anxiety of our times. We are social animals, the Universe's creativity is within us, and there is an even larger creative potential that lies largely untapped between us. This creative potential lies in the between, awaiting us.

Resilience

The Universe has exhibited one characteristic of a living system that accounts for its resilience: its use of energy. The Universe is the biggest energy event we have ever known. Science cannot even begin to account for all of this energy. How did it appear out of nothingness? How does it manage to keep expanding at a constant rate? According to our current understanding of the laws of nature, the Universe should be slowing down, growing colder and dimmer. This is what should be occurring; the second law of thermodynamics dictates that energy is finite and that all things run down. But there is no evidence this is what is happening. Instead of entropy, the Universe seems to be conserving and growing its energy by becoming more complex, something we believe only a living system can do.

Is the Universe alive? This question is not as preposterous as it once was. The energy signature of the Universe offers a tantalizing hint that life might be much more ubiquitous and complex than we have ever imagined. This same energy signature reveals just what a resilient, ceaseless phenomenon we are a part of. Because we are a part of this larger whole, this ceaseless, seamless, emerging, energy event, we partake of its overall ability to creatively overcome obstacles, and to persistently pursue life. As agents and extensions of this enormous and ancient process, we are endowed, individually and as a species, with the resiliency of the whole. We need not cower before the complexities of life, for we have been endowed with the energy, creativity and persistence required to meet and embrace them. It seems that fate has prepared us to meet all challenges and to discover the opportunities inherent in them.

Implications for a New Psychological Approach

I am not a cosmologist so my descriptions of the marvels of the Universe are incomplete. But I understand enough of the story of our Universe to know that there is scientific reason to believe that leaving our holonic embeddedness out of our psychological considerations leaves us cut off from a legacy of creativity, strength and resilience that can sustain us. It is important therefore, that I enumerate the powers of the Universe because they have consequences for our understanding of ourselves, for what we believe is possible between us, for what we believe is possible, period.

As extensions of the Universe, we partake in all the traits and features that characterize the evolution and development of the Universe. These qualities lie within us. They can be drawn upon to more fully understand our own capacities. For too long humankind has operated as if the only factor that determines the quality of life, of self, is based upon the kind of nurturing one receives in childhood. But in seeing the forces of creation, the powers innate in the Universe, as part of the nurturing one is receiving, the picture changes radically.

To adequately perceive our true nature, our psychological and social potential, we need to factor in our interrelatedness. Without properly locating ourselves in the context of the unfolding Universe it can be difficult to access the qualities that convey fully our possibilities. We are truly lost, cut off from a vital source that is positively vibrating with energy, potential, and creativity. We act like orphans, left alone to create for ourselves a meaning and purpose for our lives.

We are not alone, however. Not truly. We are a part of something larger, something that to us seems ancient, something that has given us life, something that has imbued us (whether we know it or not) with its qualities. As a result, those qualities lie within us. They are a part of our potential, the part of human potential that remains untapped, even largely unexplored, at least by modern humankind. We are social animals. We are products of an evolutionary process, of a Universe that is sociable, which has relied upon cooperation and collaboration to create life.

What we must dare, in the near future, is not likely to be attempted without experiencing that we are surging with the momentum of a bigger body. This is our truest nature. To fully realize our own humanity, to overcome the obstacles that we our-selves have created, we need only rely upon that with which we have been endowed, the capacity to interact with each other for the sake of the whole. What promises to emerge is a more confident, more mature human species.

Conclusion

The Universe was a sociable place from the beginning. After the initial burst of energy that set this soon-to-be enormous Cosmos underway, there were protons, neutrons and electrons flying freely around. Neutrons are notoriously short-lived, lasting about 10 min-utes, unless they are able to partner up. In the early moments after the great exploding into existence, the components of existence scrambled to make alliances. This initial burst of energy then was accompanied by a burst of relationship activity. This set a pattern of sociability, which until just recently was ignored by the reductionis-tic eyes of science. Now we know that the Universe, in fact the whole process of evolution, has been an erotic dance, a coupling process of enormous magnitude, gracious subtlety, and enduring magnetism.

Unlike the cold, forbidding and barren vastness where our exis-tence is some random circumstance that is bound to be snuffed out by equally random inevitabilities, there is a pattern of relationship that generates the emergence of life. This is our real legacy, a modus operandi that relies upon mutual attraction, cooperation, and the emergence of ever more functional novelty. We have overlooked this creative thrust too long. It is time to consider how our worldview, choices and lives are altered when we consider the possibility that being connected, and connecting, is not only how we got here, but how we optimize our presence in this cosmic dance.

CHAPTER 2

☙

Evolution in Living Systems

This spontaneous emergence of order at critical points of instability is one of the most important concepts of the new understanding of life.
— Fritjof Capra

This, then, is Gaia's dance — the endless improvisation and elaboration of the same elegantly simple steps into the ever-changing awesomely beautiful and complex being of which we are the newest feature.
— Elizabet Sahtouris

Introduction

The endowment we receive does not end with what is going on in the Universe. It is more personal than that. In the following pages we will look at how the ceaseless thrust of the Universe, through evolution, transformed "inanimate" matter into living substance, into complex life forms like you and me. It is a miraculous story, one that took millennia to unfold and is fraught with many obstacles, suspense, and uncertainty. It is a fitting beginning for a species that has been endowed with enormous possibility. To truly understand our possibilities, our untapped social potential, it is important to see how we, you and I, are the recipients of this 13-billion-year-old legacy.

Evolution, as stated before, began right at the very beginning. Even before life, as we usually define it, came onto the scene, it appears that the conditions that would enable life were evolving. No scientist can explain this. This has led to religious assertions of purposeful creation and intelligent design, assertions which, if they were to prevail, would seem to remove the mystery that makes this legacy so compelling. Science offers some insight into the how of evolution but offers little regarding the why. It has added some of the puzzle pieces, and they reveal what we need to know: we are not accidents. In fact, as the evidence comes in it becomes clearer and clearer that the process of evolution seems to be reciprocal and relational, that we are co-evolving with our environment.

The claim that humanity might play a role in the evolution of the Cosmos is an audacious one. Were it not for the fact that new science is emerging that points in this direction, one would be loath to suggest anything that would aid this species' apparent narcissism. What makes this story so compelling, and this claim so likely to lead to a new more balanced perspective, is the level of mutuality involved. I hope by the end of this chapter that the actual level of relationship, of interdependence, involved in the evolutionary process will make clear that our best chance to actualize our species' potential lies in aligning ourselves in relationship with evolution.

Evolution in the Pre-biotic Era

The Earth existed for a billion years before any forms of life emerged. This prolonged period of time was anything but inactive. The Earth cooled and developed a solid crust. The first rocks appeared. Carbon combined with other elements to form a great variety of chemical compounds. There were long periods of rain that created vast bodies of surface water. Volcanic activity slowed. The atmosphere settled down. The Earth bore little resemblance to the world we know now, this was before it was terra-formed by life. Still, evolution was working slowly to create the conditions that would lead to the emergence of life.

Science cannot agree upon the exact nature of how animate life emerged from the inanimate chemical environment that prevailed on the early Earth, but most scientists believe that there was a form of pre-biotic evolution that took place. The exact mechanism is a matter of much scientific speculation and laboratory research. The speculations are all based on the notion that basic chemistry and physics can account for the advent of life.

One theory that is getting widespread attention holds that bubbles formed naturally as a result of the combination of chemical conditions and a restless environment. By providing a rudimentary membrane, these bubbles became a kind of microenvironment that protected and allowed special chemical unions or reactions to take place inside. This resulted in the formation of the first complex chemical systems capable of growth and development. Eventually it is likely that the conditions arose which generated the first protocell, capable of minimal life.

All that was left was the evolution of proteins, nucleic acids, and the genetic code. These developments remain a scientific mystery. The chemical networks that grew out of pre-biotic evolution are poorly understood. They await the development of a better understanding of non-linear dynamics to shed further light upon the exact processes that led to life. Suffice it to say that pre-biotic evolution took place, which involved chemical interactions enduring enough that patterns of relationship took place. These patterns of relationship then became the building blocks that supported later, more complex, patterns. The emergence of life followed.

The Early Biotic World of Bacteria

Scientists cannot agree about whether several lines of protocells occurred in different times and places, but they do seem to agree that they all gave way to a supercell that was the single cell that is the progenitor of all the Earth's life forms. This cell, according to Humberto Maturana and Francisco Varela must have been autopoetic, "self-making," enough that it spawned what would amount to a completely new era of life. It is important to note here that the dawn of the Bacterial Age, which was to last for 2 billon years, was an emergent event. Life was a novelty, a qualitatively different phenomenon than anything that had come before, an expression of chemical relationships plus a mysterious new quality that, as yet, cannot be explained by science.

Emergence-born, Life proliferated, and re-shaped the environment of the Earth so that it became even more hospitable to life. During the following two billion years, bacteria, starting as single-celled creatures, learned all the tricks that complex life forms like us would need to survive and thrive. Bacteria learned and invented as they evolved. They transformed the Earth's environment. They practiced, and perfected, the most important coping mechanism of all. Every subsequent life form to this day relies upon "coupling" with its environment for its survival. This strategy, as we shall see, is essential to the process of evolution, to life's resilience, and reflects the basic inter-dependence that permeates nature.

This coupling is important enough to our story that we should spend a moment to fully understand it as a phenomenon. Coupling here refers to a close relationship between an organism and its environment. One that is so close that any perturbation in the environment generates a response in the organism, a response that is unpredictable to an outside observer, but that is consistent with the pattern of organization of the organism. The organism's response then impacts and shapes environment. What occurs is a mutually reciprocal relationship that leads to the changing of both organism and environment. In essence, they co-evolve toward greater and greater alignment. This kind of cooperation is one of the primary characteristics of evolution, a trait we overlook at our own peril.

Bacterial life is amazing! In the two billion years while they transformed the planet, these single-celled creatures also invented the manual of cooperation. Bacteria went so far in their drive to couple with the Earth's environment that they developed a method for sharing their DNA. Some scientists have likened this feat of cooperation to the World Wide Web. Bacteria exchanged genetic information whenever they interacted, thus allowing widely dispersed organisms access to the latest genetic innovations. This cooperation made it possible for bacteria to rapidly adapt to their environment. This characteristic makes bacteria, even today, one of the fastest, most thoroughly adaptive organisms we know. Bacterial resistance to our arsenal of pharmaceutical drugs is a continuing problem that vexes medical scientists.

The Bacterial Age saw single-celled organisms, called Prokaryots, invent all the biological capabilities that would later make the diversity and profusion of life possible. In addition to transforming the Earth's environment, Prokaryots developed a means for sharing genetic information, a kind of re-combinate biological technology and photosynthesis. They were so successful in their life strategies that they created an ecological crisis even more pervasive than today's global warming crisis.   Here's how it happened.

The early atmosphere of the Earth was primarily composed of carbon dioxide. Prokaryotic cells thrived on it. The only problem was that they were so successful at adapting to the Earth's environments that they proliferated into every ecological niche. Their success, like ours, created an environmental problem. The end result of their metabolism produced a waste product that was toxic to all life forms: oxygen.

Oxygen is a highly unstable gas. The success of the Prokaryots transformed the atmosphere, filling it with oxygen, and threatening all life on the planet's surface. This atmospheric crisis created an imbalance in the relationship between life and its environment that threatened the extinction of all life, an early termination of the experiment of life.

Bacteria probably died by the billions, but they also found a new and innovative way to capitalize on this self-generated change in their environment. Through a process of cooperation and emergence now referred to as symbiosis, Prokaryots joined forces with each other and formed multi-celled organisms that were capable of respiration, the conversion of oxygen into vital energy. This opened a whole new stage in the evolution of life. Eukaryots, or nucleated cells, soon took over the evolutionary stage.

The complex organisms that were to follow would not exist were it not for this self-generated crisis. As we shall see, cooperation leading to the emergence of a more functional and complex pattern that solves self-generated problems, is a recurring theme in the evolutionary process. It occurs whenever re-organization is needed, be that at the level of organisms, psyches, relationships, communities, or large cultures. This is a way that evolution works, a way that can offer us guidance and surcease as we face the self-generated crises of our times.

Evolution in Complex Life

The bacterial solution to the ecological crisis posed by an oxygen-rich atmosphere set the stage for the rise of complex life, although it didn't happen overnight. Over time, Eukaryots took the advantages of cooperation to creative new heights. Evolution played this new theme out, as Eukaryots, nucleated cells, formed new syndicates of more complex cooperation and organisms with specialized capabilities began to emerge. Like their single-celled ancestors, they, too, coupled with their environments, and took the process of co-evolution even further.

Soon, to make a geologically long story short, the Earth was populated by a host of complex organisms that were resiliently coupled

with their environment and the other organisms that now made up
that environment. The success of single organisms depended upon
the success of the other creatures that they shared their ecosystem
with. In this way there were linkages that resulted in complex adaptive systems, or networks. This formed a whole, which we would
call an ecosystem, where the well-being of the whole ecosystem is
intricately interwoven with the well-being of its parts, the creatures
that make-up the ecosystem.

Thus, as we shall see, the relationship between each level of
organism, from nucleated cell to more complex organism, or organism to eco-system, and even eco-system to more complex regional or
planetary environment, is a relationship between parts and wholes.
We'll return to this pattern later on, but it is important now to see
how interdependently linked to everything else life is. It is all a
by-product of relationship. This is a hallmark of evolution, a hallmark we have failed to heed in our psychological orientation. As a
result, we live lives impeded by unnecessary anxiety and we suffer
from un-actualized potential.

Complex organisms, through a process of cooperation called
"symbiogenesis" by biologist Lynn Margulis, soon occupied the
planet's ecological niches. They formed a matrix of ecosystems,
which were so tightly coupled with the Earth's environments that
they formed a resilient whole. This supersystem of interdependent
relationships was thus able to survive major catastrophes and the
mass extinctions that followed. Life took a licking at the hands of
cosmic events but used each circumstance to its creative advantage.
As we shall see, the combination of diversity and its paradoxical
opposite, unity, made the living systems of the Earth not only highly
resilient and adaptable, but very creative.

And as years passed by the millions, and the dinosaurs were
wiped out by the collision of Earth with some smaller interstellar
body, our mammalian ancestors emerged. They took the multi-cel-
lular endowment into new creative realms. Hominids arrived on
the scene relatively recently. With us, nature has crafted a multi-cel-
lular being with differentiated organs and the emergent property
of consciousness. Not the ordinary consciousness of pattern recognition that exists everywhere in nature, but with the capacity for
self-reflection.

The Biology of Being Human

So we are left to reflect not only upon the fact that we exist, but that we seem to exist for some evolutionary purpose. Each of us is composed of some 75 trillion cells, cells that cooperate with each other so well that they require none of the emergent self-awareness we are gifted with. Nature has endowed us with bodies that are so finely crafted, so exquisitely complex and integrated that we do not even fully understand our own biology. We know this much, however. Nobody exists without the coordinated effort of a whole community of smaller organisms. Furthermore, all of this coordinated effort generates something extraordinary, a kind of consciousness that we have not found anywhere else in nature.

Why? We don't really know. All we do know is that the finely crafted meshworks we call our bodies are far more advanced than we are. We don't understand them. We can't even replicate their capabilities. And yet, we are endowed with them. Only recently have we begun to look at the cooperative genius that our bodies demonstrate at every moment. Science has been mired down in a worldview dominated by a fascination for the mechanism. This has recently begun to give way to a new scientific interest in the organism, the way nature works, the practices of life itself, which has led to a focus upon how life, including the human body, is organized. Suddenly, the qualities of relationship, cooperation, and mutuality are not only in vogue, but are offering compelling new insights about the evolutionary process and about our prospects as a species.

Our bodies have a lot to teach us. I'm not talking about the information about how our lived experience is enfolded in our emotions, although that, too, is important. I'm suggesting that the biology of being human has a lot to teach us. If we as a gathering of individuals could do something like what our cells have done, we would have new confidence that together we could socially generate some possibilities for our evolutionary success. What do I mean? Let's take a quick look at cellular life in the human body. By doing so, I can demonstrate what I mean and simultaneously show how evolution has endowed us with what we need.

We take this brief excursion into cellular life not because cells provide us a prescription for how to live, but to show the social potential we are endowed with. If we move closer to these capabilities, we may discover a variety of options that have not existed previously. The cells of the body have had billions of years to perfect their social skills. We can learn from them, but we would be mistaken to believe we should, or could, be just like them.

The quality that most accurately characterizes the cells of the human body is how deeply connected they all are. They are so thoroughly coupled with each other that it is amazing that they retain their own differentiated identity, skills, and capabilities. While every cell of the body works for the welfare of the whole (coupling), and through molecular messengers communicates with every other cell, they continue to function uniquely. Each can perform unique tasks and combines with others to create innovative ways to accomplish mutual benefits.

Cells are flexible, constantly adapting to the environment and to each other, never forgetting who they are and the functions they serve. They are also very efficient, utilizing the smallest possible energy (typically a cell stores only about 3 seconds worth of food and energy within its cell walls). They exist for each other, recognizing and giving to each other. They spend their lives maintaining the integrity of all the other cells and the superorganism they make up. They reproduce to pass along all their knowledge, skills and experiences, and they die to protect the body.

Every cell in the body is interdependent with every other. This interdependence, this dance of relationships, this symphony of cooperation is how we are composed. We exist. We can look around and think about our existence, even wonder at our purpose in being, because we are party to, and expressions of, the constancy of this dance. To maximize our potential, to ensure our ongoing existence, to live fully, we need to dance along. We each have steps of our own, but it is time to value our partners in the dance and the dance itself as much as we do the freedom to dance the way we want to.

The human body is a compelling and complex organism. It offers each of us a chance to experience life. And now, thanks to some scientists, it offers us guidance about our own possibilities. The human body is the product of billions of years of evolutionary endeavor and thus offers us a key to the processes of evolution. It can serve as a daily reminder that evolution moves not only through us, but as us. Like the cells of our own bodies we would do well to organize ourselves accordingly.

Cooperation Throughout the Ages

From our current vantage point it seems improbable that we have come so far without recognizing the basic cooperation that underlies all things. Indigenous cultures have known this for a long time. But the scientific legacy handed down to us was based on a worldview that, not surprisingly, was only partial.

That worldview came to prominence when science was harnessed to the rising industrial age. Machines and their capabilities fascinated humanity. Everything changed, work could be done tirelessly, faster, and more efficiently than ever before. The mechanism, which seemingly promised freedom from the drudgery of repetitive work, and the possibility of new forms of wealth and ease, became the central metaphor for organizing all human activity. This worldview solidified with notions of "survival of the fittest" and the advent of a competitive capitalist market. The individual and the machine became the core fixations of this worldview.

We are still living in the shadows of these fixations. They have served us. That story is still unfolding. And what I want to highlight here is the fact that the evolutionary emphasis upon cooperation went unnoticed, not because it wasn't happening, but because we were not prepared to see it. Recently, some parts of science, the parts mostly interested in living systems, have made it possible for us to see that the Universe, and life itself, functions more like an organism than as a mechanism.

This change in viewpoint is amazing and necessary for our survival. Whereas before everything was composed of parts, now we see wholes. While mechanisms need to be taken apart to discover how they work, organisms must be viewed as wholes in order to discover how they work. The focus is thus on the relationships between the parts of organisms, which most frequently are smaller organisms, and the larger whole that they comprise. This reveals the connections between organisms and their larger living environment. Suddenly relationships, processes of interaction, the dynamics of cooperation, and the essential interdependence of all things become visible.

With these dynamics now visible it has become possible to look back at the process of evolution and see the indispensable sociability of creation. Remember, evolution started at the beginning with the basic elements seeking partners. Along the way, interactions created new opportunities. Protogalaxies formed as elements coalesced. Stars were born, thrived, and exploded, seeding space with heavier molecules. Masses cooled into planets and solar systems bound by attractive forces. The Earth cooled and chemicals interacted themselves into rudimentary life forms. Life thrived by coupling with its environment, and co-evolution became the principle factor in the resilience of life. Complex organisms emerged in response to a self-generated crisis, taking cooperation to creative new heights and eventually this cooperation became so fine-tuned and nuanced that complex awareness emerged.

It is now evident that we owe our being to the interactivity of the evolutionary process. We are the products of a social Universe. We are the living extensions of the restless life force of that Universe, played out through evolution. Sociability, to some degree, defines our being. Thus, we can ill-afford to ignore our social nature, our potential for cooperation, and the possibilities that could emerge if we simply collaborate.

Emergence

From out of nowhere, nothingness, the Universe emerged. So it was in the beginning, and so it is now. Life, a qualitatively new phenomenon, emerged from chemical interactions. Complex life emerged from a crisis generated by the success of bacteria. Our mammalian ancestors emerged from the planetary crisis that killed off the great reptiles that had dominated for so long. The evolutionary process, noted for its long periods of stability, has also seen extraordinary periods of punctuated equilibrium when variations appeared via natural selection, and brand-new life forms, with astonishing capabilities, emerged quickly as if from nowhere. All along, the evolutionary process has made use of the mystery of emergence to further the unfolding of life.

We are examples of that mysterious process. Science has not yet accounted for the emergence of the complex, self-reflective, consciousness that distinguishes us (as far as we know) as the self-aware animal. We are recipients of the benefits of emergence, and we are expressions of it. Later on, when we look at how human consciousness develops, we will see how emergence continues to take us beyond ourselves. But for now, it is important to note that emergence has shaped our destiny as a species, and how it has been an outcome of creative interactivity.

Relationships seem to call forth, from the between, a kind of creative potential that we cannot account for. We have chosen to ignore this happenstance, perhaps because we cannot understand it, but more likely because we cannot control it. Like no mechanism we know, evolution defies us and asks us to forgo our insistence that the Universe, that Life, operates on terms we understand, rather than on Life's terms that remain a mystery to us. Like it or not, we must learn to adapt to a reality that contains emergence, and we must align ourselves so that our relationship with it is generative.

Natural Therapy

The issue of alignment, I have found, turns out to be of utmost importance. For life, like the ceaseless Universe it was born in, surges like a rising tide through each and every life, delivering us to our places of limitation in the service of evolution. We need to align with this movement to actualize our potential, to become the purveyors of the evolutionary process that we are, to join as partners in the dance of creation.

It is no exaggeration to say that our actual well-being depends on this. Part of our natural inheritance is the ceaselessness of creation; the way evolution touches each of our lives in an ongoing way. Because of our individualistic bent we have failed to perceive the operations of evolution as it sweeps us toward the limitations we like to pretend we don't have. We live in an age where psychotherapy has been an agent of the predominant culture, where the movement of evolution sweeping into our lives and unbalancing us is viewed as an illness, as something "wrong" instead of something "right." This disheartens us, perpetuates our isolation, and disables our capacity to work creatively and cooperatively with what wants to transform us.

We are the recipients of what developmental psychologist Robert Kegan calls "natural therapy." We have not been simply left here to fend exclusively for ourselves; we are the recipients of evolution's ceaseless tide. It is gradually moving us toward a more complex and functional consciousness. This movement is inherently de-stabilizing; it upsets us, alters our lives, changes our outlook, and runs us smack up against our limitations and discrepancies in our world-view. As a rule, we don't like it. But that is mostly because we live in a cultural time frame that views all of these indications of relationship with larger processes as failures of the individual to adjust, as deficiencies to be masked and overcome.

Yes, we are confronted by hard choices, by difficult transitions, but it is usually in service of evolution's need to evolve us, to make us better agents of creation. So, we are never really left alone; we are accompanied by a powerful agent of change that not only bids us to alter our lives but provides us the raw materials to do so. There is usually, however, resistance to the movement of life. This resistance is the cause of much of our pain. Life doesn't usually adhere to our plans, to cultural ideals, even to our religious beliefs, and then we are left to pick up the pieces. It doesn't help us that the prevailing belief is that we brought this difficulty upon ourselves and that it is an indication of our inadequacy.

Nature seeks to change us. Evolution never lets us alone. Like it or not, we are coupled with our environment. That means not only that we can change the atmosphere with greenhouse gases, but that the larger processes of the Universe (such as climate change), of evolution, of life, influence us and alter our way of being in favor of greater alignment and richer relations. This is natural therapy. We have largely ignored it. Or we have chosen to view it with suspicion, turning it into a weakness or illness, instead of seeing it as part of the legacy of rich relations with which we have been endowed.

Natural therapy is an important phenomenon that deserves more attention. Chapter 12 will give a much more detailed look at how the processes of evolution break through the lives of individuals, relationships, and social systems. The awareness of our part in the Universe's evolutionary drive is one of the distinctions of a psychology of interdependence. That chapter will make clear that because it responds to the evolutionary opportunities that life unfailingly presents, this orientation is a strength-based, non-pathologizing approach to psychological health. Natural therapy is viewed as a gift and respected as a way-shower. For now, however, suffice it to say that a part of what we have been bequeathed is the constant nurturing demand of the evolutionary process. As sure as our hearts are being beaten for us, we are being grown by life for purposes that remain a mystery to us. We would do well to cooperate.

Implications for Psychology

The ceaselessness of the Universe has never been factored into our psychological picture. Humanity, at least in Western cultures and those they have influenced, has seen itself as separate from Nature and separate from the animating forces of evolution. Because we did not expect it, we have not been aware of the sociability of the Universe. Science was primarily focused on the mechanics of life until recently. It took everything apart to see how it worked. The worldview that has prevailed has blinded us to the wonders of relatedness.

Psychology has largely participated in this myopic vision. The psyche has been conceptualized as atomized, isolated, skin-encapsulated, a singularity. For years the individual alone has been the focus of all of the field's attention. As a culture we have benefited enormously through our single-minded attention to the freedom and autonomy of the individual. But, like our bacterial ancestors, our success has backfired and now threatens our well-being, and even our viability as a species. Our current crisis requires a more balanced and complex approach.

Such an approach does not require us to go back to the drawing board. Rather, like the natural therapy that is constantly knocking on our doors, we are merely required to incorporate a previously unseen and misunderstood dimension of our nature. We are interdependent beings. We are products of a social Universe, so much so that our bodies function as communities. We are each interwoven into a matrix of relationships that extends from the quantum level to the vast reaches of space, a matrix that both supports us and asks things of us. We have wrongly assumed we could have one without the other.

Our species' success has brought us to an age of new challenges and new opportunities. To make the best use of the opportunities we have, we need only remember that the evolution of life has followed the same patterns all along. We must turn our gaze to relationship, to collaboration, to the synergetic relations that evoke new, more functional ways of being. We must re-learn how to interdepend. We must stop looking askance at everything that knocks us off balance and give up some of our precious control, so that we can be transformed by the larger (and smaller) systems we depend upon for our well-being.

Psychology needs to change. This doesn't mean throwing away the hard-earned wisdom of the past. It does mean transcending the focus on the individual and incorporating that focus into a more complex view of life that takes into account the interrelatedness of all things. We are at the dawn of a new time. We can ill-afford to ignore the reality that is emerging before, and between, us. It is time to value our social nature for what it is, the legacy of life, the key to the door of the between and what waits to emerge there.

Conclusion—Evolution in the Uterus

Our perspective is shifting. As we look more closely at evolution, at the life we are currently living, there is accruing evidence that things are different than what was assumed. What has always passed as conventional knowledge, about who we are, about genuine healthy-mindedness, about our social potential, about human potential in general, is giving way. This is good. Natural therapy is at work with lessons we need to know now if we are going to come of age as a species. But it is also de-stabilizing, anxiety-provoking, and just plain scary. Nature is enlightening us about our place in the larger scheme of things.

This shift in perspective is coming now in many forms. Global warming is changing the climate. I believe that the climate change is both an external and an internal event, it is the beginning of a shift in our respect for the complex, living inheritance with which we have been endowed. I am referring here, not only to this marvelous blue planet, but to our own nature as living embodiments of all of evolution's creativity, strength and resilience.

Oddly, it is just at this moment that neuro-scientists are finding, and further exploring, the structures in the brain that confirm the role of sociability in our species development. In Daniel Goleman's book, *Social Intelligence*, he reviews the growing body of neuro-scientific evidence that shows that we are not only a social species, but that our sociability played a role in the evolution of the complex consciousness that characterizes us. We are extensions of the sociability of the Universe, extensions of a reliance upon relationship that characterizes evolution.

Perhaps the most striking example of our evolutionary inheritance is what takes place as we make the journey from a single cell to the human form in the womb. In the course of nine months every human being makes a journey through roughly the last billion years of evolutionary development. Starting as single cells, we divide up until we become a colony of cells like those found in the early seas. Soon our cells differentiate into more specialized cells and we become multicellular creatures, opening the door to more complexity. Slowly, surrounded by the warm, salty, amniotic sea, we re-trace many of the steps of evolution. We develop a head, tail, and the gill slits of a fish. Later the embryonic journey includes resembling the embryos of frogs, chickens, pigs, and a host of other animal ancestors. Even after we lose the tail and form arms and legs, the human embryo is hard to distinguish from other animal embryos. Finally, in the last few months, we grow a human-sized brain and we begin developing distinctly human features.

Perhaps Elizabet Sahtouris says it best when she summarizes all of this movement in this way: "How fascinating that this memory of the Gaian life dance is relived by each of us, reminding us of just who we are, where we came from, how we are related to all other species and to the whole dance of life…"

This reminder is fixed in each of our lives. It places us within a context of life that reveals just how much we are extensions of Life. This reminder is the memory of Life itself playing out as each one of us. It is time to bring this memory back from our cosmological unconscious, through our scientific acumen, to an awareness that as the sons and daughters of Life, of a Universe that throbs with creative energy, we partake in all of this profusion. We are evolution incarnate and our lives are deeply embedded in a matrix of relationships in which much more is possible than we currently imagine.

CHAPTER 3

❧

Synergetic Relationships

True innovation occurs when things are put together for the first time that have been separate.

—ARTHUR KOESTLER, *Beyond Reductionism*

We have the intellectual capacity to understand the cosmos and our place in it. We are in fact the legatees of an awe-inspiring history, and the golden thread of that history has been synergy. Synergy sustains us, but it also presents us with a plethora of opportunities...

—PETER CORNING, *Nature's Magic*

Introduction

Reality isn't what it used to be. It is disorienting, and it is also free-ing. It has taken us three or four decades to begin to believe that human actions are disturbing the balance of the atmosphere. The climate is changing. As I mentioned earlier, I think there is an internal dimension to this event. We are changing along with the climate. As we recognize our impact upon the climate, we will be recognizing the climate's impact upon us.

Will it take us another thirty or forty years to recognize the degree to which we are linked with Life? I don't think so, at least I hope not. The scientific evidence is starting to show us now that reality, that Life, like the Universe, is a multileveled phenomenon, and that at every level relationship provides the glue that holds it all together and makes it coherent.

So it is that we turn to synergy. For synergy demonstrates just what a sociable place we find ourselves within. No attempt to describe the necessity for a change in our psychological orientation, no effort to place an emphasis upon relationship, can hope to prevail in our world of individual striving without recognizing how much synergy forms the backbone of evolution. "Synergy," as system scientist Peter Corning says, "is all around us and within us; we are completely dependent on it. We often take it for granted or fail to appreciate its gravitas, its weightiness." We can no longer afford to do so.

Defining Synergy

Actually, awareness of synergy has been around a lot longer than I realized when I first started this project. My own awareness grew when I found that a Greek word, *synergos*, was the root for our current term. Apparently, the stereotypical meaning that is given to synergy, "the sum of the whole is greater than the sum of the parts," goes back to Aristotle. Through his definition of synergy, the first biologist might have inadvertently contributed to making synergy so hard to see.

My awareness of the essential synergies that shape our day-to-day realities grew more precise when I recognized that synergetic effects came in many forms. I'll give some common examples in a moment. But for the sake of this discussion, let's assume that synergy is not the effects, "the sum that is greater," but the relationship that exists between "the parts." I am interested in the effects because it is those effects that have so enriched our lives, but I reserve the term "emergence" for these effects. What is greater is what emerges; it is a product of the relationship, but not the same as the relationship.

Synergy, composed of the prefix "syn," meaning "with," really refers to two (or more) things, processes, or occurrences happening together. These form the parts; the whole that emerges is an unpredictable product of the relationship between wholes that do not start out being parts. These wholes become parts through the emergence of a larger whole that exists on a new level. Synergy, then, is the relationship between entities that, because of the quality of their relationship, become parts of something larger that emerges on a new level.

Relating can be highly synergetic, or low in synergy. Synergy, therefore, is also a way of describing the qualities in a relationship that produce the likelihood of a greater or lesser whole. A good example of this difference is one that most people have experienced. Some groups generate positive synergy; the way the members interact makes the group smarter than any member alone would be. Conversely, the way group members interact can create a negative synergy, which makes the IQ of the group lower than any given member. Thus, synergy describes a qualitative characteristic of a relationship that results in larger-than-the- sum-of-the-parts effects.

Typical synergistic effects are:

- whirlpools, which are produced by the combination of gravity, water and air pressure and rotational or centrifugal forces;
- salt, which is composed of two toxic substances that when combined become edible;
- alloys, which are combined metals that have characteristics no single metallic constituent has;
- medicines, some of which when combined with other medications are made more effective or more toxic;
- recipes, which often combine the same ingredients in different proportions, or add or delete certain ingredients for different effects.

All of these effects depend upon these substances or processes combining through relationship with each other. No relationship, no effects. This is the golden thread that is referred to in the quote above. This golden thread reveals itself at every stage in the evolution of life. It also runs through human biology, cultural development, and our present tense un-actualized social potential.

Synergy at the Beginning

We have already described how sociable the early Universe was. What may be less evident was the role of synergy. From the combination of quarks and gluons, to the pairing of the neutron and the proton, synergy added capabilities that didn't exist before these relationships began. Matter itself, the essential ingredient for all material development, emerged from the energy event that began everything because of synergy. Even gravity, the mutual attraction of everything to everything else, is a synergistic effect of the relationship, the mutual attraction, between protons and electrons.

What we know now, thanks to the new science that has been done in recent years, is that the physical Universe is a multi-leveled phenomenon that has emerged level-by-level thanks to synergies that took place at each level. What we need to know is that the sociability of the Universe is directly associated with synergy. The process of creatively combining different, formerly separate, things is the primary means that the Universe, through evolution, has used to proliferate.

Synergy and Living Systems

In earlier chapters we talked about the fact that no one knows for sure how life began. Science has not yet been able to penetrate that mystery. But every scenario that has any currency amongst modern-day scientists suggests that it was through the combined effects of chemical reactions, perhaps in the specialized environment of a bubble that life began. In other words, early life was an emergent, synergistic effect of the way these chemicals interacted. Synergy, the quality of that early set of interactions, played a role in the beginnings of life!

Synergy has also been present throughout the ascent of life. It was mainly synergy between chemical systems that allowed single-celled organisms to emerge. When these organisms coupled with their environment and co-evolution began, it was synergy that played a major role in determining which of these combinations cooperated the best, thus winning the competitive advantage that made the natural selection cut. More obvious is the role synergy played when bacterial success formed the first major environmental crisis created by, and faced by, life. It was synergy, created by the cooperation of formerly separate single-celled organisms, which generated the emergence of respiration and complex life. Multicelled organisms relied upon synergy for their very existence and employed it as they coupled with the environment and continued the dance of co-evolution.

There is reason to believe, as Peter Corning, Ph.D. advances in his Synergetic Hypothesis, that synergy, or cooperation, played a major role in the processes of evolution. This new formulation of Darwinian Theory posits that natural selection also favored organisms that won competitive advantage through their synergetic ability to cooperate. In this formulation of evolution, cooperation or synergy existed side-by-side with competition and played as major a role as competition was once assumed to have played. This is just one of the major changes that is taking place in the scientific worldview. It is no longer heresy to talk about cooperation, group selection, or other forms of relationship dynamics.

Is this just a form of wishful thinking? Does the desire to see relationship everywhere, to believe that connections exist between the larger processes of Life and our basic human concerns, simply obscure the truth? No. There is a simple test for the presence of synergy: just subtract one ingredient. If the absence of a single part collapses the whole, then we know synergy is happening. Apply this test to all that has been referred to thus far and you can see that without the right combination of chemicals interacting in the right kind of environment you couldn't have rudimentary life. Similarly, complex life required just the right set of organisms to create a viable life-form, one that could withstand the rigors of a pretty hostile environment. We still don't know how all of these relationships evolved, but the fact that relationship was involved is no longer a matter of dispute.

We know a good deal of the rest of the story. Complex life formed synergetic bonds with the environment. This carried the co-evolutionary process even further. Eco-systems emerged from these synergetic bonds. These complex adaptive systems brought together the diversity of a variety of organisms that were tightly bound through coupling into a network of highly synergistic relationships. In essence, the synergy of formerly separate organisms generated the emergence of more complex multi-celled organisms. Then these more complex organisms coupled, forming synergistic bonds with the environment and the other lifeforms in it. Out of this synergy emerged eco-systems, super-organisms capable of greater feats of energy efficiency, resilience, and adaptability that none of the constituent organisms could achieve alone.

Over the intervening millennia these eco-systems synergistically bonded with the environment and formed bioregions that were organismically complex, diverse while being very resilient. Thus, this rich network of interacting parts created a super whole, a living world that was capable of absorbing the blows of ice ages, meteors and volcanoes. Approximately 95% of the species that once populated the Earth are now extinct. The biosphere, however, remains intact and as richly diverse and resilient as ever, because of the synergies, the relationships that bind organisms one to another, and the overall linkage of each organism to its environment.

We know that this rich pastiche of lifeforms gained complexity and new capabilities over time. This resulted in the emergence of organisms with differentiated organs, and specialized capabilities. Nature was the first to employ the division of labor for the paradoxical specialized benefits that could be derived from re-combining labor synergistically to create effects that had never been seen before.

Eventually this resulted in the ascent of our hominid ancestors. There is reason to believe that the consciousness that gradually distinguished our hominid ancestors from the other great apes was a result of the synergies created by the use of language and a gradually complexifying social repertoire. In fact, Daniel Goleman, in his groundbreaking book *Social Intelligence*, asserts that "those who would say that social intelligence amounts to little more than general intelligence applied to social situations...might do better to reason the other way around: to consider that general intelligence is a derivative of social intelligence." In other words, the interactions of our ancestors and the bonds they formed with one another created synergies that most likely accounted for the emergence of the self-reflective intelligence that renders humanity unique, as far as we know, amongst nature's kind.

At every level of the evolutionary journey we can see that synergy, or relationship, played an integral role. No different than the gluons, quarks, neutrons, and protons that combined to make matter and gravity, we rely on mutual attraction and synergistic relations for the social surround within which we thrive. Like the chemical relations that spawned life, we rely upon a kind of bio-chemical synergy for our reproductive relations. And just as bacteria ensured their survival by cooperating and learning to share labor and other capabilities by forming more complex lifeforms, we live in cities and rely upon social and economic interactions for our well-being. Relationships, and particularly synergistic relationships, are essential to us as lifeforms and define our well-being and unique consciousness.

Synergy in the Human Body

We have already looked at the cellular community that makes up each human body. This community lives and functions mostly beneath our conscious awareness, but it is totally reliant upon synergy, the success of ongoing relations between individual cells and within the community as a whole. Synergy is the relationship quality that made it possible for the human super-organism to emerge. Even more amazingly, it is the coordination of some 75 trillion cells, through highly synergetic relations with the cells in other bodies, through the synergies of coordinated social interactions that created the conditions that made the emergence of complex consciousness possible.

Synergy in Human Relations

It is likely that what has defined human nature the most, what distinguishes humans from the other great apes, is not tool-making but the range of social coordination and meaningful interactions we are capable of. Language, a highly synergetic phenomenon, emerged from and abetted social coordination. Language is a form of synergy, a type of social coordination that allowed for a growing repertoire of complex social behaviors, which in turn created more complex meaning-making opportunities for the rapidly evolving human mind. Dan Goleman points out that after looking into the emerging field of social neuroscience, there is reason to believe that it is our social nature that accounts for our rare form of consciousness.

When one looks deeply at the role synergy has played in evolution, it is not surprising to see how central it is in the development of humanity. Neuroscience, with its new tools such as the functional MRI, is beginning to recognize how the human brain relies upon a certain quality of interaction for development. This reliance upon synergy for relatedness and connection extends from the development of the brain to that of human culture. At each level relationship is a big factor, a factor we can ill afford to keep ignoring as we do. Western psychology is the most individualistic-oriented approach to human meaning-making around today. It, too, needs to evolve, and this age, with its changing climate and cultures in conflict, is calling for an emergent new way of seeing the patterns that connect us one to another, and to the cultural and environmental surroundings within which we are embedded.

Up to this point we have stayed primarily within the realm of the objective; that is, how evolution has played within matter, from the formation of the basic elements to the human organism. Science is unveiling a Universe that has employed its own sociability to create an unsurpassed unity and diversity of cosmological events and processes, life-forms, and a rare (as far as we know) socially-spawned, complex self- reflective consciousness. For this spectacle we have science to thank, because this unfolding story of relationship forms the backdrop for all that follows.

To further the story of relationship's role in the development of humankind we need to look at the importance of synergy in the intersubjective realm. This is less easily done because the Western penchant for placing the individual in the pre-eminent role has obscured and distorted the role of mutually-created dynamics. Systems thinking, the way of seeing wholes instead of just parts, is still new. The systems viewpoint, which makes social systems (fields of interaction) visible, has been around for almost 70 years. It has been only relatively recently, however, that this vantage point has been applied to the intersubjective realm of human relations.

Every form of human relationship is subject to synergy. Families, marriages, organizations and cultures rise and fall based upon the kind of synergy they generate. What does this mean? Early in the last century, cultural anthropologist, Ruth Benedict, pointed out that some cultures were high-synergy cultures while others were low-synergy. She could see how social structures in various cultures impacted the culture's ability to produce true individuals who were not defined solely in cultural terms. Her definition of synergy, however, reflects the myopic individualistic bent of the times and is insufficient for our current formulation (more on that later). Nevertheless, she noticed that the quality of relationships typical of a culture had an impact upon those involved. This is true at whatever relationship level one looks.

The IQ of a group goes up or down based upon the interactions of its members. As we shall see, the ability to actualize both the human potential for individuation and the social potential of individuals embedded within a social system rise and fall based upon the quality of interactions that take place within a family, marriage, organization, or culture. We will look more closely at relationship behaviors and contexts later on, but suffice it now to simply say that relationship, and in particular, relationship quality, has a lot more impact upon the human venture than we have previously assumed.

Synergy and Emergence

Throughout the history of evolution, synergy has played an important role. We live in a Universe that is sociable, which has used relationship, the combination of formerly separate things, to create new, unexpected things. Just as the Universe seems to have emerged, becoming something out of nothingness, so it has used relationship to keep emerging. There is some kind of link between synergy and emergence. What is it?

Some scientists conflate the two, arriving at the idea that emergence equals synergy. I don't agree with them. As stated above, synergy is a term that describes a quality of relationship that increases the likelihood that something new can emerge, but not guaranteeing it, nor predicting exactly what will emerge.

Synergy, then, is a kind of relationship precursor. Certain high-quality interactions increase the probability that something new and innovative will emerge. What emerges is not just something new, but an entirely new level, some kind of new wholeness that was not thought to exist previously. How does this happen? We don't know yet. This is the provenance of theoretical physics, and no satisfactory explanation has yet come forth. There is a great deal of speculation about the primary conditions in the quantum realm, there is no theory that explains how quantum potential becomes a form of new, unpredictable wholeness.

All that we do know is that synergetic relationships seem to increase the likelihood of this event. We might think that this knowledge would be enough to alter the emphasis we continue to place on the individual, but this has not yet happened on a large scale. So our species' social potential still languishes un-actualized. Because it has the power to bring forth innovations, synergy is more than a value-added component of a corporate-merger strategy; it is an integral aspect of the evolutionary process. It is time for synergy and the relationship qualities it represents to become an essential ingredient in human relations.

Implications for Psychology

The time for a renewed interest in relationship is here. Not just because we have placed too much emphasis upon the individual—we do need extraordinary individuals—but because we cannot get to truly extraordinary individuals from here. There is a whole range of human potential that is largely unreachable because we try so hard to wring it out of the individual. It takes extraordinary relationships to produce truly extraordinary individuals.

What is extraordinary about human nature still lies largely untapped because we have chosen to ignore our own social nature. The synergies that have contributed to the multi-leveled Universe are inherent in our being. Much of our potential as individuals and as a species, is tied up in what cannot emerge because we have not really understood and honored our social capacities. We cannot afford to squander the opportunity presented to us by our own nature.

Synergy, and its ongoing role in the emergence of wholeness, shows us something of what we are capable of as social animals. But in order to make use of our own capacity we need to shift our focus. Perhaps equal to the Copernican shift from believing the Earth was the center of the Universe to realizing the Earth revolved around the Sun, we must now shift our focus from the individual being the apex (and focal point) of evolution to what exists between two (or more) beings. Our focus must shift from acting as if I, the one, own "my" life. We must make the shift away from the question "What does life have to give me?" We must move towards an inquiry like "I am alive, a living part of a greater whole. I am receiving the gift of life from that larger whole. I wonder what life asks of me?"

That latter question changes everything. With it life goes from being little more than a mall full of shops or an amusement park full of entertaining rides, to a mysterious presence that now asks something of us. With it we move from being a consumer passively engaged in shopping for a thrill or a bargain to being in an engagement with a challenging other. With it, it doesn't matter what state our credit is in, how much we make, or how educated we are—we are still confronted by something that wants something of us, of our being. Suddenly, we are in a relationship.

A fundamental part of this new psychological approach is based on the recognition that without relationship there is no synergy, no emergence. Living asks something of each of us. If we are prepared for a relationship with life and with the others we find living around us, then we can begin to bring ourselves to each other, to life, in ways that are synergetic, in ways that stir and liberate emergence.

One of the important characteristics that distinguishes a psychology of interdependence from traditional Western psychology is its recognition that larger processes of life exist, that we are linked to them, and that from time to time they ask something of us. That something usually has to do with evolving. Natural therapy takes place. Life alters our lives, and in so doing frequently introduces us to our limitations, attachments, and refusal to take more responsibility for ourselves. Life asks much of us and we usually don't like it. Rarely do we recognize it as something "good" and "right." Rather, we feel unbalanced and believe something is "wrong" with us, or our relationships, work situations, or locations.

What is often wrong is our orientation, the belief too often promulgated by traditional psychology that these troubles reflect only our shortcomings, deficits in our nurturing, or some other trauma. It is true that all of these things happen and hurt us, but they are not the only reasons we experience pain. Sometimes, more often than is currently recognized, we suffer because we are connected to the larger processes of life.

Why would these larger processes cause us pain? There are many possible reasons, but some common ones are that life wants more alignment, diversity, complexity, or unity of us and/or our relationships. Evolution is continuously surging through us, upsetting us, creating chaos in our well-ordered lives, or never letting us settle because our potential is so high and the Universe is restless. And, of course, our attitudes and beliefs about what is happening contribute to our suffering. The story we tell ourselves to explain our current or ongoing travails can reinforce and deepen our suffering.

That is a partial reason why this story, with its additional complexity, needs to be told. Pain is a part of life, it doesn't always mean something is wrong, in fact, more frequently than we imagine, it means something is right. Life is calling us to step into some additional potential, to discover more about our endowment. Sometimes our pain can become joy when we discover, through the difficulties of our own lives, the actual resources of liveliness we have inherited.

Up until now our ideas of healthy-mindedness have been primarily focused upon the needs and wants of the individual. This in itself is not bad. We have come a long way toward ensuring the rights and well-being of the individual. We still have further to go. Nature, the evolutionary process, thrives upon as much diversity as possible. But it also thrives on as much unity as possible.

Nature, the evolutionary process, has shown a strong propensity to favor, through natural selection, organisms that cooperate well, which are embedded in larger wholes and relate thoroughly. Synergy is the relationship process by which this happens. Nature has shown that it knows how to create, by combining the great diversity individuality has generated into innovative new wholes, organisms, and processes that forward evolution and enhance life's prospects. We can be willing or unwilling participants in this process of evolution. From the vantage point of a psychology of interdependence we will experience pain either way, but only our willing participation will lead to the possibility of new wholes and emerging joy.

Conclusion

Synergy is a part of our capacity, of our potential, a frequently too unused part. You would never know of our synergetic potential here in the West, where we suffer a high divorce rate, fractured families, an absence of community and a declining sense of civility. The litigiousness of our culture is not a product of trial lawyers, but of an over-emphasis upon individuals. We all too frequently don't trust each other. These are the by-products of rampant individualism unbalanced by the bonds of significant relationships. It is time for us to correct a pattern that has served us, but now presents us with a significant problem.

Our synergetic potential presents us a momentous opportunity. Improving our human-to-human relations will change the quality of our lives. Further improvements could lead to the emergence of innovative new ways of getting along, of making life more meaningful, of creating a future worth having for our grandchildren. Coupling more closely with our local ecosystems and with the global environment could generate myriad options that we sorely need as a species.

If we were to take seriously the universal application of relationship in the evolutionary process, we would turn toward each other instead of away. We would also recognize the value of the social and environmental surround we are embedded within. These changes would totally alter the human experiment, making it more sustainable, more congenial, and more meaningfully linked with the adventure of evolution. All of these changes are within our grasp. They are part of our natural expression, benefits of our natural inheritance. Moving toward each other, something we naturally do in crisis and disaster, will not come to us as easily in our everyday lives. But it is helpful to know that we are capable of this movement, that relating is part of our endowment, and that life is always moving forward as inexorably as the tide, combining separate beings into new, and innovative, wholes.

SECTION II
THE PATTERN THAT CONNECTS

❦

Take your well disciplined strengths
and stretch them
between two opposing poles
because
inside human beings
is where
God learns.

— RAINIER MARIE RILKE

SECTION II

ᭉ

The Pattern That Connects

Introduction

Making a departure from the past means entering a New World. Modern science has disclosed to us a world that differs significantly from the one Freud and his followers occupied. Where once it made sense to think of each human living in a mechanical world dominated by random forces, now we are beginning to realize there is very little that is random about our world, and that the order in the Universe is one of the things we have failed to take account of in our psychological considerations. Once vast indifferent distances separated humans from one another. Now, we find ourselves linked by previously unimagined patterns of connection.

It has taken a long time for science to recognize any pattern that connects. Some of the story I am about to tell is still in dispute scientifically. Just as there are scientists who dispute that global warming has a human cause, there are those who maintain the vision of a mechanical Universe where gigantic random forces determine everything. In some ways (we will see how later) living in a dynamic Universe, where there is a connection between our choices and the well-being of all things, is an anxiety-provoking thing.

To see the pattern that connects, and to recognize it personally in one's own life, is a daunting thing. One's sense of personal responsibility expands, along with the sense of being part of something, of belonging. The journey to this point, to recognizing and enjoying the pattern of connection that links us all, might seem like a desirable cakewalk, but in fact it has required that we humans embrace more complexity than we are used to. Connecting, when we have

ostensibly been separate so long, can be a fearful thing. This is especially true when connecting entails newfound complexity.

In the following chapters I focus attention upon the new picture
of human existence that is emerging. This emergence is as mysterious as those that have come before. Evolution is simultaneously
providing for us and pushing us. Alongside the recognition of how
connected we are with the larger processes of Life, we now have the
responsibility to settle ourselves down and discover the benefits of
fitting in. Life, as we shall see, provides for us, but also asks something of us. The pattern that connects, winds us into a 13 billion-year
dance, which requires that we find a sustainable rhythm so we can
continue to participate.

The Pattern That Connects

In the following chapters I intend to tell the story of how a new psychological orientation is emerging alongside a systems view of the
human project. What I mean is that systems thinking, looking at
life through the lens of wholes instead of the parts that have been
important to traditional science, discloses another way of making
sense of our prospects as individuals and as a species.

This is a story primarily about tension. It begins in the tension that
exists within every holon (previously mentioned in the introduction)
due to the holon's dual nature. It continues through looking at how
that same tension plays such a significant role inside and between
us human beings. Here we will look at differentiation theory, a psychological viewpoint that grew out of biology, to see how these twin
forces shape the human experience. And finally, we will look at the
arc of human development to see how these same dialectical forces
drive human development, on both the personal and cultural levels.

As mentioned earlier, this is a story about two fundamental
opposite, equal and connected tensions. They are invisible forces
that nevertheless shape all things and that particularly bedevil
human life. As we get more deeply into the story of holons, we will
see that we have Arthur Koestler to thank for naming this fundamental pattern that joins all things (the holarchy), and especially
for describing these two contradictory and complimentary forces
(agency or self-assertion, and integration or self-transcendence)

that define all of Life. These forces are as important and as invisible as gravity. They are the universal forces that heretofore have gone unrecognized, or have been undervalued, that complexify and coordinate human relations.

Describing the holon, and the importance of hierarchical structure to all of life, is essential to the understanding of how we might be folded in as a continuous part of the greater whole of the Universe, but that story only represents an attempt to describe objectively a phenomenon that seemingly exists outside us. But to really grasp the significance of what is being described, we must make the move from the objective discussion of holonic forces (a description of the surfaces, as Wilber points out) to the subjective experience of these same forces inside each human life and between us.

By happy coincidence, the psychological approach called differentiation theory has done exactly this, describing the complexities of the human experience of trying to balance the twin desires for belonging and autonomy. By spending some time absorbing the way these urges shape our experience of self and relationship we begin to recognize ourselves as extensions of the connective tissue of Life. The story of the evolution of differentiation theory is the story of humanity awakening to its own potential, a potential that is currently unfolding as we begin to realize just how interdependently we are intertwined with all of life.

This is no more evident than when we look, as some social scientists have done, at the entire arc of human development. Our final destination in this section will be to look at the role the twin forces of self-assertion (autonomy) and self-transcendence (integration, communion, or belonging) have played in the evolution of human consciousness. The very way we see ourselves and the world we live in, is molded by these invisible forces. Not only that, but the social reality we inhabit is also constructed by our mutual responses to these forces. In other words, our capacity to create hospitable cultures, high synergy cultures, is defined by how well we can balance our desires for autonomy and belonging. By looking at how human development, indeed human cultural history, has been shaped by these twin urges, we reveal how important these forces are, and how necessary it is that we give them their psychological due.

Conclusion

Essentially, the psychology of the future has to come to terms with a reality that is far more complex than previously realized. There are many advantages to re-orienting in this way. Humanity need no longer feel at the mercy of a meaningless existence in a Universe of random and disconnected forces. There is a whole realm of relationship and social potential that remains to be explored. There is the possibility of allaying a lot of anxiety and fear about the sustainability and viability of human life by simply aligning the life-force within us with the evolutionary process of which we are a part.

But all of these advantages lay before us as only potential without some basic recognition of the forces that are at play in our lives and a willingness to take responsibility for the choices they present us with. Knowing just how connected we are charges us with a fresh set of responsibilities that go along with newfound freedoms. The story of the holon is a story of self-transcendence, of fitting in, of becoming part of something larger. It is a story of Life standing before each one of us. It is a story about how Life addresses and tests us. This is the ultimate pattern that connects.

〰

CHAPTER 4

❦

The Story of the Holon

The hierarchy of relations, from the molecular structure of carbon compounds to the equilibrium of species and ecological whole, will perhaps be the leading idea of the future.

—JOSEPH NEEDHAM, *Order and Life*, 1936

Introduction

Tension. That is not what we want more of. Certainly, it can't be the thing that sets us free! But, it is! Tension, it turns out, is the thing that most clearly distinguishes living things from the non-living. It is a ubiquitous quality of the Universe. For every force, there is an equal and opposite force.

This isn't just something to be learned in High School physics, but an aspect of Life that connects us with everything else, and that reveals a whole set of long-ignored possibilities for human social life. How can this be? Isn't the good healthy-minded life one of peace, resolution and confidence? Yes, and strangely the way toward healthy-mindedness and social potential is through learning to deal with the normal tensions that characterize life. Let's look at these tensions and how they shape our well-being.

The tensions that seem to have the greatest impact upon our daily lives, our struggle to have a functional self of our own (the traditional concern of psychology), and our unrelenting struggle with our loved ones, are all natural ones. They come from being alive. In the past these tensions have been viewed as suspect, as if something were wrong, a person wasn't well adjusted, or a relationship was dysfunctional, instead of operating in accordance with Nature.

Now, however, we know that tension is a sign that we are alive and participating in the largest, longest lasting dance there ever was.

These tensions, as uncomfortable as they are, really indicate that we are engaged in a larger pattern of interactions that have been going on since time immemorial. These tensions reveal our role in the process of evolution. How so? Let's look at this pattern as it was first described by Arthur Koestler in 1970, when he used the metaphor of the holon to describe the Janus-faced, dual nature of the pattern that evolved with creation.

The Pattern That Connects

There are two elements of the pattern that need to be identified and understood if we are going to really grasp the forces at work in our lives, the forces that shape us, and the forces that bind us to the larger drama of evolution. These two elements are hierarchy and tension. Here I am referring to natural hierarchies, not the man-made kind that have been employed to establish elites and to maintain privilege. Natural hierarchies exist, they bind us all as parts of a larger pattern, and they help us see not only our place in creation, but how creation unfolds. Tension, most notably holonic tension, manifests as the complex dynamic energy that shapes the evolution of these natural hierarchies. Let's look at how this is so.

Natural Hierarchies

I'll start with natural hierarchies. The word hierarchy is so laden with negative association, so connected with the abuse of power, that Arthur Koestler coined another term to try and circumvent the usage of the word hierarchy. Koestler used the word holarchy to describe the way all things seemed to be nested. The negative association with hierarchies persists today and frequently obscures the real value of natural hierarchies, but recognizing the way nature has used the increasing complexity of natural hierarchy to further the creativity of evolution is important.

Koestler knew that all things were wholes made of smaller parts, such as molecules, automobiles, recipes and humans are. He also knew that all things are also parts of other larger wholes, such as organisms, freeways, meals and families. Thus, he could see that all things were nested or embedded in a matrix, a natural hierarchy of both smaller parts, that at their own level were wholes, and larger wholes, that at increasing levels were merely parts. Each thing, each aspect of reality was a whole/part, what Koestler came to refer to as a holon. Furthermore, each holon was embedded in a holarchy, nested in a natural hierarchy of increasingly complex levels.

This description is important because it reveals the underlying pattern employed by all of Nature, which ensures that everything fits in, adheres to the whole. Until this pattern had been identified science had been caught in a polarity that had greatly limited humankind's ability to fit in. Before Koestler's time, scientists fell into two camps, those who primarily saw parts, and those who saw only wholes. So-called modern science—the science that prevailed during Freud's time—was dominated by reductionists, analysts of the parts. Holism, embraced by the few who still valued the whole, was relegated to the periphery.

The situation began to change in the 1930s when system thinkers, who were primarily interested in wholes, came on the scene. These scientists, who would become responsible for the advent of weather satellites, computers, and world-wide communication, were to re-establish holistic or systemic thought. But they too saw the world too simply. The pattern that connects evaded them, because they were still caught up in thinking of everything like it was a machine. So, while they helped us advance materially, technologically, they only made the world more complex while doing little to help humankind develop the essential skills that are needed to align with the processes of evolution.

It was left to Arthur Koestler, and a few of the eminent scientists of his age, to reconcile this polarity and to put forth a new scientific vision that brought the wholes and the parts together. He developed a new language, a new way of referring to things that had been observed, to highlight the distinguishing characteristics of what he saw. So it was that the concept of the holon, the recognition of the dual nature of all things as whole/parts, became evident. It is amazing and shocking to think that this fundamental realization had eluded mankind for so long. Now, however, thanks mainly to Arthur Koestler, we are beginning to recognize a pattern that folds us into the larger whole of the cosmos in a way never before grasped.

Holonic Tension

Koestler posited that all living things are holons. A holon is simultaneously whole in itself AND a part of some other whole. For
example, the whole atom is a part of a whole molecule, and a whole
molecule is a part of a whole cell, and the whole cell is a part of a
whole organism, and so on. Each of these entities is neither a whole
nor a part, but a whole/part, a holon. All living things, including
human beings, are not merely wholes unto themselves but parts of
something else; there is no whole that is not simultaneously a part
of some other whole.

Since every holon is a whole/part, it has two "tendencies," or
"drives"—it has to maintain both its wholeness and its partness.
Thus, one characteristic of all holons, no matter what domain they
exist in, is that they have to maintain their own wholeness, their
own identity and autonomy. This is described by life scientists as an
organism's ability to retain its own agency. Agency is a holon's capacity to face environmental pressures that would otherwise absorb or
obliterate it. Koestler first described this force as "self-assertive." As
we shall see, we human beings, as holons, are constantly involved in
the process of discovering, establishing, losing and re-establishing
our capacity for self-defined, self-assertive autonomy.

A holon is also a part of some other system. It is not enough that
it simply preserves its agency. It must also maintain a capacity to fit
into its environment. As Koestler put it, a holon also was compelled
to be "self-transcending," to maintain its partness. So a holon, be it
a molecule, animal, or human, must also maintain its capacity for
communion, or "self-transcendence," the ability to fit in and belong
as a part of a larger system. For a holon to survive it must maintain
this partness in the face of environmental pressures that would try
to separate it out from a larger whole and thus destroy it.

These twin drives, the urge to merge into a larger whole
(self-transcendence) and the desire to maintain a sense of autonomy
and distinctness (self-assertion), underlie the human experience.
They create a dynamic tension that shapes our evolution as individuals and as participants in the social systems in which we are
immersed. Our nature is fundamentally dialectical. As whole/parts,
our lives are forever being lived out in a dynamic tension between
our desires for communion and for autonomy.

This tension isn't just incidental, it is essential. Koestler described twin forces that pervade nature that are design elements as fundamental to the development of the Universe (and, as we shall see in Chapter 6, to human development) as gravity, and just as invisible. Like gravity, these twin forces and the tension they create, can be experienced. It is with direct experience (the focus of the next two chapters) that the importance of holonic tension becomes most palpable, and most evident. Before we turn to the direct subjective experience of this tension inside human lives, let's take some time to review the implications of natural hierarchies and holons upon creation and particularly human existence.

Implications

No one has done more than Ken Wilber to map out the implications of the pattern that connects. Wilber, who is a student of knowledge, is the philosopher of our times. His work features an integrative look at the big picture of human personal and cultural evolution. In mapping out the evolution of human thought, consciousness, cultural development, and understanding of nature, he has revealed how all of these areas, formerly seen as specialized areas of knowledge, are related. He has made the practice of integrated inquiry essential.

Before Ken Wilber could offer his crowning insight, which came in the form of his highly integrative four quadrants model, he had to really understand the implications of Kostler's perception of the pattern that connects. To grasp what distinguishes a psychology of interdependence we need to make the same kind of mental journey. Wilber makes it easier for us because he chronicles in his writing 20 tenets of the holonic structure of creation (see Chapter Notes).

We will employ some of Wilber's tenets to seize a richer understanding of this pattern and to see how awareness of this pattern changes everything. This is not a comprehensive review of Wilber's 20 tenets, rather it is a description of those facets that Wilber has identified, that are relevant to an emerging understanding of the interdependent relationships that prevail as a formerly unknown hallmark of creation.

Natural Hierarchies and Holonic Tension

What we need to understand is the basic pattern that pervades all of creation. Understanding this pattern will make it more visible so that it will be possible to see it at work in human lives and social systems. By making the invisible visible, we can begin to see how interconnected we are with all things and begin to grasp why it is necessary to re-formulate our psychology to reflect more accurately the reality we find ourselves within. Finally, by understanding holonic tensions and natural hierarchies, we better understand ourselves, our own experience, and our untapped potential. As noted earlier, these are the characteristics of the natural hierarchy and holonic tensions that are important to know:

- Evolution has directionality;
- Reality is not composed of things and processes, but holons;
- Holons display four fundamental capacities: self-preservation, self-adaptation, self-transcendence, and self-dissolution;
- Holons emerge holarchically;
- Each emergent holon transcends but includes its predecessors;
- Each successive level of evolution (holarchy) produces **greater** depth and **less** span;
- The greater the depth of a holon the greater the degree of consciousness;
- Holarchies co-evolve;
- The micro is in relational exchange with the macro at all levels of its depth.

These traits of creation, as Wilber describes them, must be understood if we are going to appreciate the true elegance of the design of the whole, in which we are a part. It is worth it then, taking a more detailed look at these observations. Wilber writes at length about each of these features of creation, but we will review these aspects only to make more palpable the holonic structure of all things, the pattern that connects.

Composition of Reality

We are confronted today with a non-conventional picture of reality. To us it has been obvious that creation is composed of processes and things. So it seemed, until the system thinkers came along. Because of their interest in seeing the whole, the relationship between processes and things began to be known. Because they were interested in how all the parts of something interrelated, what had been obscured by the reductionists' preoccupation with the parts became theoretically visible. Today we can say that although they recognized relationship as the glue that all wholes had in common, they failed to grasp the significance of this recognition.

That awaited the work of Arthur Koestler and his metaphor of the holon. Koestler made it obvious that relationship was a first principle, that nothing existed in a vacuum, and that all things existed by virtue of being holons, by fitting into something larger even as they were composed of smaller whole/parts. Holons were most essentially composites held together and connected by relationship forces.

Thus, it has been left to us to re-formulate our picture of reality. Reality, which looks like it is composed of things and processes, is actually composed of something even more subtle and complex—relationships. This isn't obvious until you go inside human experience, then it becomes subjectively obvious. We will be going there shortly, but for now take a moment to grasp the shift that is required to make this apprehension of reality available. Each of us must overcome the insistence of mainstream science that only the objective is real. It has taken the evolution of a truly integral perspective, which incorporates inner and outer, subjective with objective, surface with depth, into a more complex vision. This shift renders the relationship dimension of reality more apparent.

As our view of reality becomes more complex, it is not parts or wholes, but whole/parts everywhere, we must develop a psychology that incorporates this more complex picture. Relationship is not just a desirable aspect of human life, it is an indispensable component of aligning with the larger processes of evolution. To ensure the survival, the sustainability, of our species, relationship must become a first principle, a way of cooperating with the directionality of evolution.

Directionality

Evolution has a direction. We can't say where it is taking us, but there are certain qualities to the way that evolution is unfolding that suggest that it is coherent, focused, and directional. This is important for two reasons. First, it seems that holons, including us humans, unfold in a certain semi-predictable way. I say semi-predictable because evolution is constantly introducing novelty, unpredictable and creative solutions to evolutionary problems. Every step, every creative move that evolution has made has nevertheless shared certain predictable characteristics with every other move or development that evolution has ever made. Secondly, knowing about the direction of evolution makes it easier to cooperate with it. We can derive a lot of benefit from collaborating with the evolutionary process, not the least of which is taking advantage of evolutionary momentum to ensure our sustainability as a species (more on this later). Understanding the direction of evolution helps us to orient and align with it.

There have been many different ways that this direction has been described. Observers in the physical sciences put it differently than those who look at human culture, who in turn use still different language than those who look closely at the evolution of consciousness. It has taken a mind like Wilber's, and an integrative vision, to begin to describe what all these different disciplines see in common. For the sake of simplicity and consistency we will look at only one of the many possible ways of describing the direction of evolution. Because it relies upon relationship, Evolution always enfolds each new development in a new emergent wholeness.

The best description of this movement comes from biology (and we will see how reliable this description is as we return to it throughout the following chapters). Evolution moves in the direction of increasing differentiation and integration. As Wilber says, in a way that reveals how this description elaborates the holonic nature of evolution, "differentiation produces partness, or new manyness; integration produces wholeness, or a new "oneness." And since holons are whole/parts, they are formed by the joint action of differentiation and integration."

The differentiating process is a necessary expression of the universal drive toward novelty and diversity. Differentiation describes the movement toward autonomy, toward uniqueness, toward becoming distinct, identifiable by virtue of originality and creativity. Integration, on the other hand, is just as necessary, giving expression to the drive toward fitting in, coherence, collaboration, oneness, or becoming unified. These two processes work hand-in-hand, simultaneously, to render an overall process that is paradoxically producing as much diversity AND as much unity as possible.

This is the direction of Evolution. Increasingly the Universe appears to strive for ever new levels of organization that are simultaneously more complex, composed of more unique and functional parts, and bound tightly in ever more efficient assemblies of wholeness. We human beings are subject to these same forces. What makes our situation so interesting, and so precarious, is that we are conscious, capable of experiencing these forces within us and around us. Consciousness is a blessing, and seemingly a curse. We suffer at the hands of these forces and have the capacity to choose how we want to relate to them. We can cooperate with the direction of Evolution or we can fight it. Either way we experience important consequences.

Tension

These consequences are no more clearly expressed than when we look at the tensions that assail every holon and the tensions that determine a holon's fitness, its ability to participate in the dance of evolution. There is a lot at stake in the struggle to balance the twin desires for belonging and autonomy.

Return, for a moment, to what we know about what is at stake: if a holon is unable to maintain either its agency or its communion it is unable to survive and simply ceases to exist. As Ken Wilber points out in *A Brief History of Everything*, holons have both horizontal and vertical characteristics. Agency (the desire for autonomy) and communion (the desire for belonging) are the horizontal capacities that all holons share. These characteristics reveal how holons are connected. Holons also share vertical characteristics, which reveal how holons evolve (see Figure 1 next page).

Ken Wilber labels these vertical characteristics "self- trancendence" and "self-dissolution." He points out that when holons fail to maintain either agency or communion they break down (self-dissolution). He also describes how holons that maintain both agency and communion undergo the reverse, that is, a building-up process in which new holonic capabilities emerge. This process is self-transcendence, in which a new, more complex and functional holon emerges. This is the mysterious process by which complexity and novelty emerge into existence.

This self-transcending movement proceeds in a predictable pattern that Wilber describes as, "differentiate, integrate, transcend and include." Each leap occurs through a process of differentiation, or dis-identification with what is, into a new form of wholeness that transcends the old and simultaneously integrates and includes the features of the old form. This movement describes the process by which all living things evolve, including individual humans, significant human relationships, and the life of human communities.

For the moment, however, let's focus our attention upon the rigors associated with the holon's experience. In addition to the tensions that we described earlier, we discover that the very integrity of the holon resides within flows of dynamic tension. Embedded in fields of relationship, each holon is constantly engaged in the process of balancing. It must withstand and balance the horizontal forces that drive it toward immersion or isolation. If it manages this task well, it transcends itself and gains access to a more daunting and subtler level of existence, as in a video game. Here the holon learns to function anew. If it doesn't manage to withstand these twin drives, it breaks down, dissolving into its constituent parts, losing functionality and becoming less complex. In either case it is subject to ongoing tensions that will determine to what degree it fits where it is.

As we shall see in the following chapters, humans, as holons, are subject to these same invisible tensions. Our well-being depends, like any other holon, upon our ability to withstand and balance these tensions. The penchant to avoid tension prevents us from discovering our own capabilities and limits our social potential significantly.

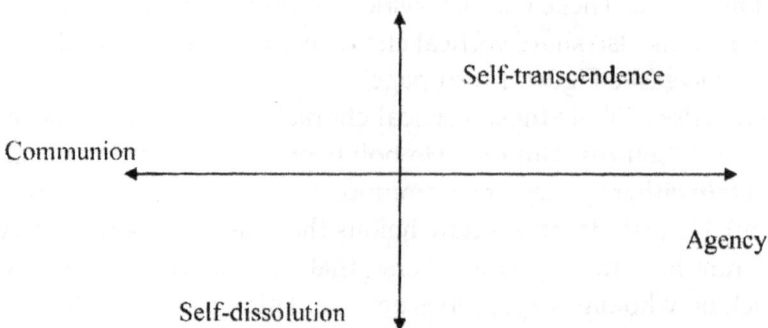

Figure 1—The Horizontal and Vertical Characteristics of Holons

To evolve more closely with Nature we are going to need to develop the relationship capacities and the ability to tolerate tensions that are inherent in Creation. This is one of the primary goals of a psychology of interdependence, to re-interpret relationship tensions from the signs of trouble they have been conventionally seen as, to the doorways to new relationship capabilities for us as individuals and as a species.

Emergence

We have looked at the mystery of emergence and, having noted that emergence seems to be the product of a high synergy relationship, the perspective provided by the pattern that connects allows us to add some additional data points to our original appraisal. By visualizing the holonic, dual, nature of all things it becomes evident that emergence takes place because several factors line up.

Yes, relationship is important. And, it is a complex relationship. Not only does it take two or more things, but all of those things must relate in such a way that they balance the urge to be a whole unto themselves with the urge to be a part of a larger emergent whole. According to Wilber and the holonic perspective, holons emerge holarchically. That means that what emerges, be it a molecule, organism, eco-system, or new type of social organization, is already itself a holon, subject to the tension between its wholeness and its partness. It is emerging as part of a natural hierarchy, a whole composed of parts that are wholes at a predecessor level.

What emerges is an amalgam of parts that have joined in a new way so that the parts have formed a new whole that operates on an entirely new level. Interestingly, the integrity of this new whole depends upon the coordination of these disparate parts AND each part maintaining its own wholeness. Each level, even the emergent level, depends upon its integrity, i.e. the ability to balance wholeness and partness of its predecessor levels for its own viability. Wilber summarizes all of this by pointing out that the process of emergence is one where what emerges "transcends and includes" what has come before.

This pattern of emergence permeates Nature and accounts for the high level of integration found everywhere in natural creation. We humans are a product of this very same process and our emergence

as a species is a product of this pattern. Our evolution as creatures of
culture adheres to this pattern. And manifesting our social potential
as a species relies on our adherence to this same pattern. Knowing
that it is by balancing these tensions that both personal and collective evolution takes place adds a great deal to the psychological picture and sets us up to move more in concert with life.

Depth

Viewing things through the lens of a multi-leveled holacharchic
construct brings into relief other important features of reality. Wilber emphasizes the importance of depth. Holarcharchically speaking, depth refers to the number of predecessor levels a particular
holon or level entails. The number of levels involved is important
for several reasons. Depth helps clarify priorities and is related to
consciousness. It also reveals the preciousness, or rarity, of a certain
level of holonic achievement.

Wilber points out that holons rely on the levels below them. If
single-celled organisms go away, so do we humans. We are consti-
tuted of single-celled organisms and if something threatens them
then the entire edifice, including our wonderful (and unique, as far
as we know) consciousness is also threatened. Similarly, if the biosphere we rely on goes away, so do we. Conversely, lower levels do
not rely on higher levels for survival. Since the biosphere doesn't
depend on us, then it could survive our departure. This clarifies and
helps us prioritize. We need to preserve the integrity of the levels we
rely on if we want to survive. Similarly, we need to recognize that
certain levels of creation, particularly social holons, depend upon the
integrity of individual human holons for their viability.

All of this applies to consciousness as well. From Wilber's considered perspective, the greater the depth, or the more levels supporting an achievement, the less the span, or the fewer the numbers of things accomplishing that achievement. As depth increases
span decreases. Since consciousness also increases with depth, then
the number of beings with that particular form of consciousness
decreases. Complex consciousness, such as our own, relies upon
multiple levels of successful relationships, and, provided we also
relate well, supports the emergence of even more complex forms of
consciousness. Wilber seems to hesitate when it comes to considering

whether social holons have consciousness, but as you will see, and as a holonic worldview would predict, social forms of consciousness exist and exert an influence upon us. That story must await further groundwork but suffice it to say that uniquely social forms of consciousness are what await us.

Finally, many humans are born. They all share consciousness. But the most conscious among us are extremely rare. They are still human, but they have achieved something extraordinary. This will always be so. The more exquisite and complex the consciousness, the fewer the humans that will partake of it. This is an immutable law that seems to limit the scope of human development. Only a precious few can achieve the highly complex forms of consciousness.

While our problems and challenges grow more complex we are stuck with a diminished capacity and a smaller number of individuals who can cope. This would seem to be a fatal limitation. But the farthest reaches of consciousness become available to more individuals when we harness our collective capabilities, our social potential. One of the primary concerns of a psychology of interdependence is actualizing the social potential of our species. This is, in part, why you will find such an emphasis upon social depth in this work. While social depth is not the same thing as the holonic depth that Wilber refers to—the depth of many levels of holons—social depth still requires multiple levels of social experience to occur.

As Wilber has pointed out, the crisis of our times is one of insufficient depth. We are used to skating on the thin ice of our cultural preoccupation with surfaces. To break through to the levels of consciousness and complexity that offer us a real shot at sustainability, we need to be capable of depth, both personal and social. Such depth is a by-product of repeated transformations, of repeatedly losing and reformulating the balance between the twin forces of self-assertion and self-transcendence at a new level.

Co-Evolution

In our look at our natural inheritance we saw that, thanks to "coupling," things, be they metabolic processes or organisms, co-evolve. We have seen how organisms shape their environment as their environment shapes them. The tightness of this fit, of this coupling, is also an attribute of holarchies. As holarchies evolve they relate to other holarchies. They shape and influence each other in their rest-less search for a greater balance and a more fine-tuned fit. What is so evident is the dynamic nature of life. There is a consistent surge of energy, constantly disturbing the status quo, upsetting the current balance in favor of the quest for another more functional balance.

It is important to remember that what we are describing here is not just past tense; the co-evolutionary process is on-going. There is a perpetual dance occurring, a flood of energy, a current pushing everything toward greater relationship, toward a more elegant fit with everything else. This is the true meaning of co-evolving hol-archies—the restlessness of the holonic search for a more dynamic balance renders all things, human-contrived or otherwise, forever in flux.

Relatedness

Rather than belabor the central point of this book, that we, like all living things, depend upon a matrix of relationships for our exis-tence, it is enough to point out that holons are also highly relational. They are, in fact, not just things, but processes of relationship, wholes that come into being as relational entities. Wilber emphasizes that it is the nature of holons to preserve and enhance their integrity through relational exchanges with holons of the same depth in their environment. As human holons, we rely upon exchanges with oth-ers in our immediate environment, as well as in our cultural envi-ronment, for the elements that enable us to maintain or enhance our integrity and to ensure the survival of our organizational structure, i.e. our sense of self and our own consciousness.

Relatedness is the rule throughout creation. There is no organ-ism, metabolic process or chemical reaction that exists on its own. Holons adhere to this pattern. Like everything else, they rely upon their constituent parts getting along in a collaborative fash-ion for their viability. Similarly, holons depend upon collaborative exchanges with other holons for their own maintenance, growth, and development. Paradoxically, the wholeness of the holon depends upon its ability to engage as a part of a matrix of relationship. There is a lesson for us in the fact that it is the self-transcending impetus of the holon that ensures the self-assertive. We would do well to notice this pattern and to give it its due in our psychological practices.

Conclusion

We have endeavored to this point to take an objective, present-time look around the reality we find ourselves within. This look has been presented because I believe we need to update our psychological practices, to align them with the vision of reality we are now capable of seeing.

The Universe turns out to be more complex and mysterious than the mechanism our scientists once conceived it to be. This is the good news and the bad news. The bad news is that we are being introduced to a whole new perception of our home, one that takes away its familiarity and the comfort of believing we knew what life was all about. Competition and the survival of the strongest, the essential pathways of the past, have offered us predictable outcomes but no real hope for a sustainable future.

We have all the technological acumen we could want, but we are still afraid of our own kind. For good reason, they (whoever they are) are our competitors. The many problems we have in getting along with our own kind reveals the actual level of shortcoming that accompanies this worldview. Ignoring this shortcoming bears dangerous consequences. So the bad news is that the worldview we have known, have become adjusted to and rely upon, is fraught with dangerous limitations that threaten our survival.

The good news isn't totally clear yet. As we are re-introduced to this home we thought we knew, we find that it is appointed with new rooms, more spacious accommodations, and new freedoms. All of this new-found possibility is delightful. And yet, to our dismay, access to these new features is not automatic. Something is being asked of us. To partake of what is so alluringly close we have to grow ourselves. Is this good news or more bad news?

The metaphor of the holon, a metaphor that was created to give us a way to talk about and see the invisible forces that deliver us to this new viewpoint, also reminds us of the new more complex beings we must be to inhabit this reality. Here again we encounter a good news/bad news situation. The good news is that we have been participating in this reality all along, organismically. We are prepared. Nature has done the biggest part of the job for us. But the bad news is that we still need to take the leap. A new world is waiting. To inhabit it fully requires us to come to terms with our own nature. We are social beings, holons if you like, and that means that we need to learn how to live within the relational flows and currents of tension if we want to actualize the possibilities inherent in our being.

What lies before us, what lies within us, now awaits our choice. The rigor of consciousness isn't something we choose lightly. All growing means loss. There is a kind of suffering that accompanies knowingly choosing to be subject to these seemingly unremitting tensions. There is a comfort associated with being only an individual. It is a lonely comfort, however.

Growing a self in the midst of relationship forces is not an easy thing. When you factor in the challenges associated with Nature's constant attempts to evolve us, to grow us through ever more complex stages, you get a real sense of what a complex organism we actually are. Life challenges us constantly, but it also offers us real support. We are capable, and the joy is in discovering these capabilities. There is a special joy in finding that some capabilities arise through relationship. By and large, this joy, the joy in our shared capabilities, resides in our untapped social potential.

Gaining access to our social capacity through relationship is understandable, but not intuitively obvious. For what is to be gained is not under anyone's control. Our wealth, the commonwealth that binds and secures us to one another, to our deepest selves, to the local environment, to the Cosmos, is not personally possessed. It resides in the between. Between the urge for wholeness and partness, between the desire to belong and the desire to be true to one's self, between the tensions that characterize Life, dwells this new wealth. It is our birthright, our belonging in this Universe. To gain access, we must stretch ourselves and live between the poles of our being, between our desires and what Life asks of us. It is this "between," the plight of the human holon, that is ultimately the concern of a psychology of interdependence. It is this between, this dynamic holonic tension, which reveals a whole new vista of human personal and social potential.

〽

CHAPTER 5

‮

The Plight of the Human Holon: As Told by Differentiation Theory

In addition to separating ourselves from nature,
we have also been inclined to regard the human
as the most important form of life on Earth,
the crowning achievement of God's creation.
Exaggerating our importance in this way has
probably further hampered our ability to see
the extent to which the human is related to all life.
—Dr. Michael Kerr in *Family Evaluation*, 1988

Introduction

If the 13.7 billion years from the Big Bang until the present were condensed into a single day, humanity would only appear on the scene in the last minute of that day. When considering how long natural evolution prevailed, it is not hard to imagine that Life might have more to say about the human being than the human has to say about Life. This is not the way things have always been, however. Until very recently, humanity has tended to rely upon a version of science that reflected humanity's narcissism. Considering ourselves to be the apex of Creation, we believed we had transcended Nature.

This was the backdrop that set the scene for the last century. And this is what makes the achievements of Murray Bowen, the founder of Bowen Family Theory, which has become known as Differentiation Theory, so remarkable. This chapter will not endeavor to tell the full story of Bowen's discoveries, but instead will tell the portions of the story that make clear the New World that Bowen helped to make visible, and the new psychological orientation that is now possible.

To grasp "the pattern that connects" requires more than an abstract awareness of it. What brings it alive, what makes it palpable and vivid in our day-to-day lives, is the direct experience of the tensions that this pattern generates. Bowen's discoveries show us the way. He was among the first to try and give words to these tensions, as such his observations and how he made them will help to reveal another aspect of who we are. His groundbreaking journey opens up terrain that we must visit if we are going to grasp more of the world we live in, and who we may be, as well as our own newfound possibilities.

Bowen and the Family Emotional System

Murray Bowen was a psychiatrist. He is deceased now, but in his professional career he was the discoverer and founder of a movement that is still being integrated into mainstream therapy. His journey, which he referred to as his odyssey, began in the 1940s. He was interested in several things that led him into an awareness that he had never imagined. He had been fully trained as a psychiatrist in the basics of Freudian analysis, but he had the realization, even at that time, that the Freudian approach lacked a truly scientific basis. He also was busy conducting research on schizophrenia. His observations led him to look deeply at the limitations of Freudian theory and to begin looking for a more scientific explanation for what he was seeing in his practice.

Bowen noticed that there was something going on between the mothers of his schizophrenic patients and the patients that seemed to have an impact upon the patients' behavior. He noticed that the patient got better, or acted out more, based upon what was occurring in the relationship with the mother. As he saw it, the relationship seemed to be the mediating factor. This was not explainable via Freudian theory, which offered only an explanation of the internal factors that could account for an individual's behavior. He was convinced he was observing a dyadic, co-created behavior, which according to Freudian theory could not exist. This observation, combined with the absence of a useful Freudian explanation, sent Bowen upon his odyssey.

He began what was to be a lifelong practice searching science for an explanation of what he observed, and he found what he was looking for. In the literature of evolution, particularly of biology, he found the concept of symbiosis. It is worth noting that Bowen, in his quest for a scientific explanation, stumbled upon the literature of living systems before there was even a field called living systems, and he was to mine this literature for explanations throughout his whole career. Symbiosis, the fact that organisms bond on behalf of increased functional capability, provided Bowen his first clue, his first insight, into what he would much later call "the emotional system." What he saw was that symbiosis could work both ways, it could increase or decrease functioning.

For Murray Bowen the concept of symbiosis explained what he was observing, and more importantly, gave him an idea how to treat what he observed. Because he had a commitment to try to treat schizophrenia and to reduce its symptoms, he began by looking for a way to create some emotional separation between those involved in symbiotic relationships. This struggle led him deeper into the phenomena and eventually delivered him to a whole new way of seeing families and the struggle for psychological well-being. But we are getting ahead of ourselves here; how Bowen came to his realization that all of us are coupled into pre-existing emotional systems, and these systems set the conditions for how we cope in the world, is important. How he reached this realization can help us to make the same realization in our own lives.

Because Bowen was as committed to treatment as he was to theory, he soon found that he didn't have enough theory to make treatment effective. This led him to look more deeply into the scientific literature for useful explanations. His observation that gaining the proper amount of emotional separation between mother and schizophrenic child led to him bringing the rest of the family into the treatment. This showed him that there seemed to be some similar kind of relationship bond, or co-created field that seemed to define the range of a family's behavioral repertoire. This observation drove him back into the scientific literature once again. Eventually, he came to the conclusion that there was some kind of system that was governing the family's behavior.

His genius was in his recognition that this was not a man-made system, such as those that had become popular in science through the mathematical models of such men as Norbert Weiner, but was something nature-made, a natural system, something evolution designed. It was not long before this led to the realization that this was a phenomenon that all families had in common. But, again, we get ahead of ourselves here. For Murray Bowen this was simply an effort to develop a theory that matched his observations.

Bowen had known from early on that the patient's behavior would improve if he or she could gain some ground emotionally. What he saw now was that the patient was linked into the emotional process of the family. For Bowen, this meant that the family must become the focus of treatment. Thus came the advent of family therapy. He also realized that treatment meant focusing upon the family's emotional system. Bowen saw that for the schizophrenic patient to get better, the family of that patient had to get better. Getting better meant gaining access to new behavioral options, options that were not available to the family members by virtue of their immersion in the family's emotional system.

Bowen went on observing and treating families. As he did so, he developed a whole new way of thinking and talking about families. He created new terminology to describe processes that would have remained invisible or misunderstood without a new conceptual framework to make them distinct. He helped create a new systemic approach to therapy, which would alter the therapeutic landscape by bringing into the picture, for the first time, the role of relationships and the emotional processes that often governed them. This is an accomplishment that is still working its way into the awareness of our times.

Bowen was the first to thoroughly describe the emotional system that links us all to each other. Although he first observed this emotional system in schizophrenic families, he knew, and asserted in later lectures and writing, that emotional systems existed in all families and society-at-large. In this way he made relationships psychologically visible.

And he did even more. He supplied new concepts derived from his observations, important concepts such as systems thinking, differentiation, togetherness-autonomy pressure, anxiety tension, the differentiation scale, and societal regression. By reviewing these concepts, I hope to make these relationship dynamics clearer to the reader and thereby reveal the underlying dynamic pattern that connects.

Differentiation

The heart of Bowen's theory is differentiation, and it is for this reason that later applications of this theory became known as Differentiation Theory. Bowen observed that the emotional system functioned better when at least one of its members could separate enough emotionally that they could act on their own terms and not be governed by the needs of the emotional system. This capacity, of one member to become whole enough to establish some autonomy while staying connected, was what he called differentiation.

Borrowing the term from biology, Bowen took as his model the process by which an undifferentiated cell separated from a mass of undifferentiated cells and became a specific kind of cell (differentiated) so it could perform a specific cellular function. For Bowen, differentiation meant separating by a few degrees from one's position in the family emotional system (the ego-mass), gaining a more solid self-defined sense of self (less defined by family relationships), and gaining access to new behavioral options. Because the family was an emotional system (a whole), anyone in the family could improve the family's ability to function and affect the whole by becoming more differentiated.

But for the functioning of a specific individual (a part) to improve markedly, that individual had to differentiate a self of their own (to become more themselves, more whole). Thus, Bowen also came up with the term "differentiation-of-the-self." This designation, along with the image of a single cell separating from a mass of cells, led to an unavoidable misunderstanding of Bowen's theory. Those who were so inclined took this to be an affirmation of the process of individuation, a validation of the psychology of the individual.

While partially true, these folks inadvertently de-natured the process, by removing the family's emotional system and de-emphasizing the natural value of this evolutionarily-designed aspect of human nature. To the advocates of the psychology of the individual, the family system might be an inconvenience; it is, however, an important part of human adaptiveness that was designed to give us a relational edge. This will become more evident when we discuss growing a self-in-relationship.

As we shall see, differentiation, a process found in nature, turns out to be important in developing psychological maturity — the ability to stand alone, to relate deeply, to balance conflicting drives—and a necessary component of individual and species-wide evolution. To get a real feel for what differentiation is, and the depth and breadth of this form of action, let's look at some of its attributes:

- ability to maintain one's separate sense of self in close proximity of others;
- knowing where one ends and another begins;
- saying "I" when others are demanding "we";
- being clear about personal values and goals;
- taking personal responsibility rather than blaming others;
- ability to separate thoughts and feelings;
- ability to regulate oneself;
- containing one's reactivity to other's reactivity;
- taking a stand in an intense emotional system;
- maintaining a non-anxious presence in the face of other's anxiety;
- being able to cease being one of the system's emotional dominoes;
- ability to tolerate pain for growth and development.

Differentiation is an important concept, a key ingredient in the development of all kinds of organisms, from the individual to the social organization. It turns out to be a lifelong process that is never settled, and determines what kind of world one lives in. This aspect of differentiation will become more evident when we can see more of the pattern that connects.

Togetherness-Autonomy Pressure

As Bowen observed relationship processes, he saw what he came to consider a fundamental dynamic that defined all relationships. He labeled this dynamic "togetherness-autonomy pressure." This referred to the tendency he saw over and over again, for individuals and members of couples and families to give up some part of self to maintain a relationship as it was, or an opposite tendency to refuse to give up any of one's self, one's freedom, for the sake of relationship. The pattern he saw was either a tendency to make the relationship too important, and thereby give up autonomy to maintain it or, to make self too important and to give up relationship to maintain self-autonomy.

An astute reader will recognize that Bowen was describing the very relationship traits of the holon we spent so much time describing in the last chapter. As a reminder, these traits are the drive to maintain autonomy (or wholeness) and the corresponding opposite drive for communion and to be part of something larger (a part). Without knowing of Koestler's work, which hadn't occurred yet, Bowen saw this dynamic unfolding in human lives and recognized it as fundamental to human relationships. He also saw that this dynamic posed a challenge for human relationships, one that defined the quality of a bond and determined the well-being of those involved.

Because Bowen was observing and describing the workings of a system, he knew this tendency to feel pressure in favor of the relationship and at the expense of self or the opposite, was altered by the level of differentiation of those involved. You may recall that differentiation was the biology-based term Bowen used to describe the degree of emotional separation from significant others that an individual had achieved. It is important to note that differentiation was not measured in terms of distance (because distancing is one common indicator of a lack of differentiation), rather it is used to describe the ability to define one's self on one's own terms while staying connected, rather than on the terms of significant others. Lower levels of differentiation, a lower capacity for self-definition, generated higher degrees of emotional reactivity and greater pressure to either conform or to separate.

Bowen also recognized that the level of differentiation determined an individual's and an emotional system's ability to balance these twin drives. Those with little differentiation found themselves bouncing between these two extremes; those with slightly more might find some temporary balance unless stressed too heavily. Those more highly differentiated would balance these forces more adeptly and would be capable of holding onto self while connecting deeply with significant others. In fact, increased levels of differentiation lead to greater access to the world and its occupants as they are.

When we explore human development, another aspect of the pattern that connects, we will see that increasing differentiation allows for deeper integration into the processes of evolution. We will return to this line of thought when we describe Bowen's use of the differentiation scale to try to make his observations more coherent.

In the meantime, let's go further with Bowen's description of the emotional system.

Anxiety Tension

Bowen knew that a great deal was at stake in human relationships. He was aware of the tension, or stress, that was constantly running through human interactions. He realized that what he saw was generated by the complexity of these interactions. Every choice, to give one's self up to protect the relationship, to give up the relationship to hold onto self, or even to find some new balance, take it, and then withstand the pull of the forces calling for one to give up one or the other, was a stressful, anxiety-provoking choice. He recognized just how much anxiety attended the fact of being human. He was the first to really see that anxiety was a form of tension that reflected what complex organisms we are.

This recognition that anxiety attends human life is just one of the significant ways that Differentiation Theory departs from conventional psychological wisdom. Instead of seeing anxiety as something wrong or a disorder, Bowen made it possible for following generations to know that anxiety was a natural component of the tension that accompanies human existence. Bowen knew early on that anxiety played a central role in determining the well-being and the adaptiveness of human beings, though he didn't express it as completely as the developmental theorists who were to come, or even as cogently as following generations of differentiation theorists and practitioners such as David Schnarch.

He could see that people could be overwhelmed by the anxiety in their lives, but he was too savvy to view this exclusively as a problem to be solved. He could see that these eras of anxiety often meant that an opportunity and necessity for growth was present and that it was time to adapt to a new, more complex situation. Murray Bowen saw, and later David Schnarch gave it more accurate language, that anxiety tension was an existential condition of human life. In Differentiation Theory, anxiety tension was something one had to come to terms with, and if one did one gained access to a more complex world and new possible ways of behaving.

Differentiation became one way, one indicator, of an ability to handle a certain amount of anxiety or tension. Increasing the ability to handle anxiety tension increased differentiation, the capacity to balance relationship desires, as well as increasing the capacity to make significant choices on one's own terms and values rather than the terms and values of others. The ability to handle more anxiety tension translates into developing a self of one's own. Because Bowen could see this complex amalgam of intersecting processes he knew anxiety was important, and he developed an understanding of how anxiety, as a reflection of togetherness-autonomy pressure, accounted for the bulk of the emotional reactivity that plagued human relations.

Emotional Reactivity

The surest indicator of the presence of an emotional system is also the surest indicator of anxiety. I'm talking here about emotional reactivity. The reader will notice that as I go about explaining the presence and the core of emotional reactivity it will seem like I am repeating much of what has been said before. This is how you will know that I am describing a system. One of the challenges Bowen faced was finding different terms for processes that were similar, that were connected, and that relied upon each other for their existence. Emotional reactivity, which can take many forms, is like the part of the iceberg that sticks out of the water. Underneath lies the bulk, the largest part, of what is going on.

I repeat—emotional reactivity is not an indication that something is wrong. A natural system is at work, and in doing so is revealing the state of the whole, the current condition of the organism. This revelation gives us the necessary cues that help us to determine how well we are actually adapting to the world within which we find ourselves. Thus, emotional reactivity is like pain, a feedback loop that if paid its due helps us find our way through a world that is complex. We don't ignore pain, because it tells us something about our world and ourselves, and how the two are coming together, that allows, and sometimes demands, adjustment. Emotional reactivity serves a similar function.

Emotional reactivity is, at its core, the center point of the iceberg, the refusal to face what life, or reality, is presenting us with. The tendency to run away from things that seem bigger or deeper than we are, is what causes us to become emotionally reactive. How is this natural? Isn't this more an indication of moral failure, or at the least a lack of preparation? No, and yes. Maybe in the lack of preparation, we do live in a world that doesn't prepare us for how complex human life really is. But we have an on-board navigational system, designed by nature, to help us with just this issue. Unfortunately, most of us haven't learned to use, or to trust, this aspect of our natural inheritance.

Emotional reactivity provides us with information about our lived experience. Information that is often not very useful. Sometimes we refuse to know these things (emotional cut-off, another Bowenian term), and sometimes, too often, we fail to distinguish emotional reactions from reality. In other words, emotional reactivity lets us know about the presence in our lives of something real, something big, but also busily tries to obscure it, by creating emotional realities disguised as thoughts. An important aspect of differentiation, as we shall see in the developmental work of psychologist Robert Kegan, is the ability to separate thoughts from feelings. We often ignore, or distrust, the usefulness of our emotional reactions because we have spent so much time being at the mercy of our feelings, or somebody else's.

Ultimately, emotional reactivity is the signal that the individual, or the system, is coming into contact with something that requires more adaptiveness than can be delivered. It bespeaks not something to be avoided, but something to be faced and learned from, for the sake of greater functionality, more confidence, and an increased sense of well-being. Life is asking something of us, and emotional reactivity is one sign that we notice and that we are uncertain about our ability to respond. We will probably remain reactive for as long as it takes us to decide that we are going to put ourselves on the line and respond. When that happens, emotional reactivity gives way to learning and growth.

Bowen saw that emotional reactivity, like anxiety, was a direct result of one's level of differentiation, one's adaptive capacity. He knew that adaptive capacity was a feature of the family's emotional system, that each of us coped with the complexity of relationships and the complexity of our own lives as we had learned in our families. He could see that two different families could deal with the same kind of emotional stressor, complexity, or circumstances, in different ways. Therefore, he created the differentiation scale to highlight what accounted for these differences in a family's adaptiveness. In so doing, without really intending to, he created not only a way to illustrate differences in the ability to cope, but a rudimentary model of human development, a model of human maturation.

The Differentiation Scale

To illustrate his ideas and make explicit the differing ways an emotional system (or an individual) could function, Bowen created his differentiation scale. The scale, ranging from no differentiation (0) to complete differentiation (100) was his theoretical attempt to show how differentiation changed functionality as it increased. Bowen never found a way to test for anyone's actual specific level of differentiation, however, since this required too much information from too many people, so he used the scale as a way to talk about different levels of differentiation and the functionality that went with them. The scale showed that at upper levels of differentiation people had a greater ability to distinguish between feelings and thoughts.

According to Bowen, those at the lowest levels of differentiation (0 to 25) have the greatest anxiety, the least ability to cope, are the most psycho-emotionally fragile, and have the greatest tendency to display physical and emotional symptoms. In his day this could be schizophrenia; in ours, it could also be cancer, ADHD, or other ailments. At this level people live in a feeling world because they are unable to separate thought from feelings.

Families and individuals with slightly greater levels of differentiation (25 to 50 on the scale) have an increased capacity to differentiate, but still suffer from having poorly defined selves. They are, to borrow David Schnarch's term, "changelings." They lack much solid self, so they adopt viewpoints and relationships that complement their emotional make-up and support their worldview. They are more adaptive and capable of growth but are still highly susceptible to anxiety-tension. They are more resilient than those lower on the scale and are likely to be impaired less. They tend to have less severe psychological problems and recover faster.

People in the upper realms of the differentiation scale (50 to 75) are more solid, better defined, less anxious, and by and large are much less emotionally reactive. They are better able to distinguish between feeling and thoughts. They enjoy more freedom and move back and forth between intimate relationships and autonomous self-defined activity. They still have some susceptibility to severe stressors, but they are much more capable of calming and soothing themselves.

Bowen saw that higher levels of differentiation were fairly rare. He nevertheless described the attributes of those who might inhabit this portion of the scale (75 to 95) as principle-oriented and value-directed. Although sure of themselves, these folks are not dogmatic, can listen non-reactively, and are secure. They take total responsibility for themselves and are capable of enjoying others who are different. They are aware of their dependence on others and freely enjoy it. They also enjoy low levels of chronic anxiety and are able to function well in intensely emotional situations.

Bowen left the 95 to 100 range of the scale as a purely hypothetical possibility since he considered this as basically an impossible achievement. Completely separating thought from feeling, self from other, and acquiring a totally objective viewpoint seemed impossible to him. As we look more deeply into the evolutionary force in human development we shall see that there doesn't seem to be an ultimate state of human development, a final state of absolute human maturity. The human species is calibrated to respond to the needs of the evolutionary process. Bowen recognized nature in humanity, but he didn't fully realize the scope of evolution working through humankind.

The scale became a theoretical tool; it revealed the complexity of what Bowen saw, his awareness that there was a continuum of functional capabilities, and showed that he was on the verge of understanding the developmental significance of his work. How differentiation reflects development became clearer later through the work of other developmental theorists and reflects another significant piece of the pattern that connects. There is no evidence that suggests that Bowen recognized, in more than a rudimentary fashion, that differentiation was an evolutionary process.

Bowen believed that one's level of differentiation could increase, though he wasn't certain it could do significantly. He seemed convinced that one's level of differentiation, and the degree to which it could be changed, was largely pre-determined by one's family-of-origin. It took the innovative work of David Schnarch, a later differentiation theorist and couples therapist, to reveal the potential for increasing differentiation in every significant relationship.

I bring the differentiation scale into the picture to show that Murray Bowen brought differentiation to the attention of psychologists as a biopsychosocial process. He mapped out important terrain that led to further exploration that is still going on. In so doing, he made possible, as did the explorers of the past, the discovery of a New World. This discovery was even more unusual and complex than that made by earlier explorers. Murray Bowen embodied a form of consciousness, an awareness, which co-evolved with his observations. He saw, and thought, in an unusual way. He became, through his observations, a systems thinker.

Systems Thinking

Bowen was an explorer with a spirit of adventure and an intrepid desire to put psychotherapy on a more scientific basis. In the process, he discovered a convergence between nature and human emotional processes. Observing this convergence closely, over time he came to realize he was witnessing something that was unknown in the human world—the operations of a natural (not made by man) system. This realization led Bowen to sharpen his observations and to develop a vocabulary drawn from biology to describe what he saw in a way that distinguished his observations from other prevalent ideas.

Soon he came to realize that what had become visible to him was invisible to others. It was at this point that Bowen realized that his observations had transformed him. He lived in a different world than others. His was a world comprised of emotional systems, and his thinking included an awareness of natural systems. He had, in short, become a systems thinker.

Bowen was not the first systems thinker, but he was the first to realize that systems thinking was rare, unconventional, and necessary. He spent as much energy trying to convey the importance of this New World comprised of natural systems as he spent upon developing his new form of psychotherapy, and rightly so. A new unknown world had materialized where it seemed nothing had existed before. Bowen's world, the world of natural systems, didn't fit into the known world of individual psychology.

He thus had to spend time helping others to see this world, to sustain awareness of it, and to be effective in treating the symptoms that are typical of emotional systems under stress. He did so, but this limited his explorations. This is why we will now turn to the work of David Schnarch and Rabbi Edwin Friedman, who further explored this new terrain, the world of natural emotional systems. Systems thinking became sufficiently established by the time of Bowen's death that his form of family therapy has survived him. Additional forays into this complex New World have now occurred. The world of natural systems, however, and awareness that humankind partakes of this aspect of nature still remains as part of our transformative potential.

What Bowen didn't know, and what we now know, is that systems thinking is a form of awareness that depends upon the achievement of a certain level of maturity. When we turn to the perspective of "the pattern that connects" that developmental theorists offer, we will see that systems thinking unfolds only after other developmental accomplishments are achieved. At present we have no psychological orientation that is designed to promote this kind of psychological sophistication, but Bowen's explorations, his work, and his consciousness, points us in that direction.

Growing a Self-in-Relationship (or Self-Differentiation)

There is a bridge that joins the Old World of traditional psychology and the New World of natural systems. It is the process of growing a self. To grasp how radically things have changed, however, consider the question: how does one grow a self in a world of connection? This isn't a question that arises from traditional psychology. There the assumption is that everything about selfhood happens within. The natural systems viewpoint makes it clear that the project of growing a self also happens between.

Murray Bowen can be considered the discoverer of this New World of natural systems. His primary concern was the family, and he provided the best map of this world he could. For him, the family was the most important reference point on his map. Others have had the courage and sense of adventure necessary to explore this same terrain. As we look at the project of growing a self-in-relationship we will turn to another explorer/mapmaker, Dr. David Schnarch.

David Schnarch has concerned himself with the dynamics of the couples' dyad. As such, he too has created a map of this important terrain, a map which points to a new way of understanding long term committed relationships. This map, alongside Murray Bowen's, describes the challenges inherent in growing a self-in-relationship, what is also referred to as "differentiating a self."

A differentiated self is one that can be unique and autonomous without giving up connection. Thus, the process of growing a self-in-relationship is a complex one that includes developing many capabilities. The primary challenge is to develop some capacity to balance the twin holonic drives of desire for togetherness and autonomy.

Early on, due to our mammalian inheritance, we had little capacity to do this; we are hard-wired by our mammalian brain's nature to seek to know ourselves through those around us. Thus, we are prone to seek our sense of self from the family we find ourselves so dependent upon. This tendency, if allowed free reign, usually results in what Bowen called fusion, a single-family identity and reality. Some families, under the duress of chronic anxiety, function as a unit and allow no autonomy. Others, under the same kind of duress, allow very little connection. They fly as far apart as possible. Both these types of families are poorly differentiated and offer their members very little room to develop selves, or realities, of their own. One of the first variables that determines the struggle an individual has in developing a self of their own, a self-in-relationship, is the level of differentiation, or maturity, of one's family (recall Bowen's differentiation scale).

So far, this map differs very little from traditional psychology, which sees the family-of-origin as the originator of many problems. The goal, however, is quite different. A well-differentiated self may still have the full range of childhood traumas that traditional psychology has focused upon but relies instead upon the strength of one's self-chosen values and one's capacity to handle anxiety. Growing a self-in-relationship relies heavily upon staying in touch with the ones who have delivered so much pain and lack of support. Staying in touch means that an individual learns to cope with pain and disappointment while staying on course with developing one's own way of seeing and being in the world.

Growing a self-in-relationship is ultimately a process of establishing your freedom to be yourself, to be self-defined, by taking responsibility for yourself. No relationship context is allowed to define you for very long: that includes your family, marriage, community, job, or society. It requires the acquisition of a capacity to be yourself even when others don't appreciate you, or even work actively to undermine you.

David Schnarch calls this capacity self-validation. He points out that humans are such complex organisms that they cannot truly fit in, or belong, if they don't feel like they are truly accepted for who they are (a greater communion is achieved through increasing autonomy). To gain this kind of acceptance one must be willing to be oneself, paradoxically, without the acceptance of others and be capable of validating oneself and staying true to one's unique viewpoint. Self-validation is an acquired skill; it is not hard wired like the reliance on others for support and safety. Acquiring this capacity means staying in contact with people who don't support you while you learn to support yourself.

As the last few paragraphs have made evident, the process of growing a self-in-relationship is an exacting and difficult process. It is a process of acquiring new capabilities, often despite others, in a paradoxical attempt to relate to them right where they are without giving up where you are. Doing this requires skill that is not acquired from a manual, but from the hard-won and bracing effort of learning through experience. The hallmark of a truly differentiated self-in-relationship is integrity. Here I'm referring to the capacity to maintain your shape, values, and ability to function in the midst of relationship tensions. Acquiring the capacities necessary to be functional even in a dysfunctional relationship context requires a willingness to stay in contact with your relationship environment. In that manner you gain a capacity to change that environment by changing yourself.

Growing a self-in-relationship is a complex and lifelong process, far too complex to completely portray in these few short paragraphs. The diversity of the human family prevents a thorough picture, but the challenges inherent in growing a self-in-relationship are the same for all humans. This is not a human-made, culture-bound phenomenon. Nature designed (and assists us with) this challenge. Growing a self-in-relationship is universally a process of increasing one's capacity for dealing with anxiety, balancing the twin holonic forces, and defining oneself in the midst of relationship tensions. Growing a self-in-relationship serves Evolution by adhering to nature's design. The more capacity we have for coupling with each other and with our natural environment, the greater the likelihood that Evolution can bind us more tightly into the whole of creation.

The Couples System (David Schnarch's Map)

Nature found a solution to the problems created by change by designing co-evolution through coupling. You may recall that coupling, a process of nature defined by Varela & Maturana, joined creatures in linkages with their environment so that each could shape the other, and they could thus grow more tightly linked. It turns out that Nature employed this same method, by way of the dyadic system, to ensure development in humans. Employing his own capacity for systems thinking, David Schnarch provided a map of this aspect of the New World, which shows that our intimate relationships form natural systems that promote growth and the evolution of human consciousness. This, too, is a complex story, too complicated for this discussion, but one that must be touched upon lightly in order to reveal just how comprehensive is the underlying pattern that connects.

David Schnarch took the spirit of adventure, combined it with his courage, his passionate nature and keen intellect, and at great professional risk explored the natural systems terrain of the couples' relationship. He integrated sex therapy and marital therapy by providing, for the first time, a systemic explanation of how personal maturity, passion, intimacy, integrity, and sexual potential were all linked. He was able to show how long-term committed relationships inevitably led to certain kinds of relationship problems, problems that were predictable, because the natural system that underlay relationships was doing what it was designed by nature to do.

He created a unique form of couples' therapy he called the Crucible Approach, which is non-pathological, strength-based and systemic. In so doing he went beyond the normal provinces of conventional wisdom. His approach transcended the focus upon safety, trauma, empathy, and reciprocity that dominated the world of traditional individual-oriented therapy. Instead he focused upon increasing differentiation, anxiety tolerance, self-definition, self-confrontation, self-validation, and solving relationship gridlock through personal growth.

For the purposes of this discussion it is sufficient to note the common characteristics of long-term relationships that reveal the underlying operations of a natural system. These are:

- problems are invariably fusion-related;
- emotional reactivity dominates the mode of relating;
- discrepancies in desire exist;
- relationships inevitably deliver participants to their limitations; and
- personal growth is required to resolve relationship gridlock.

A long-term committed relationship is an emotional system. Schnarch saw that when a primary relationship reached a level of significance comparable with the interdependencies of the family-of-origin, the unfinished psychological work of the past became available in the present. Remember that Schnarch, like Bowen, saw this psychological work systemically.

Long-term relationships become places of anxiety and emotional reactivity because the underlying natural system is signaling that there is something impeding its functioning. That something is invariably a form of fusion. Fusion, for both Bowen and Schnarch, is the degree to which the partners in a relationship are at the mercy of each other. Not only do they lack clear boundaries (a traditional psychological term), but they are like an emotional pair of Siamese twins—when one twitches, the other jumps. They lack selves of their own and each relies on the other to function and refuses to take responsibility for themselves. This creates a lot of difficulty in dealing with the natural interdependencies that are common to long-term relationships and there is usually a struggle amongst poorly differentiated couples regarding whose reality is the correct one. This is essentially a struggle to see who is going to give up self.

This struggle creates a lot of blaming, anger, resentment, and complaining, and tends to generate arguments and hostility. Unfortunately, whether it leads to overt reactivity or not, this struggle frequently results in differences in desire. No one desires, for very long, a relationship for which you have to give up yourself. The loss of sexual desire is a clear indicator of the demand for a partner to de-self. Recall that the well-being of the human holon depends upon balancing the desire for connection with the desire for autonomy, to be oneself. One can only give oneself up for just so long to maintain an important relationship, and doing so has inevitable sexual consequences.

This pattern of giving up self or demanding that the other give up self is the root of fusion, and is a substitute for real growth, for learning how to function on one's own. Because the relationship system is a natural system designed by the evolutionary process, it soon delivers both partners to the place of their own limitations. When this happens, traditional psychology—and couples themselves—tend to think something is wrong. A natural systems viewpoint sees it quite differently. Something is right! Yes, there is probably pain and anxiety, but these are indicators that additional growth is required, that Evolution has come knocking.

At this stage, relationships are in gridlock, a term both Bowen and Schnarch use to designate that there is no room for anyone to move in the old reliable ways. To a couple it feels terrible, like an old fight is haunting them. Gridlock breaks out in many forms: it could be a fight about sex, money, in-laws, religion, or child-rearing. No matter what the form, whether super-hot or like an old familiar pet fight, gridlock always involves the refusal to take responsibility for oneself and the tendency to focus upon the other as the obstacle to well-being. At this point many people will choose to leave or have an affair. Each choice postpones growth and ensures the re-occurrence of the issues involved. These efforts to avoid growth are abetted by traditional psychologies focused upon dysfunction and individual pathology.

Gridlock, Risk-of-Self and Growth

Schnarch has demonstrated that the only way out of gridlock is through it. This means that members of the relationship must grow themselves by turning their attention away from their partner to themselves. Gridlock dissolves when either partner takes responsibility for themself, becomes more self-defined, and is willing to risk placing the relationship in jeopardy by being themself. The move to greater responsibility for self is invariably a move toward self-confrontation, self-validation, greater tolerance of anxiety and pain, and a realization of existential aloneness. Paradoxically, this is also a move toward greater freedom, intimacy, and potentially deeper connection.

Not surprisingly, this shifting of focus from the other to the self is exactly the same movement that is needed to grow a self-in-relationship and to increase one's level of differentiation in the family. For this reason, it is worth devoting more attention to the necessity of risking yourself to become yourself. Growing a self-in-relationship, just like dissolving gridlock, is a process of giving up one way of defining yourself (via something or somebody outside yourself, like a job or a relationship) and choosing a new, self-defined ground upon which to establish your new sense of self. This kind of shift is inherently anxiety provoking and risky.

For a period of time, while you are becoming more solid about your new position and your new orientation, there is going to be more anxiety than you are accustomed to. This is one way you know you are on track; another is that those you are in relationship with— family members, relationship partners, co-workers—are all going to accuse you of being selfish. Weathering the anxiety storm that gets kicked up, both inside and outside, is what enables you to become more solid, and to acquire the capacity to handle more anxiety. Now you have more choices, know more about yourself, and are freer to be yourself while connected to others. Growing yourself, becoming more differentiated, requires you to put your old self on the line in order to develop a new, more functional self. This is Nature's way. Nature, through Her evolutionary restlessness, is pressuring everyone for this kind of growth.

Leadership and Societal Regression (Edwin Friedman's Map)

Evolution is also working through human society. No individual, family, relationship, community, organization, or nation-state is immune to it. The pattern that connects binds us at all levels. What that means is that emotional systems, natural systems, underlie all human activity, shaping the choices that are made (at all levels), and push us toward greater complexity and functioning. Bowen witnessed how societal processes were often governed by natural systemic dynamics. He was able to refer to what he saw but died before he was able to adequately describe how this was so. This was left to one of his greatest adherents, Rabbi Edwin Friedman.

Rabbi Friedman is another adventurer, a New World explorer, and a mapmaker. His focus started out with pastoral counseling and family and marital therapy, but eventually his explorations included the emotional health of congregations and organizations. Finally, just before his untimely death, he recognized the role of leadership in helping emotional systems function well and preventing societal regression.

According to the natural systems theorists, societal regression is a by-product of ambient anxiety. It is the social system being run by the lowest common denominator, the most emotionally reactive and least differentiated elements of that social organism, be it family, organization or nation. Bowen experienced this as he tried to convey the concepts he had derived from his observations. He found that people low on the differentiation scale defined his concepts in the most general and loosest way to avoid the anxiety specificity generated.

Friedman saw societal regression as much more insidious than that. He could see that emotional processes often defined what was possible for organizations and entire nations, just like families. He knew that a culture's level of chronic anxiety determined how functional that culture was and the range of the culture's repertoire of behavioral choices. Seeing the way emotional systems operated and their effects upon organizations, he began to focus upon the role of the leader.

From his perspective, leadership served an entirely different function than had been previously conceived. Rather than emphasizing vision and persuasive ability, the traditional ways of envisioning leadership, Friedman asserted that leaders served best when they were well- differentiated, self-defined, action oriented, and capable of buffering the ambient chronic anxiety of an organization. Instead of focusing upon insight, information, technique, or persuasiveness, he focused on emotional qualities such as maturity, depth, presence, and the ability to recognize what was really at stake.

Friedman mapped out important leadership aspects of the New World. His map, like Murray Bowen's, like David Schnarch's, like this one, is only partial. The map, as they say, is not the territory. These maps do, however, point the way. A New World is coming into view. It is challenging some of our precious assumptions—the world is not flat, and we are more connected than we ever assumed. We could occupy this new way of being, but to do so we must be ready to do two things: give up the comforts of the Old World and brace ourselves for adventure. Nature is calling.

Implications for a Psychology of Interdependence

A New World is here. It has always been here, waiting for us to perceive it. Now, recognizing the possibilities (and responsibilities) that are coming our way, we have a new opportunity. But to take full advantage of how awareness of the presence of natural systems alters everything, we must change our practices.

This especially applies to the field of psychology. The one-sided emphasis upon the individual has got to become more complex. Individuals are important, but as we have seen in the work of Rabbi Friedman, leaders stabilize whole social systems through the power of their maturity and presence. In order to accomplish this feat, however, a leader must be in emotional contact with the social system they are part of, and this requires the skills developed through growing a self-in-relationship, and requires the appropriate valuing of our connections with each other.

A new realm of possibility awaits humanity. The irony is that this realm is already shaping the world we live in. The psychological practices of the current day strive to adjust us to a reality that doesn't really exist except, as Einstein said, as a kind of "optical illusion." When we are buffeted about by the effect of the natural systems in our lives, traditional psychologists often convey the impression that something is wrong with us as individuals. Unfortunately, well-meaning people who want to help frequently do things that are harmful. This tendency, to interpret the effects of natural systems as individual pathology, has got to change. It is time we begin to align ourselves with the natural systems that Nature has designed, so that we can maximize our social potential, our evolutionary potential.

Whatever the psychology of the future is, hereafter it will have to consider these characteristics and adopt the following viewpoint:

- self is relational;
- differentiation is essential;
- anxiety-tension is existential and systemic;
- growth occurs through self-risk, and
- involves the balancing of autonomy and belonging;

- relationship is omnipresent and the primary context for all growth;
- Nature induces psychological anguish; and
- Nature provides the strength and resilience to meet these challenges;
- Evolution is always at work transforming us and our society.

Notice that this viewpoint extends from, and includes, the individual, relationships, social contexts, and the processes of Nature and Evolution. This is a hallmark of a systems perspective. Systems thinking reveals the "pattern that connects." It leads us into a New World, disclosing untapped social potential, and indicating new practices, practices that align us more closely with that which spawned and supports us.

Conclusion

We have only begun to focus our attention upon our natural inheritance. The natural sciences have just begun to reveal to us the magnificence of Evolution's designs. No doubt we still have a lot to learn. We are as yet a young species. If we can find the wherewithal to survive, to stick around for the sake of discovery, then we might yet become the real servants of the evolutionary process. Before this is likely to happen, however, we must learn first what Life asks of us.

What is Life asking us? There are a lot of questions being asked, myriads of challenges that humans have to face. Life is behind most all of them, asking us to grow ourselves, to adapt to reality, not the reality we prefer, nor the reality that we create, but the one that knocks upon our door. We have learned to resist, to assert our independence, our individual wills, believing that our wholeness, our personal dignity is at stake. In the world of separateness, the world where self is a skin-encapsulated being, this makes a kind of heroic sense. Unfortunately, this leaves one going it alone, looking within for the strength to persevere.

The New World offers a very different set of options. Everything is connected. Even going it alone is different. The strength to persevere is a given. Evolution has persisted for billions of years. Life is a partner, not an adversary. We are challenged, but it is in the service of Life, by a process of creation that has endowed us with

all the latest innovations. Life has prepared us with well-tested biological capabilities, with cellular technologies our life scientists are
only beginning to describe. The full consciousness of the Universe
may actually be available to our endeavors. Developmentalists are
beginning to see that Evolution is co-evolving human consciousness.
There is a wealth of riches available to us now, perhaps enough to
ensure our survival. But not on our terms, on Life's terms.

The New World is not waiting to be occupied. We have been
occupying it to our limited ability. We are convinced by our own
narcissism, our own science, that we are alone in a cold, distant
and disconnected Universe. Some intrepid explorers have begun to
show us maps that reveal another world, another Universe that exists
overlapping this one. We already occupy it. But it is like a ghost-
land, haunting us, creating effects we cannot account for without
harming ourselves, while invoking our traditional ways of seeing.
To really live fully in this unknown world, to really enjoy the possibilities that are here, we must develop ourselves, acquire the sight
that comes with increased consciousness, go beyond our limitations,
and risk ourselves for the possible selves that could make this New
World palpable.

ﻉ

CHAPTER 6

🌾

The Developmental Embrace

The perfect state for the human being is not bovine placidity, but the highest degree of creative tension that can be withstood.

—A. L. KROEBER

We do not know yet to what extent the principles operating within man (in the psychosocial world) are identical with the general principles which operate elsewhere in the universe.

—GARDNER MURPHY, 1947

Introduction

There is a story, an old indigenous story that goes like this. Once all the creatures in the world gathered in a great council to clarify the jobs they each perform in the service of Creation. One by one they step forward. The beaver is here to look after the wetlands and to monitor how the streams flow. The worm is here to burrow through the earth so that the roots of plants may find air and nutrients. The deer is here to slip through the woodlands, to watch what is happening.

The council is progressing well, but one poor creature stands away from the fire, in the shadows, uncertain of its role. This is the human. At last this being steps forward and haltingly addresses the assembly, "We are confused. What is the purpose of human beings?" The animals and the plants, the insects and the trees, all are surprised. They laugh, but then the laughter gives way to stunned silence. "Don't you know? It's so obvious!!" "No," replied the human, "we need you to tell us." And the other creatures of the world all responded, "Your purpose is to glory in it all. Your job is to praise Creation."

It is hard to praise Creation when you are divorced from it. This is the unfortunate wisdom in the Western world. Nature is no more than the backdrop, the stage upon which the progress of nations and technology takes place. Emphasizing a hyper-rational world-view, dominated by a scientific narrative that has humankind at the top of the food chain, competing with Nature and separate from it, humankind has lost its moorings. Humanity, and Nature, have suffered from this artificial separation. It is really hard to appreciate the elegant design of Nature when you have to compete with it instead of being one of its beneficiaries.

That is the bad news. The good news is that although most of humankind seemingly has walked away from Nature, Nature has not walked away from us. We are still in the position to praise Creation, to marvel at the wonders of our inheritance. But doing so means that we must answer Nature's call and live on Life's terms instead of our own. Fortunately, the shift from focusing primarily upon the world we construct for ourselves to the world of Life's construction, is part of Life's contingencies. We have been designed to make just such a shift, to know our own place within Creation. This shift is part of "the pattern that connects," a part of our endowment. It is a manifestation of how Evolution surges through our lives, upsetting and disturbing us, and slowly, if we don't resist too much, re-aligning us. If we can organize ourselves so that Life can have its way with us, we can live with the winds of Evolution at our backs.

I am asserting that this shift, a qualitative shift from the concerns of the individual to the concerns of Life, the whole, the Evolutionary process itself, is built into our kind and is available to us if we are willing to cooperate with the designs of Nature. How so? This is the story of human development, the all too unknown story of how Evolution surges through our lives in predictable ways, transforms our consciousness and changes the world in which we live.

This chapter will tell the story of human development, of how it has been described thus far. It is simultaneously the story of how Evolution kneads us into beings that are aligned with the dance of the whole of Creation. Every nook and cranny of human development will not be examined. What matters to this thesis is the overall sweep, the movement that takes place and the driving force, not so much the details of each map. The details are important, they reveal the nuances that can make a life interesting and workable, but it is the big picture that shows best the movement of evolution, the pattern that connects.

There is a grand scale to what is happening. Without knowing it, it is impossible to orient our efforts, to align the psychological project. Here we examine the big picture to capture the majestic elegance of what moves us, of what we must relate to, if we are to become the beings who are not only capable of praising Creation, but who are capable of sustained participation in it.

Development: A Life-long Process

The arc of human development is a long and complex one. To tell the story adequately one must incorporate the whole of a human life, as well as the journey in consciousness that our species has made. I am primarily interested here in conveying the sweep of this arc; the complexities of this movement, though important, are not the major focus of this thesis. I am interested in showing what has languished obscured by the details, the role Nature has played in generating and shaping this arc. My intention is to reveal this ongoing relationship.

Thanks to Jean Piaget, the transformations in cognition that happen as children mature is fairly widely recognized. He was aided in demonstrating the reality of these changes by the fact that the changes of childhood are fairly dramatic and readily observable. It is relatively easy to see the difference between a seven-year-old's awareness and a twelve or seventeen-year-old's. Even with these obvious differences, it took a Piaget to make it possible for humankind to consider how best to support the changes of a growing mind. Now we have largely adopted an educational curriculum that is aligned with these predictable changes.

For a long time, the final stage of Piaget's schema of childhood development was considered to be biological maturity, the final stage of the development of the human mind. This is no longer the case. Starting in the 1960s, developmental scholars have researched the way that human adults think and make sense of the world. What has emerged from their studies is a picture that shows that the human mind goes through many possible transformations (there is a life-long potential), each of which presents a new way of thinking, new possibilities, and a new view of the world. Now a developmental perspective of a range of human possibilities is beginning to emerge.

It is to this picture we are now turning, because in addition to revealing the potentials inherent in human beings, this picture shows the role that Nature plays in the developmental process.

Think about it. We are presented with naturally occurring dilemmas. Life isn't what we thought it was. Our relationships ask the seemingly impossible of us. Our careers, or our family lives, are thrown off by behavior patterns that once worked but now mysteriously produce just the opposite results. The communities and organizations we once relied upon suddenly close in on us, losing their vitality and integrity, leaving us to make sense of the world in new ways. More often than not we just get depressed or feel anxious for unknown reasons. All of these dilemmas are elegantly designed by systemic forces, which are inherent in Nature. They pose challenges for us that are finely honed to disturb our lives. They also offer us a way to comprehend the world anew!

This is what the developmental perspective reveals. How so? Researchers have found that the world we are capable of seeing is a product of our state of mind. As New Agers are prone to say, we create our world with our minds. What they don't say, and often overlook, is the other half of this truth: the world also creates our minds. There is a vital reciprocity that has the world shaping human consciousness and human consciousness shaping the world. It is this relationship, this interdependence, between human awareness and the world, where each affects the other. That is the untold story. The developmental perspective reveals this aspect of the "pattern that connects." Let's see how.

Development as a Stage-by-Stage Construction of Reality

Human development is a life-long adjustment to the experience of Life, whereby the relationship each of us has with Life changes us. These changes in turn alter the life we have, and the way we see Life. This process of being altered by Life is predictable and leads each of us toward a closer identification with Life. In a step-by-step, stage-by-stage process, human awareness unfolds in a direction that starts out with primarily personal interests and moves toward an interest in the whole of Life, indeed, with the Evolutionary process itself. This isn't just something programmed into our genes; it is a process of relationship that occurs as an interaction between Life and individual awareness.

Looking at the shared attributes of the developmental models shows us something about the way Life courses through our lives and alters the way we see the world, ourselves, and each other. These shared attributes are:

- Language
- Differentiation
- Stage-by-stage evolution
- Increasing complexity
- Balancing evolutionary drives
- A more objective embrace of reality

Language
This unfolding is first seen in the very language we speak. The way we think, and the language we use to describe our thoughts, or how we make sense of the world around us, reveals the structure of our consciousness. This turns out to be an important discovery. The way we see the world is shaped by our consciousness, our beliefs. The world looks as it does, not because that is the way it is, but because it is what we can see. In essence, our sense organs, which give us vivid impressions, are governed by what we believe is possible—the structure of our consciousness. It is this fact that has energized the old spiritual idea that we create the world we live in. It is true that we do live in the world we create. But that world is not the world; it is a partial version, a construct of the world.

What psychologists such as Dr. Robert Kegan of Harvard University, Dr. Jane Loevinger of Washington University, and Dr. Clare Graves of Union College in New York, have found, each in his or her own way, is that human consciousness is very pliable. Each discovered that by examining language (again, each in their own way) they could capture the way an individual mind makes sense of, or constructs, the world. They developed different schema, but agreed that consciousness unfolded in a predictable direction, describing development as a stage-by-stage process.

Differentiation
You may recall during an earlier discussion of Evolution, that it had direction. Not surprisingly, that direction is identical to the direction in which human consciousness unfolds. Using sophisticated methods, instruments developed and tested cross-culturally over

the last 40 years, developmental scientists have shown that human consciousness unfolds through a series of partial constructs of reality toward a more differentiated, more complex, and more integrated apprehension of reality. In essence, over time and under the right circumstances (see the section headed The Driving Force) human consciousness and Life gradually embrace each other in a tighter and tighter embrace.

The primary characteristic of this direction is increasing differentiation. Remember Bowen's Differentiation Scale. It was designed to show how as differentiation increased, individuals, families, and organizations gained ability, had a broader behavioral repertoire to draw upon. His work has been confirmed, and elaborated upon, by developmental psychologists, such as Robert Kegan.

Dr. Kegan looked at differentiation and, like Bowen, could see that it was a life-long process that involved separating feelings from thoughts. Kegan, however, went on to show that differentiation also included distinguishing the field of relationships and meaning in which one was embedded in from the self. He developed a viewpoint (see Table 1), that emphasized the tendency of the human mind, at varying places along the continuum of differentiation, to construct reality.

Kegan's research showed that at varying levels of differentiation one is subject to certain aspects of one's environment. This changes as one grows more differentiated. As growth occurs, one gains new freedoms and new capabilities. One transforms what one is subject to or what one is unable to reflect upon, to something one is able to reflect upon or think about. One makes a recurring shift from what one is to what one has. Kegan's theory became known as Subject-Object Relations, but it always rested upon the notion that one's construct of reality was based upon one's level of differentiation. The essential thing that this aspect of Kegan's work revealed was that as differentiation increased, so grew the human mind, gaining access to more and more complex and adaptive ways of dealing with reality.

Remember, differentiation is a biological process in cells. Bowen used the term to describe the same struggle for identity in humans. Differentiation refers to the degree of self-definition that an organism achieves while being embedded in a matrix of relationships. As self-definition increases so does the capacity of that organism (be it a cell, human, or social organism) to integrate itself more fully, and

Stage Name	Subject (S) Description of Stage Object (O)
Impulsive	**S – Impulses and perceptions O – Reflexes (sensing and moving)** My impulses drive me. Others are good or bad, important or unimportant, based upon impulses and perceptions. Social relations are defined by impulses and no distinct other exists. Conflicts around impulses and perceptions are governed by punishment or by obedience to those with whom one feels attached.
Imperial	**S –Needs, interests and wishes O – Impulses and perceptions** My needs and wishes are everything. Others are instruments that may assist or impede the fulfillment of needs. Social relations are organized around .need fulfillment. Others exist only in relationship to one's needs. Your needs conflict with mine; resolution of this conflict requires fairness or quid pro quo relations.
Interpersonal	**S – Mutuality and reciprocity O – Needs, interests and wishes** I am what I become when I am with another. How I see myself is determined by the relationship contexts I am embedded in. Others are providing the relationship contexts where I get to exist. Social relations are organized around mutuality. The social agenda is organized around being liked and included so that one can have a sense of self. Committed to mutual expectations for preservation of good feelings.
Institutional	**S – Self-authorship and identity O – Mutuality and reciprocity** I am my own being. I am defined by myself and I am distinct I am organized around the principles I have chosen to live my life by. I am complete unto myself. Others are distinct institutions of their own. Social relationships tend to revolve around the need to preserve one's instituted sense of self. The social agenda is defined by one's need to assert and maintain the integrity of one's principles. Conflicts which exist between my self-organization and another's are mediated by principles that transcend relationships.
InterIndividual	***S – Interpenetration with other O – Self-authorship and identity*** *I am distinct. I am whole unto myself and I am incomplete. I am my own being and I am the world's being. I am what I know about myself, and what I am discovering about the world around me. Others are both distinct and aspects of oneself. Social relations can be intimate and the agenda is to gain more complete access to reality, to more fully integrate it, and to more fully integrate oneself into reality. Conflicts are mediated by the assumption of responsibility for the well-being of all, as aspects of self.*

Table 1—Kegan's Stage Conceptions
(Italics indicates a post-conventional perspective)

in a mutually beneficial way. Increases in self-definition, in this case, mean increasing relationship skills. This is the direction of human development, as well as the direction of evolution.

A Stage-by-Stage Evolution

Each of the aforementioned developmental psychologists developed a stage-by-stage formulation of the unfolding of development. There is agreement that human development unfolds in predictable and structured ways. Developmental theorists, however, do not agree on the specific details. Their instruments differ and give them slightly different pictures of what the stages look like. Each of them has a different conception of the stages, but they all agree that human consciousness unfolds in a stage-by-stage way, and that each stage represents an increase of differentiation and a consequent qualitative shift towards greater adaptiveness.

This stage-by-stage movement shows the mutually tightening, ever-aligning embrace of Nature and human consciousness. Each step increases our uniqueness and furthers our integration into the surround we find ourselves within. At first, we are born into a body and all awareness is in the sensations in that body. Then as our brain develops we become aware that we are more than our mere sensations. The early stages of development are primarily about being more than before—more than an extension of mom, more than an extension of the family, more than an extension of my age-cohort, more than my local community of relationships, more than my local culture.

Later stages, though less often evolving, seem to include more awareness not only of being more, and out-growing something, but of becoming more, and gaining something. One becomes more than a member of the culture, one becomes a citizen of a nation-state, and one can become more than a member of a state, one can identify with being a citizen of the world, and one can outgrow even that iden-tification and become an extension of the species. This, too, can be outgrown and one can identify with all of life, with Evolution itself.

All along, as Kegan and others describe, the movement through the stages is from one form of being embedded—for instance, iden-tifying with your family's reality—to another broader form of being embedded, such as our relationships with peers. What the stage-by-stage conception of human development shows is that the same movement that occurs in adolescence happens throughout a human life, making it clear that human beings are capable of change, and of achieving identification with larger-and-larger relationship contexts.

This stage-by-stage view is important for several reasons. In addition to revealing the predictability of the natural evolution of the mind, it reveals some of the difficulty with communication that crop up between individuals, within organizations, and between social entities, including nation states. We will look at this hidden diversity later, but for now we simply point out that each stage of awareness constructs reality its own way and one believes the world is as it is seen from this place on the developmental spectrum. Nature toler-ates this conflict early on, but as we shall see, She has created a mind-set (an identification with evolution) that is capable of embracing all of these differences. This, it turns out, is in the direction Evolution is headed.

Increasing Complexity

The stage-by-stage formulation reveals another aspect of human growth: movement along the path of development involves a step-by-step increase in complexity. Identifying with your family's reality, no matter how engaged they are with others, is a lot less complex than identifying with the amalgam of realities that make up a culture, or the world-at-large. These increases in complexity are by-products of an identification with larger and larger relationship contexts. Recall that Wilber pointed out that each transformation of consciousness, each dis-identification from one relationship context to an identification with a larger one, is a process of transcending the smaller context and including it in the larger. Evolution moves us from one complex relationship context to another more complex one. This is how we gain access to new behavioral options, new ways of seeing, and new choices.

Increasing complexity brings with it new freedoms, but also brings additional burdens. New freedom invariably means new responsibilities and an increase in anxiety. This is one reason why every human does not utilize all of the potential available to them. Traditional psychology seems to agree with the conventional sentiment that additional anxiety indicates that something may be wrong. A strength-based approach, on the other hand, assumes that humans are endowed by Nature to handle additional complexities and additional anxiety and views this as a step toward greater maturity.

No matter what orientation one takes toward this process, it goes on. Nature has an agenda of Her own. A person can choose to try to avoid the more complex, more anxiety-provoking reality that one is being thrust into, but the consequences can be harsh. Nature seems to be intent upon evolving. Humans like choice; more specifically, they like control. Nature seems to prefer that humans be as adaptable as possible. When we get into the myriad forms of natural therapy that knock us off balance, we will look more intently at how Nature unsettles us in favor of evolution and growth. One way this happens is that Nature introduces us to new complexities as she grows us.

Balancing Evolutionary Drives

A hallmark of Nature's involvement in human growth is the presence of the sometimes contradictory, sometimes complementary, twin drives of belonging and autonomy. Bowen was fond of pointing out that these drives were so fundamental that they were characteristic of all living protoplasm, and that they also appeared as a tension in all relationships. Not surprisingly, these same tensions are central elements in what developmental scientists are finding in the evolution of human consciousness. Systems thinkers would call these tensions isomorphic—forms that exist across levels. At all levels of human endeavor, the desire to fit in and the desire to be freely oneself play a central role.

In the process of growth, humans struggle with these irreconcilable opposites. This rarely feels good. It keeps us on edge. It is never satisfied. It keeps us unsettled, off balance, and constantly pursuing something that keeps moving. As Robert Kegan points out, no matter how well one manages to balance these twin urges, the balance is always a little unbalanced, temporary, and sure to lead to another period of instability. In essence, these twin urges drive us. In pursuit of fitting in and in maintaining the desire to be ourselves we restlessly change how we function.

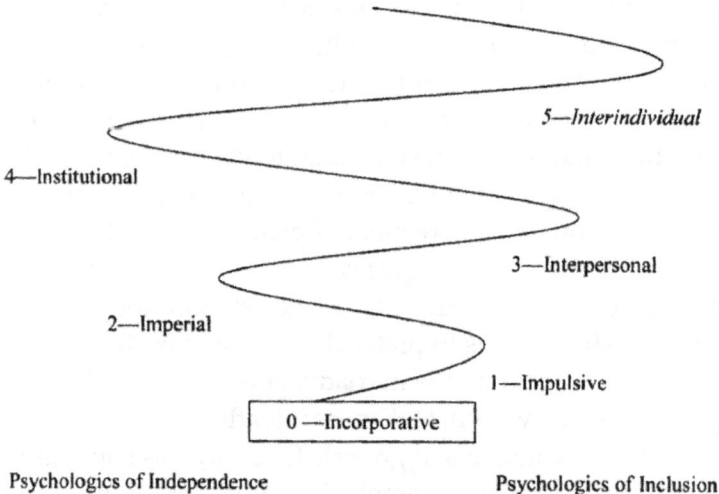

Figure 2—S. Kegan's Spiral of Development
Italics indicate post-conventional development

Each of the leading developmental scientists observed this pattern, although again each saw it in his/her own way. Kegan, who described it best, developed a stage-by-stage model that viewed each stage as a temporary truce, a tenuous balance, between these drives (see Figure 2). In his view, each stage is skewed toward one of these forces, with growth involving temporarily balancing these twin desires in new ways.

Loevinger tended to see the early stages of development as governed primarily by differentiation, a gradual process of slowly dis-identifying with one relationship context in favor of a broader one (see Figure 3). For her, the early phases of growth were more about defining a self as separate from a relationship context. The early stages were primarily about getting away from fitting in, of becoming autonomous, and the later stages as being more about integration. Here she recognized the paradoxical reality that further differentiation allowed for greater integration. In her view then, the urge to be connected to something larger, to belong, was a by-product of increased development.

Overall, Loevinger presents a picture of growth that reveals the twin urges at work. Unlike Kegan and Graves, who saw growth as a back-and-forth, stage-by-stage process of trying to find a better way

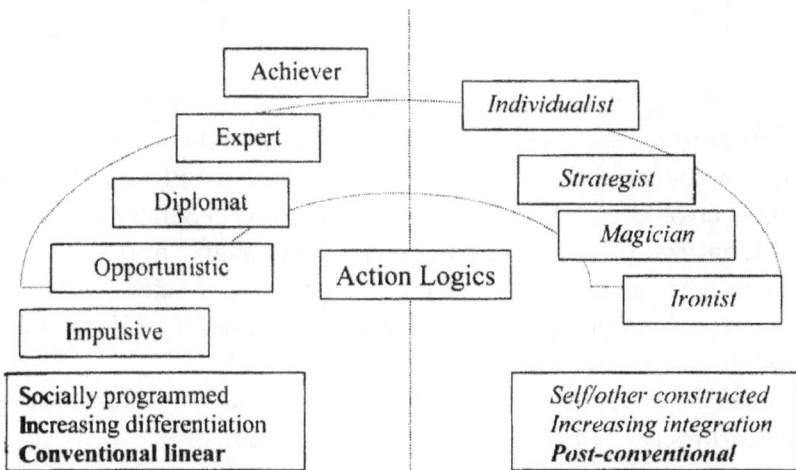

Figure 3—S. Cook-Greuter's Conception of Loevinger's Conventional-Post-Conventional Divide in the Leadership Maturity Framework
Italics indicate post-conventional development

of balancing these tensions, Loevinger embraced a slower, longer wavelength that balanced these tensions over several stages. It isn't really important to this thesis to determine which of these conceptions is most accurate. Here it is only important to show that each of these major theorists recognized, each in their own way, that Evolution had built these design parameters into the process.

During the 30 years that Clare Graves studied human development he was impressed by the regularity with which the questions of self-sacrifice and self-expression appeared. Through diligent study, he found that the urge to sacrifice self gave way to a desire to express self, and vice versa. Human life, according to Graves' early research, was a constant struggle to find a way of being that either didn't sacrifice too much, or express too much, self. He formulated his theory accordingly, stage-by-stage. Humans tried out new strategies that allowed these preoccupations—self-sacrifice and self-expression—to better co-exist.

In so doing, Graves was incorporating into his conception of human development, his realization that belonging, i.e. fitting in, while expressing just the right amount of self, and autonomy without sacrificing too much self, were important human concerns. He was able to see that these concerns were not just relevant now, to his subjects, but had always been important to humankind. Thus, he recognized that there was an important parallel between what he saw unfolding now, and what had transpired in human cultural history (see Table 3).

In making the leap from the exclusively personal, psychological, to the cultural, the collective, he showed not only, that the twin urges played a role at both the organismic level of the individual, but at the collective level of the social. The world, Life, generates and alters (think natural therapy) human consciousness; and human awareness, in turn, alters the world (i.e., perceives and interacts with it anew). This happens in a stage-by-stage way, revealing Life coursing through human consciousness.

Later in Graves's career he came to see that the stage-by-stage growth process not only delivered better ways of handling these urges but generated larger patterns. Thinking systemically, he saw that there was a relationship, a dynamic link, between the progress of human consciousness and the existential conditions that humankind had to deal with. In other words, there is a reciprocal

Stage Name % of population	Ego Development Belonging/Self-expressive	Description of Cultural Stage
AN – Beige 0.1%	**Autistic** Self-expressive	**Semi-Stone Age** - Natural order and natural law prevail
BO – Purple 10%	**Magical Animist** Belonging	**Tribal** – Mystical spirits, good and bad, swarm Earth leaving blessings, curses and spells which determine events. The spirits exist in ancestors and bond "the people" in supportive relationships. Kinship and lineage establish political links. Liaisons form across tribes by marriage.
CP – Red 20%	**Egocentric** Self-expressive	**Exploitive** – Big Spirits, dragons, beasts, and powerful people (chieftains) dominate, set boundaries, punish, and reward according to their whims. Feudal lords protect underlings in exchange for obedience and labor. Pacts of convenience expand influence and control. Control and expansion of turf.
DQ – Blue 40%	**Sociocentric** Belonging	**Authoritarian** – The unfathomable System, Truth, or Force rules the universe, sets human destiny and limitations, prescribes what is "right" and "wrong," gives meaning and purpose to human existence, and rewards the faithful. Treaties, doctrinal alliances, and borders. Diplomacy and sectarianism.
ER – Orange 30%	**Multiplistic** Self-expressive	**Entrepreneurial** — The world is a rational and a well-oiled machine, and has inner working and secrets that cannot be learned, mastered, and manipulated. The laws of science rule politics, the economy (invisible hand) and human events. The world is a chess-board in which games are being played as winners gain pre-eminence and perks over losers. Marketplace partners, strategic alliances.
FS – Green 10%	**Relativistic/Individualistic** *Belonging*	**Communitarian** – Each entity in the human population or in the meta-physical realm is unique, yet belongs to the same cosmic community and should be seen relative to the same field of equals. The bonding impulse within everything and dispersed everywhere rules the world. Human rights issues, collectivism, and reciprocity.

Table 2—Grave's Ego and Cultural Stage Conceptions
Italics indicate post-conventional perspective

A'N' – Yellow 1%	*Systemic* *Self-expressive*	**Systemic** – *The prevailing world order is a function of (a) the existence of different realities and (b) the inevitable movement up and down a dynamic spiral in response to the problems of human existence. The command and control center facilitates the emergence of entities through levels of increasing complexity.*
B'O'Turquoise 0.1%	**Integrated**	**Holistic** – *Universal forces permeate all forms of life, energy, and existence, ordering their movement, changes and patterns. Preservation of eternal truths and forces of the Cosmos.*

Table 2—Grave's Ego and Cultural Stage Conceptions
Italics indicate post-conventional perspective

relationship between human awareness and the environment/society one finds one's self within. Each affects, or alters, the other. They are, to use a term we are now familiar with, coupled.

Graves revealed a link between human consciousness and the world we live in. He also showed that it is a dynamic link, a relationship. The world, Life, generates and alters (think natural therapy) human consciousness; and human awareness, in turn, alters the world (i.e., perceives and interacts with it anew). This happens in a stage-by-stage way, revealing Life coursing through human consciousness.

A More Objective Embrace of Reality
Each step of the way delivers us to a more objective grasp of reality. This is Nature's way of helping us adapt to the complexity of the situation we find ourselves in. Although this has been noticed by several theorists, none has seen it more clearly than Robert Kegan, who reiterates Piaget's sense that with each stage of human development comes an increase of the overall ability to grasp the Truth as it is, in the environment in which we live.

As we proceed to grow, there is a corresponding transformation of awareness that increases our ability to adapt and to integrate more completely into our environment. This is the movement of Evolution, the product of human consciousness coupled with the existential conditions of Life. Each stage of development introduces us to an even more accurate apprehension of reality.

Along the way we are always handicapped by a partial version of reality. Within each stage of development Evolution provides us with a more complete version. The movement of Evolution carries us, whether we are willing to go or not, from concerns that are primarily personal (egocentric) to concerns that are related more to the whole (world-centric).

The Movement

Human development reveals Evolution at work within consciousness. Each successive alteration serves Life's cause. There is a direction to the movement. There may be differences in the stage-by-stage models of different theorists, but there is agreement about the general direction of the movement. What becomes evident as we look at the movement is the direction and intent of Evolution.

Figure 4 shows the relationship between two ways of describing the overall direction of developmental movement. The top boxes contain Kohlberg's description of moral development. He described the development of moral sensibilities as a journey from a primary obsession with bodily needs through the typical attempt to fit into the prevailing culture and play by its rules. He sees that human beings can acquire a capacity to root their sense of morality in self-chosen principles, larger and more complex principles that go beyond the social contract to a deeper sensibility (post-conventional). The lower set of boxes describe yet another way of viewing this movement, by Carol Gilligan. Here we see that the center point of belonging shifts as development takes place. Again, the movement starts with a basic concern for the organism, as defined by the body and its sensations and needs. As growth takes place however, the sense of the organism one belongs too expands and shifts outward to include larger and more complex relationship contexts.

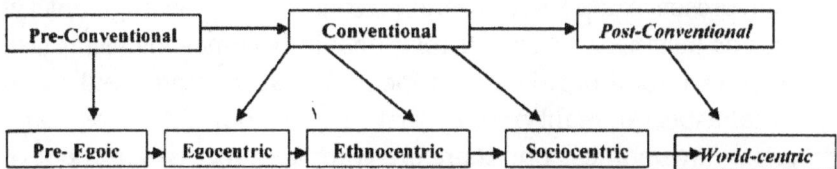

Figure 4—The Movement of Developmentn from Pre-Conventional to Post-Conventional and from Pre-Egoic to World-Centric
Italics indicate post-conventional perspective

By combining these two viewpoints, we gain a picture of how Evolution shifts the focal point of human consciousness toward, and then away from, individual concerns. The aim of Evolution seems to be to construct an individual in service of a larger, more encompassing, world. This figure also reveals that Evolution seems to take aim at a totally different way of organizing the self from the more common viewpoint. It is important that we consider the possibility that Evolution actually seeks to develop human consciousness beyond conventional considerations to an awareness that transcends those concerns and includes them in an even larger, more complex world. That is described in this figure as post-conventional, and as world-centric.

What does that mean? It means that maturity isn't what it used to be. It used to be assumed that humans reached maturity when they became adults (when they left their teen years). Then there was the realization that there was more to adulthood than that. Maturity then was conceived in more conventional terms, such as marriage, family, or an established career; in other words, when one found a place in society. And maturity was always considered solely in terms of the individual, which is a conventional consideration. Now, once again, the idea of human maturity is changing.

The discovery and subsequent mapping of post-conventional forms of consciousness have shown that human awareness is pliable and constantly evolving. In addition to revealing new capabilities (see Table 3), post-conventional awareness has brought with it the realization that there are human possibilities that are, as yet, un-actualized. The picture of human growth that is emerging, is one that shows new post-conventional capacities and a New World to be occupied. It now seems that there is no end-state, no ultimate maturity to be attained. Instead, what is becoming evident, is that human awareness is plastic, subject to being altered by Evolution.

The presence of post-conventional consciousness changes everything. For instance, the role of relationship becomes visible at last, not just as a good option as it appears in earlier states, but as an essential aspect of reality, a way that Life functions. Also, as many theorists have pointed out, there are complex processes in modern life that require more complex forms of consciousness. It has become axiomatic amongst developmentalists that leaders, therapists, teachers, and parents cannot facilitate change that is more complex than

Conventional	Post-Conventional
	(includes conventional and adds)
70% (Loevinger) to 98.9% (Graves) of pop.	*30% (Loevinger) to 1.1% (Graves) of pop.*
• reliance upon external validation	• *reliance upon self-validation*
• finds self-esteem through others and externalities	• *self-esteem is internally generated, motivated by own principles*
• susceptible to external definition	• *self-defined*
• little self-confrontation	• *ability to self-confront*
• tendency to play to the lowest common denominator socially	• *interested in the highest common denominator socially*
• linear, cause & effect formulation of reality	• *systemic thinker, sees relationships, formulates reality more complexly*
• experiences the twin urges as opposites and generally generates anxiety tension	• *experiences the twin urges as complimentary and generally generates excitement and creative tension.*
• objects clearly defined and separated from context	• *focus on process/context rather than objects, sees cycles, and natural systems*
• Life is a problem to be solved, and all problems have solutions	• *Life is a mystery to be lived; there is an element of mystery and serendipity.*
ª science has all the answers, or will have them	• *lives with ambiguity and paradox, seeks many forms of feedback/information*
• knowledge is accumulative, value-free, and objective.	• *likes to question assumptions and seeks multiple explanations*
• leadership is charismatic, personal, and vision and persuasion based..	* *leadership is based on presence, maturity, depth, solidity, and principles*
• leader's "selfishness" destroys community	• *leader's self maintains integrity of community.*

Table 3—Conventional/Post-Conventional Comparison

their own consciousnesses. So the leap to post-conventional awareness is a leap to a greater behavioral repertoire, a form of effectiveness that is sorely needed now.

In his book, *In Over Our Heads*, Robert Kegan points out that we live in an age when the complex demands of modern life are greater than what we are prepared for. We lack the curriculum, as he points out, to develop the forms of consciousness we really need. This is true. As a culture we have not as yet sufficiently encountered the New World.

The important idea to take away from this discussion is that new forms of awareness, with new capabilities, are becoming available to us just at the time we really need them. Right now, we do not have the cultural supports to promote this awareness. That doesn't stop Evolution from pushing us towards development of these capabilities anyway. The surge of Evolution creates a lot of disruptions and pain that could be rendered more meaningful and useful with a therapeutic approach that perceives this movement as something desirable and healthy.

The Helix

Finally, the developmental embrace, this stage-by-stage movement by which human consciousness unfolds and adapts more and more closely with Nature, has been captured in an illustration adopted by several developmental theorists. It is helpful to see how Evolution moves through human consciousness in a graphic form. An illustration makes the abstract more palpable and conveys complex information in simple ways. For this purpose, I'm going to call back Figure 2, Kegan's Spiral of Development.

Instead of focusing upon Kegan's stages, I want to draw your attention to the helix, the spiral. The spiral portrays the movement of Evolution by its ever-expanding nature. By growing, the spiral shows that Evolution expands consciousness by never covering the same ground twice. Instead of focusing solely on the past, it reaches to a larger, more expansive future. The past is embedded in the reach toward a future that holds new possibilities, a future that requires movement. The spiral shows that new perspectives include and go beyond old ones. This accounts for the familiarity and the sensation

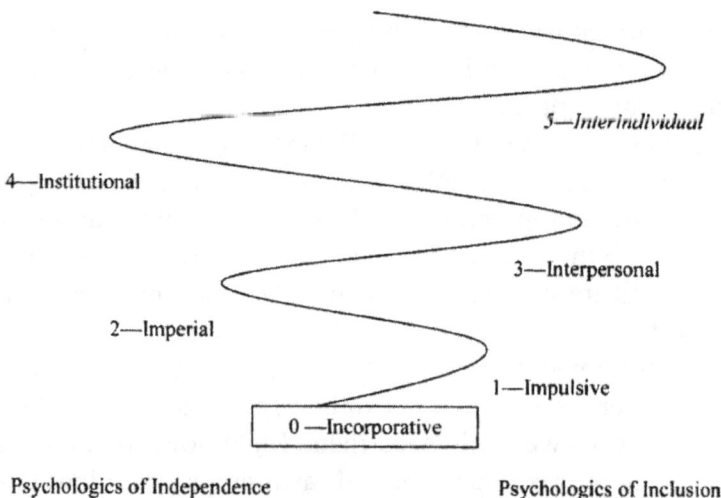

Figure 2—S. Kegan's Spiral of Development
Italics indicate post-conventional development

of a recurring cycle, while demonstrating that something new is present to be integrated. The ever-widening gyre conveys the ongoing nature of this movement, the restlessness of Creation.

The spiral captures the movement of Life coursing through us and pushing us into the future. Life is constantly playing through our lives, disturbing us, and delivering us to new challenges that require new ways of operating. The relationship with Life and the role that Life plays in shaping us is made even more obvious later when we look once again at Clare Graves' double helix model of human evolution (Figure 5). In the meantime, it is important to consider the motive force that drives Life and human consciousness toward each other.

The Driving Force

Life is a miracle. It is predictable and wild; predictable because we have identified some of the dynamics that lead to growth; wild, because Life stimulates growth in unpredictable and unforeseen ways.

Early on it seems like the developmental project is defined mostly by a need for an effective construct. Always, it is a partial reality, subject to being tipped over by Life. Growth goes through a series of partial constructs that expand the world you identify with (by expanding the world you no longer identify with or are subject to).

Each of these steps results in a "sealing up," a taking for granted that this world, the world you are now introduced to, is the world. This assumption is cause for a lot of conflict. A developmental perspective reveals that this is not necessarily so. I call the well-meaning and confusing cross-talk that often happens between people who occupy different worlds (developmental stages), the "Babel effect." There is a hidden diversity that often impedes communication and arouses distrust.

Sealing up is inevitable; having a stable world depends upon it. But this world, too, must be forsaken. It must be, as Robert Kegan says, "hatched out of." Each forsaken world gives way to a larger, more complex world where a new self-identity waits. Each successive world is deeper and takes in more of the complex social, environmental, and existential surround, resulting in a corresponding complexification of consciousness and the evolution of a new self.

Each step is anxiety-provoking as it involves becoming a stranger in a strange land. This is why growing the ability to tolerate anxiety is so important. New Worlds do not become available to those who let anxiety dominate them; instead, they get what traditional psychologists call "anxiety disorders."

If one learns to tolerate anxiety and can bear existential aloneness, a person can become a true individual, as we in the West would describe it. This is the birth of the true self. Evidence suggests that most people never reach this level of development since most people do not give birth to their own unique selves. Sadly, we live in a cultural world that does not support this much growth. And most unfortunately, we as a species, and the world at large, suffer enormously from thinking that when this does happen, it is the end of the story.

The birth of the psychological self is not the apex of development. Evolution has other plans for us. Birth provides access to other stages of growth. There is a great deal more uncertainty to be integrated and additional New Worlds open up beyond this point.

Sometimes it is the wildness of life that delivers one to a New World. Hardships, such as my stroke, cancer, an accident, or some incurable disease, will tease one out of one world into another. These transitions have their own rigors, but they can deliver one to a New World just as surely as a more orderly life process.

Eventually though, the process of growing and giving up one's world and self leads to a more enduring sense of self. This is the self that is a pattern of consciousness. It is both whole and incomplete, mirroring Life in that it is predictable, still human, and wildly connected, part of something larger.

There is an idiosyncrasy to what happens as a person becomes more themselves, more unique, and more able to join in something larger. This is differentiation at work, the place where paradox becomes a way of life. All along the way, through each stage new capacities to balance the twin urges go online. But here in the post-conventional realms of human potential, Life is embraced more completely, and we fulfill more of our holonic potential.

What drives all of these changes? Life does. Early on it punctures our narcissism by putting others in our way. It also topples our constructs of life by breaking into them, introducing complexities we cannot deal with without growing. The basic pattern that developmental theorists and therapists see all the time is discrepancy. There is a conflict between the way things or people behave and the way they want things to be. These discrepancies reflect a worldview that is incongruent, inaccurate, and incomplete. They frustrate and impede our will, and they transport us.

Sometimes growth is brought about by internal contradictions or conflicts. As Life introduces us to more complex situations, we ourselves grow more complex. We find ourselves torn between two or more options and aspects of who we are or can be. These moments often confront us with gut-wrenching choices where, as experts in differentiation recognize, we are torn by choices that eliminate possibilities as they define us.

David Schnarch eloquently describes how anxiety in conjunction with significant long-term relationships creates natural emotional systems that lead inevitably to difficult, often painful, self-defining choices. Family life, marriage, even friendships can generate these types of dilemmas. They are predictable and elegantly designed.

Often, refusal to take responsibility for one's self will lead directly into painful confrontations, with consequences unforeseen or long avoided. Simple choices to preserve self or valued relationships as one has in the past, can backfire. In each case, the natural systems created by our emotional make-up in conjunction with others, will create specific dilemmas that confront us, like it or not, with our own limitations. These confrontations, as unsavory as they seem, represent the call of Nature as Life invites us to grow ourselves, to become more complex, to be more fully capable.

The odd, often compelling thing about these dilemmas that Life confronts us with, is that no matter how we respond to them, we are shaped by them—whether we choose to get married, have kids, have an affair, stop being sexual, make others pay for our unhappiness, or live with integrity. Life uses these choices to create fresh opportunities for growth. We are transformed by our own choices, not because we live in a vacuum as disconnected beings as traditional psychology assumes, but because those choices create impacts on our surround, and because we are connected, those impacts eventually rebound upon us.

There is an ongoing, reciprocal relationship between Life and human awareness. No matter what we do, we do not fall out of this matrix of relationships. We are shaped by it. Our choices impact it, resonating outward, activating systemic forces that come back to us in ways that are specific to our original behavior. We are met by the consequences of our choices. Sometimes we are confirmed, and sometimes we find ourselves challenged, but in each case, Life cajoles us onward toward a deeper embrace of our responsibility to be ourselves and to connect as deeply as we can with the larger surround of which we are a valuable part.

Transition: A Relationship Process

An important aspect of the story of human development involves transformation—of what happens when one makes the transition, the journey between one world and another. We should know that we are not abandoned to random forces, not weaklings who have lost control, not psychologically defective, but we don't. Why? Because the theory of the lonely, disconnected individual makes such occurrences breakdowns instead of breakouts.

Breaking out happens all the time. Every human life is subject to this kind of metamorphosis, yet we tend to think it means that something is wrong, labeling it a crisis instead of a natural expression of Life at work in us. Thus, we resist Life. We fight our own evolution, and we experience lots of unnecessary suffering because we are not willing to suffer necessary suffering. Thankfully, none of this angst stops the tide of change, the surge of Evolution. But it does slow change and makes us feel bad and alone instead of good, healthy, and accompanied. So, understanding that human life includes periods when natural therapy is at work is extremely important.

How is it that a human life can be wrested from one world and delivered to another? Well, it isn't as a result of random forces, chaos assailing our orderly world. No, development is more predictable than that. We may not know the exact moment when Life will intercede, nor the exact nature of that intervention, but we do know that it can and will happen, and that when it does it is an expression of our evolutionary potential. Emergence, a power of the Universe, a way that Evolution and Life unfolds, breaks us open and enables us to find ourselves anew, not only for our own sakes, but for the sake of Creation.

It looks as if Life wants something of us. It puts us through big, sometimes unimaginable changes, as it restlessly searches for new creative ways to unify and diversify everything. These changes enhance us, they don't always feel good, but they render us more adaptable, more adept, more human. These changes, which are necessary for Evolution to proceed, offer us an opportunity to know our place in the whole procession of Life.

The Biopsychosocial Nature of Life

What this journey into the developmental realm has shown is that Life courses through us. We are living extensions of Evolution. None of this is intuitively obvious. In fact, the new developmental perspective makes it clear that the picture of what is really at play couldn't even be accurately perceived until adequate development took place. The systemic thinking that brought this whole adventure into focus is not a by-product of learning (i.e., it can't simply be taught), but of the structure of consciousness.

Development indicates that some of the world is always imperceptible. This is not a handicap to be overcome, but a fact of life, a way that Life grooms us. If, as in the indigenous story at the beginning of this chapter, we are really going to be open to the wonders of Life and praise Creation, then we have got to know that we are participating in an unfolding miracle. Only hubris leads us to believe that we can know everything we do. We are the conscious animal, but we haven't evolved as much as we tend to think we have.

This, however, isn't the whole story. Evolution is proceeding. And because it is, we have been introduced to a New World, a world that contains an additional complexity for us to embrace. This world is more integrated than our thinking has been. Here, we bump into Ken Wilber's essential message: to grasp the nature of the wonder we are participating in, we need an integral approach. And so the ungainly word "biopsychosocial" was coined. It refers to the connection that exists between biology, psychology, and sociology. It refers to the elegance of the pattern that connects us.

We are biological organisms, subject to the same processes that have characterized the evolution of all life forms. We are also psychological beings who bring a consciousness to play, a consciousness that simultaneously apprehends the world and constructs it. We get in our own way (not to mention how we obstruct others and Life itself), but we have the capacity to get out of the way, to collaborate.

And we are social beings, capable of interdepending, of opening up and being ourselves, of embracing others, of collaborating, of sharing our unique ways of perceiving and responding to the exigencies of Life.

We are all of this at once, and possibly more. So we need a psychological approach that embraces all of what we are. Evolution continues, an orientation that expects the buffeting around, the raw painful emergence of Life.

Clare Graves set the stage for this realization. He had the rare insight that systemic forces were at work in human development. He depicted this through his double helix model of human development (see Figure 5 duplicated below). In it we can see that there is an ongoing relationship between existential conditions, the environmental, social, and mind-set prevalent in our culture (the existential helix), and the development of the structure of human consciousness (the black helix). Graves saw that this was a reciprocal relationship, that consciousness affected existential conditions, and these conditions, in turn, affected consciousness.

Graves' recognition showed the way Nature had once again coupled human life to the environment, so each could affect the other in order to become more tightly aligned. This is an important development in human awareness, and a timely one. As the climate changes, so must, so will, our consciousness change.

Conditions in the world, the larger systems of Life, are changing; and as they do they will impinge upon us, asking us to change too (natural therapy). If we have good sense, we will change now to minimize the suffering we can expect as a species. If we delay we only increase the likelihood of greater suffering. In either case, there will be suffering until we bring ourselves, individually and as a species, into better alignment with the conditions we have co-created.

This is our ongoing task, to bring our selves, relationships, and social organizations into alignment with the evolutionary thrust. A new psychological orientation, an orientation toward Life, is only a part of the overall adjustment that is taking place. Ken Wilber espouses a new integral vision, which could, if it were considered, lead us into an era where integrity, personal and social, means embracing Life, and acting accordingly.

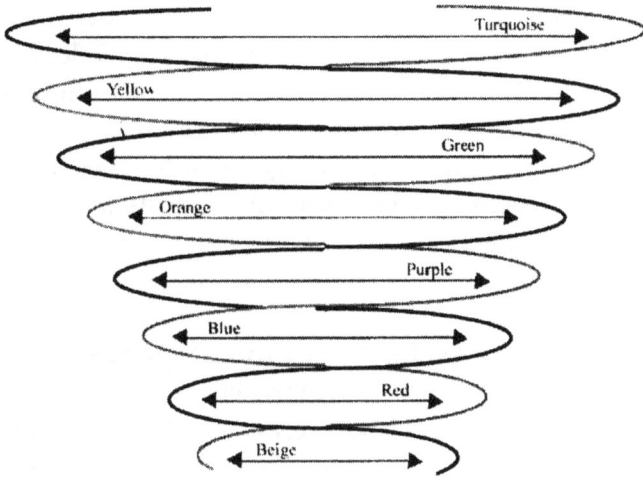

Graves Double Helix

Self- Expressive (autonomous)   Self-Sacrificing (belonging)
Existential Helix represents Existential Conditions   **Black Helix** represents Structure of Consciousness

Figure 5—Graves Double Helix Model of Human Development

Multidimensional Integrity

We are entering an era where environmental limitations will threaten the viability of the human experiment. As the ancient Chinese scribes knew, such periods of crisis represent periods of great opportunity. As the green helix shifts, so shall our minds. We have a chance to put the winds of change, the surge of Evolution, at our backs. All we need do is to go through the hard work of redefining integrity. We can no longer afford to consider integrity as only a personal, individual quality. Now we must find a new meaning for integrity, one that aligns the considerations of the individual with the needs of the whole and aligns our relationships with the environmental and social surround. Integrity must become multidimensional.

It has been said that no man is an island. In an era when islands are disappearing, where the ground is literally being submerged beneath our feet, these words and the awareness they convey are very poignant. The age of disconnection, from each other, from the world around us, from the Life of this planet, and paradoxically, from ourselves, is over.

We still need extraordinary individuals, but now we need people who know how to be whole unto themselves while staying connected deeply with what is going on around them. Communities and other social organizations, including multinational corporations and nation states, depend upon the emergence of connected individuals whose integrity ensures and requires the integrity of the whole. This is what Life is asking of us.

Implications for a Psychology of Interdependence

A new psychological orientation must reflect what we have discovered about our nature, about Nature, and about the interrelationship between these two aspects of the whole. Relationship is the norm in the Universe. There is no aspect of human development that is not impacted by the fact that we are connected, that we are tightly woven into the fabric of Life. We are coupled, joined with our surround—existential, societal, or familial. This is a fact of Life that is only now emerging into our awareness. It is a timely and ultimately hopeful realization. And it brings with it not only new possibilities, but new responsibilities.

The developmental perspective is important by itself. We need to know that Life is knocking upon our doors, that the restlessness, anxiety, and depression that afflicts so many is not weakness or moral turpitude. Change happens. Not because something is wrong, but because Life is pressing us towards Evolution's needs. To know this, to be prepared for it, to feel accompanied, and to have someone who knows these white waters and their cross currents makes the whole adventure more meaningful personally, and potentially more useful to the whole.

The developmental perspective reveals more than the dignity of humankind's participation in Evolution. The complexity of human relations also comes into view. We are so complex that we carry the hallmark tensions of the pattern that connects. We are, after all, human holons, beset with twin desires that keep us on edge. We have urges that frequently contradict each other, and we restlessly search for a tenuous balance, that doesn't last for long, all in service of Life's need to grow us. Because we live in an era that doesn't yet know about these natural forces, we tend to think something is wrong. We blame upbringing, or a permissive culture, and resist

Life. And so we suffer a divorce rate that is too high, relationship distrust, and the death of desire, never knowing there is something right going on, and that potential is locked away in these conundrums.

Add to this the complexity seemingly imposed upon us by virtue of our ongoing relationship with the existential conditions we literally find ourselves within. The developmental perspective makes it clear that there is a reciprocal relationship between the structure of human consciousness and the conditions of Life that impinge upon us, asks things of us, or brings home the consequences of our personal and collective choices. Adaptation is an exacting process. It can leave people anxious and depressed, afraid of living, seemingly victims of existence. This is a kind of suffering that could be rendered meaningful, as more than just a personal failure, if we had a psychological orientation that really considered what is at stake in human relations.

Life has created us. It has made a complex organism that is capable of embracing the complexity of Life. We are not orphans. Life is still with us. But it is asking something of us. It upsets and disappoints us, it breaks us open, by breaking apart our precious lives, all in service of a more complex awareness. Life unfolds each of us by teasing out the necessary complexity through hardships and initiatory ordeals. So much resides in these crises/opportunities that we need a psychological awareness that does not settle for a return to functioning but seeks the kind of reorganization that serves the whole. Life forces transition upon us, but cultural attitudes see misfortune to be treated, rather than as an opportunity to be revered.

The reverence for Life, for the Evolutionary process, for the level of connection that alters the whole psychological project is itself a product of a developmental perspective. A psychology of interdependence is a product of the systemic awareness that only comes from a post- conventional perspective. Graves, Wilber and others have all said that a concern for the viability of the evolutionary process, as well as an understanding of the contributions of all the stages of development that characterize human evolution, is a developmental achievement. The viewpoint born of this development that informs this psychological perspective. A new post non-conventional perspective offers us a way to support the kind of development that is so sorely needed now. It also offers a way of reframing

many of the dilemmas that afflict us as a species and, in the end that
has always been one of the most valuable contributions any psychological perspective could offer.

Conclusion

This chapter, and those preceding it, have set forth the way Life
surges through each of us in a pattern that is predictable, and shows
how connected each of us is with the Evolutionary Process. The pattern is ancient—predating life. Starting with the big picture, the Universe worked our way down to individual consciousness in an effort
to show how the big picture and the details of our lives are related.
All of this was done to demonstrate the pattern that connects us all
to the processes of Life.

Each of us is an extension of Evolution and is the beneficiary of
the relational means that Evolution uses to fulfill its purpose. Life
unfolds us in the service of Evolution, sometimes in deeply unsettling ways, and asks us to open ourselves (and to become ourselves),
and to grasp Life more closely for the sake of the whole.

This is the pattern of connection, the movement of Life through
each of our individual and interconnected lives, impacting us
through relationship from all directions. Each of us generates relational impacts that resonate far beyond our awareness and sometimes rebounding upon us, and each of us is impacted in turn.
The developmental perspective reveals how we humans, like other
organisms, are coupled with our surroundings and involved in a
dance that is completely improvisational and interactive. The choices
we make, both individually and collectively, change the world, and
the world, in turn, changes us.

This is the way of Evolution. Life has been patterned on the basic
processes of Evolution and we, despite our hubris, are privy to these
same patterns. It is time to acknowledge this, and to orient our helping professions accordingly.

At the same time that we are slowly grasping that a pattern
of connection prevails in the world, a New World is emerging. It
is still largely unknown and we have only just begun to access it.
Early explorers like Bowen, Graves, Schnarch and Freidman have
offered us new ways of considering ourselves, each other, and what
is possible between us. This New World currently exists beyond the

conventional world we are so attached to. Like the Old World of the past, which was once a new world, this New World, full of post-conventional possibilities, holds new norms, new conventions for us.

We are not yet organized culturally to support the emergence of this world, but that doesn't stop Evolution from proceeding. There is a lot of pain and confusion, heartache and despair occurring because there is no support system for this emergence. This is one reason a new psychological orientation is needed.

Besides minimizing the harm that occurs via misunderstanding the evolutionary impulse at work, a new psychological framework is needed to provide the necessary supports for the enormous potential that lies untapped. Exploring the New World means unleashing all of the human energy that has languished on the social side of our holonic nature. We have gone as far as we can go emphasizing only the individual; we can go further, but not until we anchor individual development to the well-being of the whole.

We have very little idea of what we are capable of accomplishing together. There is widespread recognition of this potential, but the challenges inherent in the twin desires for autonomy and belonging tend to prevent its actualization. No psychology of the individual is going to be adequate to the task of supporting the emergence of vibrant, wise, and healthy networks of human beings. The magic lies between us, in the realm of relationship, in the potential of emergence. It is going to take an emphasis upon interdependence to release this promise.

❦

SECTION III

TOWARD A PSYCHOLOGY OF INTERDEPENDENCE

❦

Again and again in history some people wake up.
They have no ground in the crowd and move to broader
deeper laws. They carry strange customs with them and demand
room for bold and audacious action.
The future speaks ruthlessly through them.

—RAINER MARIE RILKE

SECTION III

🌿

Toward a Psychology of Interdependence

We are not a crazy, misfit species! Yes, we have soiled the nest and hurt the planet, jeopardized Life and our own kind. We have lived out the evolutionary imperative that we understood in the West as the preeminence of the individual. But in so doing, we have been faithful to the part of the life force that was easiest to embrace. The dignity and importance of the individual was so compelling, so freeing! Who could blame an adolescent species for being fixated upon self-expression?

The road that beckons, however, asks something more of us than we would like, more than we are sure we can deliver. Hesitation is natural. Anxiety and uncertainty are natural. There is no way to avoid choosing, however. Inevitably, consequences will be generated. With climate change we have come to such a time. The green helix is shifting, and we are going to change with it or forgo further evolution.

Evolution is an exacting process: we fit in, or we don't. The time in between—when we aren't fully formed and don't quite fit in, still holding onto the moribund practices of the past—is inherently anxiety provoking. It is also enlivening. Confidence grows with hardship faced. The actual adaptability of our species, of our own individuality, becomes obvious when we undergo challenge. In addition to challenge is support, with hardship comes discovered resources, and with self-sacrifice comes new forms of self-expression. The future demands this kind of growth and offers the challenges that promote it.

Evolution Knocks

The great secret, the realization we have gone too long without, is that we are part of Nature. We partake in all the processes that have created us and have led us to our current state. We are not alone with our own problematic elements but have been the beneficiaries of 13 billion years of creating and solving such problems. Nature has prepared us for this eventuality by exploring over and over what creates synergy, enables the greatest fit, and ensures the continuation of Life.

We have faithfully served the one-sided picture of reality that science and our most prevalent form of consciousness offered. The individual has reigned supreme, following the overly simple dictum of "survival of the fittest." The desire for a more realistic picture of what is going on, however, has offered a different view.

As a species, we are already undergoing a kind of mass initiation. No elder is dragging us off to the forest or a cave to help us see the world anew. But we are being dragged off! Life is assailing us, transforming our lives, our work places, relationships and viewpoints. Life is asking increasingly difficult things of us, shaking us, undermining our confidence and leaving us wondering about ourselves, marriages, governments and species. Life is what is happening to us, as we make other plans.

Relationship with Life, however, asks something of us. To access the New World is going to take more than watching the news reports, more than googling information about how to live a green lifestyle. It is going to take a change of consciousness, not in what we know, but in who we are. This kind of change is already afoot although we would rather not notice. It is too inconvenient. Giving up the illusion of control is anxiety provoking, looks hard, and leaves one feeling vulnerable and fraught with uncertainty.

This is exactly what the knocking of Evolution is like. Increasing personal risk and becoming available to Life, means knowingly giving up the driver's seat—not abandoning our direction, but choosing to go into a world of connection instead of going around it. This choice is very difficult and there is precious little cultural support for connecting us with what is really going on. But everything around us, passing so quickly, keeps calling to us, keeps creating strange failures and anxious feelings.

Because we are part of the pattern that connects, we are subject to forces beyond ourselves that have a life of their own. They are inside and outside of us. The helping hands that Life offers, the resources that are our birthright, are unavailable to us because we have been taught to fend for ourselves as if Life has no stake in our successful adaptation to the rigors of Creation. But Life does! Thankfully.

Science is slowly noticing. Biologists studying the organism, and social scientists studying humankind as social organisms, are reporting another side of the story. We evolved differently than we have believed! We are connected to the larger processes of Life, we are extensions of Universal forces, we are beneficiaries of an Evolutionary Heritage that has prepared us to adapt. We have been endowed with potential we don't even know we have and we are at a time that is calling for us to discover what is already within us. Existential circumstances and developmental opportunities are preparing the stage; now we need guidance and cultural support.

A New Orientation

What is being called for is not simply relationship as it has been known in the past. What Life wants, what it relies upon and uses to forward growth, development, and evolution, is high-synergy relationships, collaborative relationships that promote emergence. This kind of relating is not a product of a better understanding but occurs as a result of a transformation of consciousness. Emerging now, if only in a few (and hopefully more, later), is the awareness that all things are linked in complex systems—in relationships that transcend our expectations and connect the choices we make with the well-being of the planet. Consciousness is creating an opportunity to reorient our cultural projects.

The move toward a psychology of interdependence is an attempt to contemporize the psychological project so that it is based upon current science, is balanced (reflecting our species social nature), and responds to the very real challenges that confront us as a species. It is a project of consciousness. Not the mass consciousness that now prevails, but consciousness that includes awareness of the values that have brought us here, good and bad, life-affirming and deadly.

Chapter 7 will describe the features that distinguish this orientation, features that are derived from a distinctly different way of seeing the processes of Life. These attributes are ways of describing an overall approach that seeks to promote awareness of how connected each of us is, while addressing the complexities that come with a life of connection. The form of consciousness that informs this perspective is a product of Life and it occurs naturally, it is available to anyone willing to submit to the rigors of metamorphosis. These rigors are constantly occurring a la natural therapy but are mistakenly seen not as opportunities to become more to serve Evolution, but as problems, suggesting something is wrong. Life is not making the mistakes; we are. In Chapter 8 we will address the many ways that Life breaks into our lives, altering them, and asking us to progress, to grow, to become more complex for Life's purposes.

But what are Life's purposes? I don't profess to know; it seems to me that the answer to that question is unfathomable, but that may just reflect my own prejudice. Maybe in time some sense will emerge. All I know is that for this species to know its place in Creation and begin to grasp the larger story of Creation itself, we have got to stick around, and continue to evolve. I prefer to believe that this story is still unfolding, that Creation is an ongoing miracle. For this reason, I am fascinated by Mystery. Chapter 9 reveals something of the way Mystery has captivated me and informed this work. In my case, Mystery has always resided in the between, so that is where I will attend.

Conclusion

I'm not worried about the persistence of Life. Nature is resilient. The complex life-systems of this planet are hearty. Rather, it seems to me that the well-being of the human experiment is at stake. I feel that the best way to preserve the human experiment, to honor Life, to pay ample respect to the forces that have cooperated to deliver to us this precious chance, is to be a good collaborator in the dance, to be a good partner.

This is what the psychology of interdependence is all about: finding the way through balancing our magnificent creative individuality with our relationship capacity, and cultivating our dual nature to find a way to fit best in the dance of Life. Aligning ourselves more closely to Evolution and coupling more closely with Life ensures that we will have the energy and the capacity to be dancing for a long time.

CHAPTER 7

❦

An Interdependent Approach

Each discovery of a new and deeper context and meaning is a discovery of a new therapia, a new therapy; namely, we must shift our perspectives, deepen our perception, often against a great deal of resistance, to embrace...the self is situated in contexts within contexts within contexts, and each shift...is a painful process of growth, a death to a shallower context and rebirth to a deeper one.

—KEN WILBER, 2000

The way we treat ourselves is the way we treat each other, our community, and the planet.

—H. H. DALAI LAMA, 1991

Introduction

In the previous chapters the case for an alternative psychological approach is made, one that takes into account our dual nature as human holons. In this chapter we have come at last to describing the essential features of such a framework. This approach is meant to be additive, to supplement what has come before and to add important elements to the psychological project.

There is a need for a psychological model that reflects as accurately as possible the conditions of the times. Science has come a long way since the time of Freud—the Victorian Age. We know a lot more about the origins of the Universe, Life, and Evolution. The life sciences have changed and we now know that living systems have played an important role throughout the history of Life. We are moving from the Age of the Mechanism, where everything from the Universe to the human brain was conceived of as a kind of machine, to the Age of the Organism, where the relationships between living things are seen as important and generative. The World has changed in the process, and so must psychology.

As individuals and as a species we have an important need for a meaning-making system that addresses the difficult issues that threaten the well-being not only of individuals but of the social relationships that comprise our marriages, families, organizations, societies, and the emerging world culture. Traditional psychological approaches are tragically limited, focusing primarily within, and are not adequate to meet the challenges we now face.

What distinguishes a psychology of interdependence is that it focuses on the between, the qualities of connection that frequently define the way one experiences what is possible. The between is the ground of emergence, as well as the place where social energies reside—energies capable of transforming relationships, communities, and our species' interactions with Life. By focusing on the between, as well as within, the doors to storehouses of human potential are unlocked. The psychology of interdependence affirms relationship, not just as something nice to be part of, but as an essential component in the evolutionary scheme of Life. The characteristics of a psychology of interdependence are all derived from Nature and reflect patterns of Life and strategies of Evolution, qualities that have recurred in the life of the Universe. As such, they demonstrate how we got here and how we can maintain a sustained presence in the dance of Creation. These characteristics make a psychology of interdependence:

- Strength-based
- Non-pathological
- Relational
- Systemic
- Developmental
- Transpersonal

Strength-based

There are three important aspects to a strength-based approach to the psychological project. The first refers to the stance of such a psychology. The second involves aiding the natural capacities of the human organism, be it an individual or an aggregate of humans forming a social organism. The third involves alignment.

A psychology of interdependence goes in a different direction. Its stance is based upon the knowledge that the human organism is endowed with capacities that are highly adaptive. Like medicine, which made a similar shift in stance in the late nineteen sixties when it realized that the most effective ways of treating invading organisms was to enhance the body's natural defenses, a psychology of interdependence focuses upon the organism's response—to enhance the organism's capacity to respond to challenges, to increase the integrity in the systems an organism is involved in, and to improve the relational exchange with the environment.

This means shifting the focus away from the circumstances surrounding one to the response of the organism. This is a move from being a victim of Life to being challenged by Life. It is a move from being an innocent stripped of coping mechanisms (or having the ability to cope distorted) to discovering that the means to cope and to adapt are not compromised. It is a move from fixating upon making externalities responsible, to focusing upon personal responsibility. The strength that is being referred to here is in the organism's ability to respond to whatever it encounters.

This strength is a power of the Universe. It is an attribute of Life, an ability to adapt that has assisted Life in occupying all of the microclimates of the Earth. Lastly, it is part of our endowment. Each of us, as an extension of the Universe, as the embodiment of evolutionary processes and is endowed with the most sophisticated learning capacity we know—the human immune system.

The immune system is a biological endowment (an extension of how Evolution operates) that ensures the adaptability and structural integrity of the individual. The immune system was formerly seen primarily in terms of protection, but more recently the immune system has come to be seen as the source of an organism's integrity. It is, as Rabbi Friedman says, "synonymous with self." The immune system distinguishes self from non-self, what threatens from what increases integrity, what invades from what enhances, and what undermines from what challenges. It grows and adapts to the challenges of Life, which makes it an incredible arbiter and source of well-being.

We are each biologically endowed with an organismic capacity to respond to the circumstances of Life. As Rabbi Friedman points out, the immune system grows and more effectively adapts and maintains the integrity of the organism when it is challenged. Life initiates change and the organism, through the responses of the immune system, adapts or fails to adapt. Whenever there is a failure to adapt, or adaptation is too slow, then trouble begins; anxiety, depression and other forms of suffering increase.

It is important to keep in mind that a psychology of interdependence also views strength as something that emanates from the bond occurring between the human organism and its environmental surround. The adaptive response, the capacity built into our immune system, is a product of Life and exists to facilitate a close-knit bonding with the living environment. Our adaptive responses are stimulated by Life and they simultaneously transform the living environment. We are coupled; each shapes the other. And the more closely aligned we are, the greater the strength of our participation and the more resilience we enjoy.

One axiom that exists throughout a psychology of interdependence is that the integrity of one level affects the integrity of another. A lack of integrity in one, say the responses of the organism, are based upon a more regressive stance (less focused upon what is happening in the moment), and leads to actions that promote the decline of integrity in the organism and in the environment. This realization is part of the systemic nature of this approach. Strengthen one part of the system and you add to the strength of the rest of the system.

We have here a three-pronged explanation of what strength-based means. Like differentiation-based approaches, a psychology of interdependence shares stance and focus on aiding the immune response of individuals and social systems. This approach differs by placing a greater emphasis upon the role of Life and the importance of the coupled relationship that exists between the human organism and its environment. Strength (or resilience) is ultimately a by-product of an increasing alignment between humanity and Evolution, the embrace with Life.

Non-pathological

The word pathology comes from medicine. It refers to a disease process, or some deviation from normal. In the early days of the "talking cure," the science of psychotherapy was exclusively in the hands of medicine. Freud was a Viennese doctor. The idea of mental illness came down to us from the early Freudians as a medical problem to be solved via medical intervention.

This medical notion focused upon the past and posited that all mental and emotional illness was derived from poor or deficient child rearing and that all these stem from the past. This assumption is currently reinforced by the insurance and pharmaceutical industries. The DSM, the diagnostic manual by which all mental health diagnoses are made, has enshrined the medical idea that disease processes or abnormalities underlie all emotional problems.

This medicalized approach applies in some cases, but it does not apply in all. And where it doesn't apply, the assumption of illness does more harm than good because it reinforces the idea that something abnormal is happening. It indicates that the source of the problem lies within, and usually in the past of the individual having difficulty.

A psychology of interdependence emphasizes differentiation and focuses upon differentiation-of-self. Essentially a focus upon the organismic response of the individual, or the social system, shifts attention away from external circumstances (and medical assumptions) that may stress an organism, to the adaptive efficacy of the organism's response.

As we have seen, the repertoire of choices that are available to an individual, family, or organization, the range of possible options that define an organism's ability to respond, are defined by the level of Differentiation. This places an emphasis upon the adaptive capacity of the organism, upon the personal responsibility for choosing what actions to take, rather than focusing upon the stressor, be it environmental or internalized. This is basically a shift away from what is wrong to what is right, to what is adaptive and capable.

Individuals or social systems that focus too much attention upon external circumstances become subject to them. This limits the options available to those that will not disturb the relationship with these circumstances. This is typically what happens in families and significant relationships, and it is also what happens in larger colonies of human organisms like businesses, communities and societies.

The fact that this happens is not an indication that something is wrong, it merely indicates that a natural emotional system is governing. Natural systems bind us, they couple us as living entities with each other and the environment. But we humans are complex organisms that are capable, albeit with struggle and growth, of becoming self-governing and self-regulating beings. We can participate in emotional systems but do not have to be subject to them. Acquiring the capacity to become self-governing is a process of maturation, of increasing the differentiation-of-self, and taking greater personal responsibility for one's actions, changing oneself in order to change the circumstances.

Acquiring the maturity to define and stay upon a self-selected trajectory requires keeping an eye upon what really matters. One of my clients, a mountain bike rider, put it really well. To cross a creek, he often needs to ride across a log. He knows that if he wants to stay dry he has to keep his eyes on where he wants to go. As soon as he looks at the creek, he gets wet.

Let us not forget that Life has needs of its own, and that we are a part of how those needs are being worked out. Life is something that healthily challenges us. Evolution keeps surging into our lives, upsetting our well-ordered plans and unseating us. This is another way of saying that we are subject to being organismically challenged because the process of Creation is going on, and it has an agenda that differs from our concerns. Life has a relationship with us that occasionally asks something of us. When Life breaks into our lives and asks things of us, like to grow our awareness, to have a more complex view, these moments are not occurring because something is wrong. These are not pathological occurrences. They may cause anxiety, depression or a host of other painful stresses. These moments are often more than merely adjustments. What is being called for is transformation—a radical remaking of outlook and world.

Forces are at play in the world that can stimulate differentiation-of-self. Pathogenic beliefs may be stirred up. But the forces of Life, such as the holonic drives that unbalance our relationships and call for new strategies for life-long tensions, are a form of natural therapy. We are unsettled, but this is not because something is wrong, nor is it some form of mental illness. We aren't even experiencing a health crisis, although there may be physical elements. The crisis is natural, generated by the demands of Evolution. All of this happens because we are profoundly connected, because we are part of the warp and weave of the Universe. Evolution hasn't given up on us, and we cannot afford to give up on it.

Relational

A psychology of interdependence recognizes that all things really are connected. Relationship is part of our condition. Connection is inherent in Life! It isn't something we choose to have or ignore. It infuses all of Nature, including us. Relationship is a prevailing aspect of Evolution, a bond that glues us into the pattern that connects the galaxies with our families, the sub-atomic realm with our thoughts, and the climate with our choices. We can't fall out of this pattern; no action or belief severs the reciprocal vitality of this connection, for this is the fabric of Creation.

Connection is the coin of the realm. It is the way things are. This may seem like a simple balm to all that ails us as a species, or at least here in Western culture. But being connected isn't simple! Being connected as we are subjects us to all of the dynamics of the Universe. This means we are subject to what Evolution asks of us. And Evolution wants us to be as unique as possible without disconnecting. It bids us grow our uniqueness in a sea of frothing connections.

Murray Bowen referred to this burdensome complexity as differentiation-of-self. I think David Schnarch named it more accurately, in terms that are more accessible, when he referred to creating a self-in-relationship. In both cases, they are pointing to the process of creating a self of one's own in the midst of a plethora of relationships. A central aspect of this process is the challenge inherent in staying in these relationships while learning how to contend with natural tensions inherent in relationship dynamics.

Both Schnarch and Bowen knew that there are rigors associated with this process. A psychology of interdependence sees these rigors, and values them as important challenges that Life has presented to build the immune system of each human. Through connective challenge, Life is teasing the uniqueness out of each of us. Standing up or standing out, being seen or being ignored, being the target of unhappiness, being disliked, losing desire, and placing one's most important relationships in jeopardy, are just some of the relationship challenges that arouse our attention. And as our relationships grow more significant to us, there is a greater likelihood that these very challenges will assail us. Nothing is wrong when this happens. It is disturbing, but Life is just growing us for its purposes.

Essentially, these rigors have to do with finding and living with a sense of personal integrity, with becoming both solid and permeable.

To manifest the greatest capacity for connection paradoxically requires the highest capacity to hold onto oneself. Life is giving us a boost because Life really wants as much conscious connection as it can muster. Our evolution as a species depends upon it, and the progress of Evolution itself depends upon us filling our niche in Creation as well as possible.

Strangely, and brilliantly, the Universe bids us to contend with paradoxical forces in order to fit all that more elegantly into an expanding matrix of Life. So, in addition to the systemic awareness that there is a pattern that connects one level of experience with another (see the next section), this approach concerns itself with the ongoing process of learning that is stimulated by the twin forces of autonomy and belonging, forces that are part of our biological endowment. As Murray Bowen pointed out, "all protoplasm" is subject to these twin relationship urges. They unsettle all our relationships, they make us anxious and restlessly ensure a constant process of growth. They stimulate a recurring transformation of consciousness that delivers us to finer and finer adaptations to the march of Evolution.

Learning is a form of adaptation. It is deeper than cognitive insight and understanding. To really learn requires action. Everything is theoretical and abstract until it enters the realm of experience. And experience requires some kind of action. Thus, Life presents us with a host of relationship challenges that require us to act, to respond. In so doing, Life awakens us and invites us more deeply into the dance of Creation. This dance is a relational one. It is a dance that thrives when you dance your unique dance. At the same time, it is a dance that connects, that magically evokes: something new emerges, something unforeseen, something more enlivening, more complex and yet more simple.

All of this relating, from family dynamics to marital tensions, to conflict between ethnicities and cultures, to our species' relationship with its environmental surround, is a concern for a psychology of interdependence. This approach accepts the burdensome complexity of all this interrelatedness because it knows that the celebration of connectedness that is our species' birthright carries with it a personal responsibility for the integrity of the whole.

Systemic

A psychology of interdependence is a systems-based approach. It relies heavily upon the perceptions and experiences of systems thinkers. Systems thought has transformed the psychological project and made the psychology of interdependence a reality. Remember, such thinking is not something that comes through education, it is a product of experience, of growth. The living systems that influence our lives become visible, real, to those who have endured transformation. What follows is one version, one map of a landscape that is only now coming over the horizon.

What I am presenting here is the big picture. Living systems have predictable characteristics. These attributes reveal systems at work and offer real guidance towards promoting lasting change. True systems thinking links the big picture with the nitty-gritty details, but I don't want too many details to weigh this overview down (see the chapter notes if you want to go deeper).

What am I talking about? The word "system" is used to refer to a group of interlocking parts that relate to each other and form a whole. This whole now can be seen as a social phenomenon, a living system that has both an internal/subjective and an external/objective dimension. This viewpoint sees individuals, couples, families or communities as living systems, having repertoires of behaviors defined by how parts interact. Each system is then comprised of interacting parts and is embedded as a part in a larger system. Thus, behavioral choices are also influenced by both the way that the larger system operates and by the composition of the embedded system.

Readily apparent in this simplified description is the complexity of relationship dynamics that influence any organism's response to challenge. Any whole/part must look up to the larger system it is embedded within, and down to the whole/parts it is constructed from, to create a response that preserves and enhances the functioning of all these elements.

A psychology of interdependence takes on the burden of this relationship complexity in an effort to support learning, integrity and Evolution (development). A psychology of interdependence is a form of action science. It assumes that all actions (including no action) have relationship and systemic consequences, and that awareness of these consequences is of paramount importance.

Action experiments, choice-making, and learning are more the focus of attention than insight, understanding, and verbal communication. Every intervention is an experiment with complexity, a learning opportunity, an effort aimed at greater integrity, but an act of approximation, almost always lacking a clear bull's eye. The focus is upon enhancing the response of the organism to the field of complex relationship dynamics that form its being; inner and outer. The method, however, is action not insight.

Essentially, a psychology of interdependence is interested in cultivating communicative actions, ecological awareness, selves-in-relationship and the ability to tolerate and catalyze systemic change.

Systems change as a result of parts acting differently. The system, be it marital, family, or organizational will likely do everything to maintain itself. When it does, nothing is wrong, it is acting consistent with its nature. The part, be it individual, couple, neighborhood, or nation-state is going to be pressured to stay in place. Only action creates change. And all transformative action requires handling great pressure. A psychology of interdependence expects this pressure and assumes these forces are always at play.

This approach adopts the value that our social evolution as a species cannot proceed without a greater awareness of the impact that social systems, particularly their internal dimensions (such as emotional systems), have upon the beliefs we hold, the way we organize ourselves, and the quality of individuals we develop. The systemic perspective is essential if we are going to align ourselves with the natural flows that will ensure that we evolve with Nature.

Bear in mind that we are talking about living systems, not mechanisms. Life flows through these organizations; they are social organisms; they evolve, die, and work to maintain their identity. Each has a living integrity of its own. Far more significantly, each is an embodiment of Life, a mysterious arrangement of living parts collectively bound to each other, carrying forward the animating mystery that drives us all.

These are exquisitely sensitive life forms, which respond to changes in their environment and are highly resilient entities. They evolve through natural emergencies that are stimulated by changes in the environment, including changes brought about by their parts. They are part of our living environment, part of the continuum of Life that includes us, part of the mystery that lives through us. Changing them is changing us.

The systemic perspective takes one through the looking glass. The world is changed. One of these changes involves a temporal shift, a shift in time. In this world the past is no longer just in the past. Unlike traditional psychologies, a psychology of interdependence holds a spiral viewpoint that makes evident how the past opens to the future through the present. This is a systemic viewpoint. The emphasis upon organismic response rivets attention on the present.

Life challenges us here in the present. These challenges are so difficult that meeting them changes the past. This means that the past is transformed through response to the present. Trauma, failures and disappointments are all amenable to change. They are reduced in significance by the adaptive response to the present, healed by present-day action. A psychology of interdependence is a hopeful approach because it knows that the present is full of potential and offers a chance for change.

As a systems-based approach, a psychology of interdependence is also integral. This means two things. First, this approach emphasizes integrity. The health and well-being of the individual, as Michael Ventura points out, is dependent upon the health and well-being, one could say the integrity, of the environment he or she is embedded within. Secondly, this approach, because it recognizes biological, psychological, and sociological linkages, meets Ken Wilber's definition of integral.

Wilber, the champion of integral psychology, in his four quadrants model refers to the "Big Three": Nature, Self and Community. These are the domains within which all development takes place. There is an alignment between the biopsychosocial nature of this orientation and the "all quadrants" emphasis of Wilber. The assumption is that an approach that addresses the inner and the outer, the objective and the subjective, is going to be more effective in generating integrity at all system levels and will promote the greatest development. This approach shares those assumptions and sees the following as evidence of alignment:

Bio	=	Objective	=	It	=	Nature
Psycho	=	Subjective	=	I	=	Self
Social	=	Intersubjective	=	We	=	Community

With this perspective comes real rigor. The difficulty of change makes a new kind of sense. Living systems link, bind, and sometimes run us. So, too, this perspective helps make clear the kind of change that really makes a difference. There isn't an easy way, but there is a way. Not surprisingly, this way requires our evolution as individuals and as social beings.

I am intrigued by the world that has come into view. I recognize that everything is changed. I am slowly being transformed by this awareness. I rely on those who have been here longer, who see better, or who just grasp this better than I. The world of emotional systems is a complex one, enough that lots of seers are needed, and in the meantime, the work of a psychology of interdependence is to provide supports that can help cultivate these seers.

This is not the end of the story. Evolution is ongoing. It will surely reveal the limitations of this approach. But for now, living systems offer us a set of stepping stones which lead to a sustainable future.

Developmental

A psychology of interdependence recognizes and affirms the connection between human development and Evolution. It views Creation as an ongoing process. One that depends on humankind, and that humankind equally depends upon. This approach views this linkage as crucial, often determining the well-being of individual, family, community, culture, as well as our environmental surround. There is, in effect, no separate entity here, just a need for distinction to make the interlocking dynamics as functional and meaningful as possible. Toward that end, a psychology of interdependence addresses the needs of both the wholes and the parts.

The Universe is continuing to do what it has always done—using relationship to create more complex and efficient interconnections. Building, through paradoxical and systemic bonds, a place that is rich with connection and diversity. As the greatest ongoing energy event, the mother of all sources of energy, the Universe is maintaining its ceaseless creativity through what we call Evolution. Human lives offer one of the arenas where Evolution continues its restless pursuit of diversity and unity, of autonomy and communion. It surges into and through our lives.

Stage-by-stage development, the manifestation of Evolution in our lives, is the source of metamorphosis, the transformation of our consciousness. Life intervenes, thwarting and propelling us, often to grow our consciousness, to complexify our awareness, to make us more malleable to Life itself, and asks us to respond in new and creative ways to real dilemmas that enhance the survivability of our species.

We tend to forget that there is a connection between the natural flow of Evolution and the dilemmas that give each human life its character. Every life is a form of Life itself. Each human life is Life's expression of its profusion and its attempt to further the procession of Evolution. In that respect, Life is involved in each life, as an invested partner. Each of us is accompanied, even shaped, by forces that have a vital interest in an outcome that serves far more than the personal interests of the individual. Each of us is steered, much like the undifferentiated stem cell, towards a fitting place, towards a shape and function that serves the larger organism of which we are a vital part.

Life, then, is an initiator. We are so busy adapting to the cultural surround, like our families, that we often forget that our lives are not our own and that we exist, in part, to further the cause of Life. We are subject to metamorphosis, to changes that Life puts us through. These momentous occasions are a concern of a psychology of interdependence because they are so often seen as psychological or emotional problems, instead of natural emergencies, naturally occurring chrysalis periods. How we respond to these challenges often determines how useful we are to Life, ourselves, and others.

This isn't predestination, a choiceless dance by an unconscious automaton. Though often, when Life intervenes and sweeps humans into experiences that overturn or challenge their interests, there is a feeling of choicelessness. When this happens, Life is asking for creativity, for us to employ our human organismic capacity to respond in our own idiosyncratic way to increase the diversity of life and to advance the cause of Evolution. Our choice about how we want to respond is our way of participating in evolution.

A psychology of interdependence knows that humans are capable, although with great difficulty, of responding in ways that lean toward advancing the integrity of the whole. It is hard, in part because there is a lack of support for adult developmental growth. Western industrial growth society is not a high synergy culture. So, in order to reach full potential, humans have to become true individuals, self-governing and self-defining beings capable of standing alone.

Currently, this happens despite cultural forces. And growth tends to stop right there because this has been considered the apex of human development. We know better now. The right kind of supports, including a psychology that values the big picture along with the needs of individuals, can lead to a more integrous human. We now know that individuality serves best when it lends its idiosyncratic strengths to the service of Life.

Humanity is involved in something much more complex, relational, and volitional than a dance of automatons. When humans undergo transformation for the sake of the whole, they participate in Evolution, in creation. Undergoing the anxiety-provoking rigors of transformation is for most humans a hair-raising prospect, but this is what Life asks of us. Each of us must choose (although sometimes Life makes the choice for us). Walking into the transforming fire is never an easy choice, but it is one that affirms Life.

A psychology of interdependence recognizes that the ability to respond is linked with development. The more stages of growth one has under his or her belt the greater the range of responses available. The further along the stages of growth a culture is, be it a couple, family, work organization, or society, the greater the range of options available for dealing with challenges. Furthermore, a psychology of interdependence not only provides supports for natural emergencies, to extend the range of responses available, but links these challenges with the big picture of Evolution, providing meaning that reconnects lives with the vital energy of Life.

A psychology of interdependence is not a product of altruism. It is born of a developmental realization. This psychology rests upon a vantage point that is derived from a place on the developmental spectrum. It is a post-conventional psychology. It is based upon the perception of, rather than speculation about, interconnection, systemic forces, the moment (responding now), relationship, and awareness of the evolutionary history of our species.

As Clare Graves would say, a hallmark of such development is a concern with aligning the spiral of development with the project of Evolution. That is precisely what a psychology of interdependence attempts to do. Finally, as we shall see in the next section, it is a transpersonal psychology, taking in the farthest reaches of human development, the exalted and little understood stages of adult development that go beyond individual concerns, as well as the co-constructed social energies that themselves have a transpersonal nature.

Transpersonal

Let's start this discussion by reiterating what a psychology of interdependence does. This approach places an emphasis upon furthering the efforts of Evolution. This involves de-pathologizing an essentially natural process, thus relieving apprehensions, and clearing the way for Evolution to take place for the sake of Life and the human host. The work is oriented toward aligning human development with the needs of Life. This perspective supports well-being in the individual (or human colony) by valuing and supporting the conditions that increase the viability of Life. This endeavor is intrinsically transpersonal.

A psychology of interdependence is transpersonal in three easily identified ways:

- it is based upon a synergetic relationship between Life and humanity,
- it represents a developmental outlook (post- conventional) that is transpersonal,
- it views collective phenomena, co-constructed energies, as transpersonal.

The perception of a synergetic relationship between Life and humanity inherently places the locus of psychological well-being between the individual (or social system) and Evolution. It is a concern for a collaborative relationship, one that goes beyond the individual but includes him or her. The transpersonal nature of this relationship revolves around the synergetic generation of a third thing, something unique and more than the two constituents which compose its parts. Transpersonal here refers to the half of our holonic nature that is always a part of a larger whole.

A psychology of interdependence is a product of a developmental outlook that is itself transpersonal. The post-conventional framework no longer privileges individuality but looks toward the needs of a larger whole. This entire approach rests upon the perception that the individual merges with the larger context of the Evolutionary process, and that the individual, if you will, is like the fruit of a larger living organism. This organism employs individuality but has needs that go beyond those of the individual. The transpersonal needs of the individual have to do with finding an appropriate fit within this larger organism.

A psychology of interdependence also views collective phenomena, co-constructed energies, as transpersonal. Here the notion of the transpersonal is slightly different because it totally abandons using the individual (i.e., the individual ego) as a reference point, instead referring to the cumulative efforts of a group of individuals. Collective phenomena such as emotional systems, group identities, and the content of the collective unconscious are seen as having a transpersonal nature

This is not a new idea. Arnold Mindell, a noted Jungian and transpersonal theorist, has described a host of group phenomena, such as group roles and time-spirits as having their origins in the collective unconscious of a group. The idea of a social brain that is generative of a host of cultural innovations is now gaining traction as a source for our species' social evolution. The social brain is an emergent phenomenon that occurs when enough flesh and blood brains are linked in a brain syndicate. Synergy enables a kind of transpersonal collective thought to then occur. This approach, through sociotherapy (explained later), takes an interest in these collective or social matters.

Conclusion

What really matters about this approach are not its attributes and qualities. Does it address what really ails us? The answer, of course, depends upon your point of view, the world you inhabit. A psychology of interdependence takes an expansive view. It looks for the patterns that connect us one to another, as well as to our cultural and environmental surroundings. In so doing it tries to address the heartache that comes from the assumption of disconnection that has left us lost and cut off for so long.

This approach is based on a different realization. It sees connection, and notices that connection brings its own challenges, many of which have been misconstrued as problems, as something wrong, and are treated as such. It focuses upon the needs of the individual, sees him or her as an integral part, and goes beyond to include the needs of the whole. This approach sees the moment and recognizes the potential for healing, change, and choice that is being ignored by a focus on the past; it considers the future. It provides support for the emergence of humanity's full potential. It celebrates how intimately connected we are with Life and works toward alignment. It recognizes a larger drama (evolution) and seeks to ensure a place for humanity upon that stage.

Ultimately, a psychology of interdependence recognizes relationship. From the living environment, the green helix that shapes our fate as a species, to our relationships with others, intimate or otherwise, to our relationships with ourselves, this approach pays attention to the quality of our interactions and knows that they can provide positive, generative synergies, full of emergent possibilities or negative, life-draining synergies that threaten our future. This approach knows we are co-creating our children's inheritance. It believes that Life has prepared us for this privilege. All we have to do, this approach asserts, is make the best of what is already between us.

〰

CHAPTER 8

ᴗ

Natural Therapy

All breakdown is not pathological;
some breakdown is breakthrough.
—R. D. LAING, 1960

Introduction

The primary thesis of this book is that relationship is central to our existence. Synergy helped forward the Evolutionary process. Cooperation led to biological advances. Nature used coupling to create an elegant fit between life forms and their environment. Even the emergence of complex organisms, such as ourselves, occurred because nature combined all of these relationship processes. We are Life having a relationship with itself.

We are not orphaned. We have not been abandoned. We are not as alone as we have been led to believe by science. The fact is that Life has an interest in what happens to us as individuals and as a species. Life has an investment in us. While this is good news, revealing a place for us in the dance of evolution, it is also troublesome for having such a meddlesome partner creates some hardships. Life also wants something of us. This chapter addresses the many ways Life intervenes in our lives to protect and add value to its investment.

Life's Investment and Motivation

We aren't here solely for our own sake. Typically, we act as if we were. But the truth is more complex than that. Life is operating though us, and if we are to truly be happy, to find some kind of contentment, we have to live out Life"s needs with our own. What are

Life's needs? It is startling how infrequently this question gets asked! The answer isn't always clear. Especially when it comes to our individual lives. Here the trick is to ask what Life might want from me specifically. But it is not so hard to think about what Life wants generally. It wants to continue and to improve its chances of continuing. Life seems to want three things:

- to optimize the fit,
- to increase adaptability,
- to advance Evolution.

Optimizing the Fit

I am starting with Life's desire, not because I think human aspirations are unimportant, but because Life's needs have typically been ignored, or treated like they were of secondary importance. Later I will focus upon the human response, the choices that are made, but for the moment I want to consider what is at stake, from the viewpoint of Life.

The whole process of Evolution operates like a mysterious jigsaw puzzle. The picture emerges as the pieces fit together. What comes into being appears because there is a relationship fit that enables something new to emerge. This fit is part of the pattern that connects. Life folds us in as part of the Universe's restless process of Creation. We, like protons and neutrons, are part of the raw materials, the media, of this huge, ongoing, creative process.

For Life to ensure a fit though, it has to work us into some kind of useful shape. For that reason, we bear the complicated stresses associated with all protoplasm, that is the holonic tensions of trying to be uniquely ourselves and trying to fit into something larger. We, and our relationships, are buffeted about by desires that are sometimes contradictory, sometimes complementary, and always changing. Life is constantly kneading us, trying to create a paradoxical combination of solidity and malleability that enables a fit.

These changes constantly upset us, they threaten our security, and they puncture any illusions of control we may have. They are the signs that Life is involved in our lives, and they represent the challenges that transform humans into full-blown participants in the evolutionary process. Knowingly or not, we are involved in a co-creative endeavor. The knock comes, we feel the rigors of Life kneading us, and we are left to respond, but not just on our terms. Life is seeking to fit us ever more completely into the pattern that connects to serve Life, to further Creation, and to bring us home.

Increasing Adaptability

It isn't easy being part of an ongoing experiment. There isn't any permanence. That isn't particularly appealing to the part of us that craves mastery, predictability, completion, and rest. The thrill ride that is Life is surprising. If we are willing, one of those surprises is that Life's desire for increasing adaptability makes us more resilient, more alive, and more responsive to the unfolding journey in which we are engaged.

Life sometimes hurts. We find ourselves in difficult, painful, seemingly impossible situations. We feel, know, no human should be subjected to this. If this suffering was brought about by human causes, there would be criminal or civil consequences! But Life gets away with it. Not because Life is immune to our response, as we shall soon see, but because Life is being driven by the imperative of Evolution.

The only assurance we have, Life has, that we are going to remain a part of this ongoing experiment, is the adaptability we acquire. Therefore, to forward Evolution and to ensure a place for humankind in this ongoing experiment, Life challenges us. We are thrust into new, more complex, anxiety-provoking, frighteningly painful and uncertain situations. The lives we knew or planned are swept away. Why? For Life's sake, the resources of strength, courage and creativity that we have been endowed with become available when we endure these hardships.

In other words, these hardships are evocative, initiatory. They evoke the creative, the adaptive, response. Life benefits because new human capabilities and shapes emerge. Human individuals benefit because they discover inner resources. And humanity benefits because the range of options, of possibilities, is expanded. The Universe is a high synergy place. There is an alignment between the benefits of the part and the whole. All of this development and growth depends upon us. Life challenges us for adaptability, but it is up to us how we respond.

Advancing Evolution

The Universe is an energetic, creative, and restless place. It is impossible, unless you're an ideologue, to say what it is up to. The awesomeness of the place we find ourselves part of is humbling. What the Cosmos has done is unimaginable. How the Universe proceeds is still beyond us in the province of mystery. But we have reason to believe it is still expanding, still becoming, still evolving.

There is an ongoing quality to Creation. The Universe, our home, our being, is still unfolding! This process, like all creative processes, is messy. Things don't always work out. Dead ends, mistakes, failures, and accidents happen. All of this impacts us. So do the successes.

In either case, it seems that things happen, Life steps in, Evolution disturbs us. There is no place to hide, no way to appease this ceaseless activity. Life, it seems, is full of possible hits. Evolution seems careless, it takes our balance so easily; but it has also prepared us, having endowed us with the very creativity, resilience, strength, and capacity for synergetic relationships that we need to be up to the challenges that evolving presents.

Life moves forward, through us, by way of challenging us. It upsets our lives, it asks us to make adjustments, it replaces the world we thought we knew with a world that operates differently. These difficulties hurt and they deliver new possibilities. At first, we just suffer, but with time and the right response, the Universe, Life, and we humans discover new capabilities, innovations in both substance and consciousness. Like it or not, we are already participants in Evolution as raw material and as Life's emissaries.

Metamorphosis

Life is predictably unpredictable. It serves up hardships unevenly. Not all acorns become oak trees. Are the ones that do the lucky ones? After all, falling or being carried to a fertile place subjects them to the forces of climate, place, and environment. This is how a tree gains its shape and its vulnerabilities. One could imagine that even the least hostile place shapes the tree. Is going through the gauntlet of adaptation really better?

We have made the determination it is, sort of. In the West we like a de-natured reality, not too wild, please. But despite the malls, the gated communities, and the insurance policies, Life gets in. So, despite our efforts and the degree of civilization we think we have achieved, we are still biological beings subject to the forces of the wild, the forces of Life.

This is a well-kept secret, an inconvenient truth. There is no cure for Evolution, for the way Life breaks into our tidy lives. It shouldn't, according to all of our cultural norms, and when it does, we are prepared to meet it as some sort of disease, or something that is unfortunately wrong. Thus, we respond accordingly, turning to the medical profession, psychotherapy or hiding. And, instead of evolving, getting stronger and becoming more adaptable, humankind grows more rigid, frailer and closer to extinction.

Life has a job to do. It places pressure upon us, tempers us, and increases our chances of surviving, of living another day to serve Evolution. Life, in its infinite wisdom, has chosen to unfold the capabilities of this complex organism gradually, in a stage-by-stage manner. This means that humans, like acorns, are pre-programmed to unfold in certain ways under certain conditions. We have within us the contingent capabilities, just waiting to be called upon.

It also means that humans, unlike acorns, are subject to a human-made environment (culture) that shapes and sometimes retards their development. We are not in the part of the story that looks at cultural supports or the lack of them. We will come to that later. For now, it is only important to know that Life is working on us for its sake and potentially our own. That work, however, happens in ways that defy our penchant for order and predictability.

Developmentalists have shown that human capabilities unfold, that they build on each other, and that they are incredibly elastic. We are early in understanding how this happens. We don't know if this reflects the unfolding of a pre-programmed set of capabilities that define the human being, or if what unfolds is a reflection of human adaptability plus the rigors of humans evolving here on this planet. I am in the latter camp for ecological reasons. But no matter the case, it is now indisputable that human capabilities unfold in a semi-predictable manner.

What is remarkable about this semi-predictable pattern of human development is the activating role that Life plays in it. This is what makes the pattern predictably unpredictable. A human life is laden with potential by virtue of how adaptable we are as an organism. But not all of that potential is realized, not only because of cultural reasons, but because Life, the initiator, does not strike everyone and seldom hits two people in the exact same way.

A metamorphosis of one's life might be initiated by a painful discrepancy or a traumatic loss. In each instance the hit we take propels us deep into the throes of metamorphosis, changing us and the world forever. This is Nature's way. Life is softening us up, re-making us so that we may become more pliable, more useful to the processes of evolution. All of us being meaning-making animals adopt a construct of reality.

Upon this construct also rests a sense of self. To most of us, occupying the world and seeing ourselves accordingly is a seamless process. What we don't know is how partial our construct of reality really is. Nor do we know how unformed our sense of self is. There is a discrepancy between the world we have adopted, the world we assumed to be the world and the world we find ourselves within.

This discrepancy is troubling. It is Life in the guise of a broader reality asking change of us, demanding that we evolve by recognizing the world anew. If it breaks through to consciousness, it forces a difficult (sometimes impossible) choice between the self and the world we know, and an as yet unknown self, occupying a strange and unknown world. So, despite ourselves, our wishes for consistency and continuity, we find ourselves between the worlds, experiencing metamorphosis.

If it doesn't break through to consciousness, this discrepancy can ruin our lives in other ways. It creates paradoxical effects that confuse and disable us. Instead of growing, we are stunted, hardened into inflexible selves, living lives based on half-truths and false assurances, creating and re-creating lives smaller than what we are capable of. Life may leave us to live out this half-life, or it may intervene in other more dramatic ways. Life might, instead, utilize other means to re-make us, such as illness, death, accidents, and other unforeseen losses. In any case we are headed into a metamorphosis, a time of transition, a chrysalis period. Life, whether we know it or not, is having its way with us

Natural Emergence

Sometimes the world we know seems too confining despite the efforts of others, and we run to the new world and the freedom it offers. This too is a natural response to how one's construct of reality, sometimes borrowed from friends, family, or loved ones, feels too constrictive. Our freedom to choose is limited by the world we occupy. So, to avoid the recurring pain and anxiety of repeating the miscues of the past, we leave behind a familiar world and enter a new one. In high school I wrote a poem that captured the feelings of the chick about to peck its way out of the egg. Today I know that poem, full of longing and ambivalence, was my first conscious experience of natural emergence.

The emergence from one world, one partial construct into another, is seldom graceful, free of pain, loss, and anxiety. But, it is natural. There is nothing wrong. This experience can be desirable, and it can happen overnight. You can be, like Dorothy, delivered to a new world by a whirlwind, or the move can take years of difficult labor. In each case there is a disruption, a breakdown in one world for a breakthrough to another. Life both impedes and transports us. It stands in our way, creating hardships to be faced, much like the riddles or impossible tasks of the fairy tales, or it yanks us unceremoniously, like the squalling newborn, into an alien world. There is always a hesitancy, a shock, an anxious discovery.

A stage of development may have been comfortable once. It probably served very well, brought us friends and loved ones, but now it is inexplicably suffocating. This is not ingratitude; it is the restless march of Evolution changing what has heart and meaning for the sake of the whole. But this unnamable uneasiness creates countless anxious conflicts between family members, lovers, church and organizational members, not to mention those who suffer knowing they no longer belong. Journeying from here to there may be desirable, but it is fraught with difficult consequences. There is seemingly nothing natural about this form of birth because it can be brutal; but it is natural, Nature's way, not our own.

Natural emergence can follow metamorphosis, but not always. It is possible to know one is coming upon a new land, a new way of operating, without undergoing a complete transformation. The desirable can come into view after years spent laboring. Emergence can happen as a result of a diligent openness to learning, a willingness to forgo certainty for the sake of growth. More likely, Life will pick you up and shake you into a difficult awareness, much like a predator shakes its prey.

Stage-by-stage, through metamorphosis or natural emergence, Life takes us for a ride, a wild ride, one that usually exceeds our plans, and introduces us, if we are willing, to a more complex world and a new set of capabilities. The nature of the ride, however, depends, in part, upon us. Life has its own agenda, but it cannot succeed without us. We are given what we need to withstand the sharp turns and whiplashes of Life but finding that out probably means being willing to go for a ride, to go where you never intended to go.

The Stresses of Metamorphosis and Natural Emergence
Life really does have its own agenda, and we are subject to it. This adds stress to our lives. Stress that goes beyond getting through school, relationship and financial uncertainties, family or job concerns. Life can come at us through all of these areas of uncertainty, but when Life gets confused with these concerns, we tend to think something is wrong instead of realizing that Evolution's agent is transforming us. By misinterpreting the stresses associated with the call of Evolution, we condemn ourselves to a life of disconnection and quiet desperation, a confusion that has typified this age. Unfortunately, there are cultural forces that are ready and eager to capitalize on just such confusion.

These stresses are caused by natural forces that are helping us to realize our full potential. Admittedly, this is a complex maneuver, because Life has a stake in the outcome. Our becoming isn't just for our sake, so we are thrust into a collaborative process without knowing it. Being challenged in such a way rarely brings out the best in us. Still, it is the strength, resilience and ability to go beyond that represents the best of ourselves, what is being asked for and activated.

We are overwhelmed at first. This is to be expected. There are significant losses. Life deals out some real hits. There is the loss of the illusion of control. The known world may become alien or constrictive. Loved ones no longer see or understand us. Worse yet, they may cause us more pain than we ever imagined, or they might seem like zombies, more dead than alive. Nothing is as it seemed. A reality that once seemed vibrant now is drained of meaning. Independence becomes dependence. Living seems like something others do while we sit and wonder what hit us, where our lives went. No one knows, so it seems, that in actual fact Life has tapped us for a new life.

Depression and Anxiety
We are not talking about illness here. This is not even a form of soul sickness. The medicalization of depression and anxiety is perhaps an understandable response to the genuine suffering that occurs when Life tips us off-balance, but this response creates more prolonged suffering than it eases. Some forms of depression, perhaps most, are developmental; they are the result of real-life dilemmas, deep dilemmas that Life has created, which may take years to become fully known and understood. Yes, as Dr. James Gordon points out in his seminal work on depression, Unstuck, there may be changes in the brain, but these changes can be better addressed using natural means, such as exercise, meditation, nutrition, and deep relationship.

Depression and anxiety accompany real change. They are natural reactions to discovering that one's nature seemingly is no longer capable of sustaining meaningful life. Depression and anxiety are also very likely to be essential ingredients in Life's transformation. Depression hurts, it takes one out of life, it reveals the unreality of what you once believed in, and as Dr. Gordon says, it sets you on a "journey." Depression is such a significant, all-encompassing experience that it cannot be ignored. It can be misunderstood and mistreated, but it cannot be ignored.

Depression, which currently afflicts so many (making it a lucrative market for pharmaceutical companies) and is likely to upset still others, is an indicator that Life is at work helping us give birth to a new self and a new world of possibilities. This outcome, however, depends upon our response. This is a collaborative endeavor that can be subverted by a response that fails to embrace the initiative of Life.

The current understanding of depression as an imbalance of neurochemistry, a disease similar to insulin-dependent diabetes, ensures a response that impedes Life and reduces our chances as a species of taking advantage of the adaptive challenge that is being presented to us. Our current constructs of depression, with a few exceptions, do not help us embrace Life, nor do they help us claim our own places in the dance of Evolution.

Anxiety is a more complex and omnipresent stressor. It is very possible to feel anxiety coming and going. In other words, there is anxiety associated with staying put or in moving. The old world or modus operandi is too constrictive and dysfunctional but is the devil you know, while the new world is unknown, scary, and makes one feel incompetent, is the devil you don't know.

The challenge, as Murray Bowen and David Schnarch know, is to grow your tolerance for anxiety so you can choose the more functional devil (world) you don't know. No matter what you do, no matter what choice you make, you are going to be anxious. Remember that anxiety is an existential condition. It comes with life, and is a reliable indicator, when it increases, that something is up. Your anxiety is going to increase when you begin to experience anything—impediment or inducement—that affects your growth and stability.

Anxiety is also a natural response to the awareness, even embryonic, that one is encountering a more complex situation than one had bargained for. Murray Bowen and Rabbi Friedman both thought we were living in an age of societal regression, a period when social anxiety tended to rule. We are at such a time when we as a species are encountering a more complex situation than we are prepared for. Regression seems like a plausible explanation when you consider how as a society we view depression and anxiety as problems to be fixed, illnesses to be treated with drugs, rather than invitations from Life, albeit hard ones, to discover new and more complex capabilities.

Instead of stepping up to our capabilities, we mistakenly view success as avoiding the hardships that actually render us fit. When the green helix moves, as it is now with climate change, depression and anxiety are going to increase. For this reason it is important to respond to the helping hand of Nature by embracing these challenges rather than viewing them, as we currently do, as problems to be eliminated. Embracing Life isn't going to rescue us from hardships, but it does give us a chance to discover through those hardships the capabilities and the place Life is making for us.

Accidents and Illnesses

Living is a terribly vulnerable experience, although most of us don't like to admit it. But no matter what we do, no matter who we are, there is no escape from what isn't supposed to happen. We can be assailed and altered by cancer or MS, or someone important to us can be killed or dismembered in an accident. Life takes a radical, unforeseen turn and suddenly we are thrust into a New World. For years after my stroke I kept having the impression I was just in a bad dream and would wake up soon. I never did. Instead, the world changed. I was in free fall, more dead than alive, for a long time. And all along I encountered a world that was much more complex than I had ever guessed.

Accidents and illnesses are tragic. But they sometimes change the course of life for the better. There are plenty of people who would swear that they have a better life as a result of how Life had altered them. I don't believe that the transformation that takes place in many lives is just a consequence of being roughed up by Life. I think that it is a combination of difficulty, such as an accident or an illness, and the way one responds.

Lucky was born not just because something bad happened to me, but because I decided early on to focus upon what was left, instead of what was lost. I am Lucky to be able to type these words, even if only with one hand. I am Lucky because Life gifted me with a hardship that is extreme enough that my outlook is changed forever, but not so extreme that I cannot relate to others. I have been introduced, rudely it is true, to what really matters. I think that having the chance to live, knowing what I know now, is a boon for which I am grateful. I know that in some way I created my luck with my attitude, but I also know that without Life altering my circumstances I would never have discovered my good fortune; I would have never known I am capable of appreciating life this much.

Life shook me, as it has others before me and as it will others yet to come. I would be thrilled if all those people felt lucky. But I know they all won't. Others will treat them like tragedies, and they will believe they are. Some people will never know that in addition to being unfortunate they are also fortunate. Life has challenged them, has altered everything, and thus made everything to be experienced anew. How they take on this challenge, how they respond, is what will define how they feel about what has befallen them.

Hardships
Life sometimes seems like a cat playing with a captive and wounded mouse. For what may seem, or even be a lifetime, we experience

hardships. It could be the duress of ill health, financial difficulty, disfigurement, or social inequality and prejudice. There are so many ways that Life seems to unfairly assail us. This is the sometimes-bitter truth that leads to the "gaze aversion" that bedevils the disabled, disfigured, and homeless. No one wants to know where but for fortune we may go. But hardships, too, have their adaptive value. There is no doubt that inequities exist and that we, as a culture, need to act to minimize the suffering they generate. But cultural adaptation, while absolutely necessary, is not the only level of adaptation that is possible, even essential. Victor Frankl, after his experience in the death camps, wrote, "The last of the human freedoms is to choose one's attitude..." — to play well the cards you have been dealt.

Life has many ways of getting at us. Few are painless. But difficult times, if we are willing, can help us grow, can enrich the chances of evolving, can make the most radical difference. The future is relying upon how we respond to the hardships that Life provides.

Loneliness
When Life takes us by the hand, it often sweeps us away from the known world, and before it introduces us to a new one there is often a long, difficult, though transforming, aloneness. Like the caterpillar in the chrysalis or the hero on his or her journey, Life confronts each of us with a time of stewing in our own juices. For us humans, social animals that we are, this is often the most painful aspect of the initiatory ordeal, the metamorphosis that Life is subjecting us to.

Loneliness is part of the human condition. Schnarch, Friedman, or Bowen would say it is existential. We are lonely because we exist. And more importantly, the paradox is that unless we come to terms with our solitary existence we cannot become fully who we are capable of being. Ultimately, who we are is determined by how we take responsibility for ourselves. Therefore, the loneliness that Life subjects us to helps us to find our most authentic selves. And how could we possibly fit in if we aren't authentic?

Through our loneliness, Life provides us with confrontation with our existence and responsibility for how we play the cards dealt to us. This in itself is an ordeal. So much is at stake: who we are, how we fit in, the contribution we have for our community, for our world. There are a lot of answers that come out of the silence that occurs when you can only hear your own voice. No wonder so many people want to dodge this aloneness; it is daunting to think the answers to my life's uncertainties will come out of my emptiness.

Few people elect to go into solitude. But go we do. Nothing is wrong when it happens. I can't tell you how many couples I've counseled who think there must be something wrong with their relationships because they feel lonely. People don't get married planning on being lonely, but they should. That way there isn't such a rude shock, so much self-doubt, blame of the other, or questioning of the relationship when it happens. Life wants us to become whole alone so we can fit in as a part of something larger. One of the great complexities we face is the fact that oftentimes we must come to terms with our aloneness in the midst of the very ones who both make it difficult and necessary.

Loneliness is much more than a burden, a hardship, or an ordeal. It is a treasure. The poet Rainer Marie Rilke said a couple should "protect each other's solitude." Life does this for us. It is, perhaps, more insistent, but as noted before, there is a lot at stake for us as individuals, as a species, and for Creation.

Responding

Natural therapy knocks us around, and in so doing Life asks for something from us. We are confronted with a challenge. Life provides the hardship, the initiating challenge, but the quality of what happens is determined by what we do next. This is the choice-point that determines everything. Our response defines the outcome.

This is how we participate in Evolution, not by directing, being in the driver's seat, but by responding, creating choices that enhance Life. The Universe may seek greater adaptiveness and fit; it may provide a host of internal resources; but all of this accumulated capacity, this human potential, is only galvanized if we respond appropriately. Life puts us in a collaborative position, and if we choose to respond in kind (collaboratively), a high synergy situation occurs, an embrace allows something new to emerge.

People get depressed and anxious and lose their balance or have it snatched away by illness, accidents, or other hardships, but these difficulties are not really the problem. Life challenges us, but that is not the problem either. The problem is how poorly we respond and how our responses deepen our quandary. To really understand the value of the difficulties that assail us, we need to look at what we do with these occurrences.

As an organism we are endowed with a capacity to respond. And this capacity is multi-layered as developmental stages. We have already described the capacities Life has endowed us with. These lie dormant in us until they are awakened. It is the actions of Life that call for us to discover the treasures within. Life places us under duress and calls for us to go deeper than we are accustomed to. We are stretched and asked to discover our own ability to respond.

The ability to respond, however, is defined by a lot of things. If a person doesn't know relationship is always going on and isn't just interpersonal, then that person is going to have trouble responding in any creative way. The world one occupies, one's level of development, is going to limit the range of responses that can be envisioned. The amount of anxiety one can tolerate will determine the capacity to choose. All in all, the ability to respond creatively ultimately comes down to how much responsibility an individual or any social organism holds for its own well-being.

This is the real problem then: How do we as individuals or as a species go deeper? How do we access the untapped capacities that enable us to respond to Life? These are actually easy questions to answer. Unfortunately, these answers by themselves aren't worth very much. We need to grow ourselves and increase our own development.

Recall that Ken Wilber pointed out that each step of growth, each stage of development accomplished, added depth. He also has said, we face a "crisis of depth." In other words, to give Life what it asks for, to discover the capabilities we have been endowed with, to know the place in the Universe that is ours, we only need to go deeper; but depth is not easily found in this culture.

Cultural Supports

Now we turn to the issue of supports. Robert Kegan pointed out how we "lack the curriculum" to support the levels of development that are needed to meet the demands of our complex culture. By that I take him to mean that we lack the cultural supports, the institutions, social practices, and settings that would support such development. I believe this is true. But it is even more complex than that. We lack supports for more complex states of realization. And we allow early states, less complex realizations, to get in the way of further growth.

What we deem as normal from the "through the looking glass" viewpoint of a psychology of interdependence, is an impediment that keeps us from developing our personal and collective potential. We have a two-fold problem. We need new supports, and we need to reconsider the supports we already have that are also obstacles to new development. There are supports for early stages of development that ensure a certain kind of natural realization and exploit it. Let's look at an example.

At first, we humans come to know ourselves through what we see reflected in the eyes of those who are significant to us. Developmental literature says that this trait, looking outside for cues about how to be and for a sense of self, typifies early stages of adult development. This is entirely normal. Early adult development involves looking outside to locate and know oneself. This is what David Schnarch refers to as "seeking external validation."

Schnarch also has a succinct way of describing this characteristic. He talks about "seeking a reflected sense of self." Early on it is a very natural human characteristic to look around for something to give one a sense of who one is and who one could be. Unfortunately, this trait is also a kind of developmental vulnerability that can be, and is, exploited.

It is a sad but true fact that the field of psychology was responsible for helping to create a system that would exploit this developmental vulnerability. This happened when American psychoanalysts joined forces with industry and created the field of public relations shortly after Freud's first visit to the U.S. Through expensive research and time these people created the corporate advertising machine.

In the years that have followed, billions of dollars have been spent on influencing the psyche. One expert pointed out that more money has been spent upon shaping the appeal to the American consumer than was ever spent by individuals or the government on mental health. He calls this practice a mass form of "therapy" designed to drive the economic engines of the marketplace.

Through mass marketing, particularly advertising, the individual is bombarded with messages that are designed to affect the self-image. People who have developed in normal ways are prone to look outside themselves for a "reflected sense of self" and are then susceptible to messages that suggest a way to look and feel good. This form of "therapy" is effective, otherwise billions wouldn't be spent on it each year. It makes people feel good about themselves and drives the economy; it also arrests development.

Commercial messages are designed to play on the normal human desire for a way to feel good about oneself. And they work! Our economy is proof of this. But our more complex abilities are amongst the hidden costs. A personally defined true individual appears only in later stages of development (see Table 2, pp.130-131). But this development is stalled, if not completely hindered, by the exploitive support that the marketplace provides. Coincidentally, it is exactly this form of development that forms an immunity to the alluring seductions of the marketplace.

This is an example of a cultural trait that supports (and exploits) the development of a reliance upon externalities and simultaneously impedes growth. It is one of many that favor a youth-oriented, developmentally immature, regressive society at the expense of more complex realizations. It is time for us as a society to encourage a deepening realization of our own personal and collective capabilities.

This is one of the missions of a psychology of interdependence. Remember that these newer, more complex realizations are not the products of education but arise in response to experience (or to hardship). Developmentalists believe that learning can lead the way, but it is experiential learning, rather than the kind that comes from books and classrooms. This is one reason why it is very important that we appreciate the opportunities that Life provides to promote growth and the evolution of depth, both personal and social.

What can be done about this? The responses are starting to surface and a psychology of interdependence is just one. It is apparent that a new way of seeing is emerging now. Cultural practices will follow new perceptions, alternative realizations, different understandings, and new practices that embrace Life. From the foregoing discussion it should be obvious that new methods that support development in those middle-aged and above could assist with the maturation of our culture. To speed maturation along there are some things we can do. We need to:

- de-pathologize the moment, and
- conduct psychotherapy as if Life really mattered.

De-pathologizing the Moment
This emerging psychology doesn't have all the answers. But it has indicated that there are stages of adult development that require periods of adjustment (metamorphosis), and when this occurs it happens for the benefit of Life and the individual organism. Today we have a very primitive response to this predictable occurrence. We act as if something is wrong and treat the whole process as a disease because it disrupts the life of an individual. This tends to strip away the adaptive benefits of organismic challenge, leaving the individual organism bereft of its own capabilities and Life bereft of the better fit that would help us adapt as a species to the processes of Evolution.

The continuing reliance upon medicine and the elimination of all suffering indiscriminately leaves us developmentally thwarted and immature. There are circumstances where a medical response may be necessary, but we, as individuals and as a society, must be aware that what is good for the pharmaceutical and medical industries may not be good for us. Doctors vow to "first, do no harm." It is time to consider how Life may be harmed, how being left oblivious of the hidden costs of medical treatment can be harmful to humankind.

Conducting Therapy as if Life Really Mattered
Psychology, like it or not, tends to be an agent that reinforces the prevailing assumptions that form the mainstream culture. The disease model of depression and anxiety is just the most obvious manifestation of how this is true. The field relies so heavily upon the medical/scientific assumptions that, along with economic considerations, have defined this age. Through the lenses of these disciplines Life is not a miracle. Mystery and deep inquiry have given way in favor of profit, efficiency, and productivity.

There are many practitioners who chafe against the limitations imposed by the insurance companies. These are caring, compassionate, and courageous practitioners who would like to be exploring the mysteries of Life but are thwarted by a health-care system that mirrors the values of our sacred cow, the marketplace. There is simply very little room for anything that does not generate profit.

Life and the Evolutionary imperative that drives it don't really care about investors' returns. It is evident that there is a conflict between the values of Life and the values of the industrial growth society. A conflict that puts us all at risk and is based on the idea that we are not really connected to Life. This is a conflict that Life will not lose, but humanity may. Life wants something different from us as a species, something it has prepared us for that will enable us to befriend the Earth, each other, ourselves, and Creation.

Right now, we are living in an age when Life matters less than profit, less than keeping the prevailing assumptions in place. We are also living in an age where all the prevailing assumptions are being questioned. This is a dynamic and uncertain time, a time where Life is exacting. Disruptions are occurring. Evolution knocks insistently. We need to answer in some way that is amenable to Life. And psychology, which is ostensibly an agent of change, bears responsibility for understanding consciousness, and must respond as if Life really matters.

Conclusion

The ways of the past will go and, as always when metamorphosis takes place, there will be disruptions. This is a good thing, painful and scary but completely natural and designed to deliver us to a New World. We need to focus on our responses. Natural therapy is already happening, already promoting the kind of deepening that freshly enables us. All we need do is be creative about how we respond, remembering that we are Life's emissaries and that we have been created for just this purpose.

Obviously, this is no panacea. Predicting hardship, disruption, and anxiety is not the way to offer a popular alternative. This is not a pain-free course. Natural therapy is free, but if it isn't responded to well it can be costly. The premium placed on personal responsibility, staying in relationship, and learning how to be collaborative is completely paradoxical. This is not an easy thing to manage. Life asks much of us. And, because it does, we know that what we do, the choices we make, are important and integral to the whole.

This is the bottom line. We cannot know our own capabilities, our own personal and social potential, without the challenges of Life, without natural therapy. And Life cannot have what it wants without challenging us and provoking our response.

CHAPTER 9

ٷ

The Between

Existence is beyond the power of words to define:
From wonder into wonder,
Existence opens.
—Lao Tzu

all things are possible
I don't mean my house or yours
I don't mean inside or out

that space between
is where I'll meet you
—Susan Windle

The mind that is not baffled is not employed.
—Wendell Berry

Introduction

Life is a miracle, shrouded in Mystery. There is so much that we do
not know. It is important to remember that we don't know because
what we don't know impacts and often defines us. I am wise enough
to know, as the Tao Te Ching describes, that no words can define the
nature of the Great Mystery. I am foolish enough to expose my igno-
rance, knowing that what exists within "the between" is a mystery
to me, but it has led me here and informs all that I have written and
seen. Essentially, what I want to convey here is the power of retain-
ing a healthy respect, even reverence, for unknowing.

To be clear, I am not advocating for blindness, for a kind of
closed-down unknowing, but rather for an openness to the demands

of staying in relationship with what is unknown, inscrutable, and unsettling. What we don't know shapes us, bedeviling us with uncertainty, and rendering us creatures that are uneasy. We don't take kindly to being rendered uneasy, vulnerable, and open, and aware that we are only partially aware, but through one of Nature's most brilliant paradoxes, not knowing is the way to knowing.

The Portal
In 1982, when I was 34, I had a dream—a great dream. During the course of one fall night's sleep I had a dream that came in four separate parts. Each part addressed a portion of my life, and during the course of the dream I aged from 34 until I was an old man. I will only retell one aspect of that dream, but the dream has given my life a sense of direction, an aura of wonder, and a kind of exasperating uncertainty. The dream was too compelling to ignore, and yet too mysterious to really grasp.

For a moment, during the course of this complex, long dream I was lucid. I knew I was aware that I was dreaming, and that in the dream I was having a vision. I saw a passageway, an opening in a rock wall. In the dream, the dream-me knew that this vision was important. I must study this passageway and learn and memorize every detail. In the meantime, the dreamer, the flesh and blood sleeping me, was somehow awake and knew that the scene I was beholding as the dreamer was important, not only to the dream me but also to the dreamer, to the one infused by a sense of wonder of having awakened in the middle of this dream vision.

I never fully came to that night and went on to dream the final segment of the dream. In the morning I had the good sense to record this dream. It has stayed with me and continued to invoke in me a sense of wonder. In graduate school several years later, I realized that the passageway I had seen was a portal between the worlds. I imagined myself as a kind of portal-tender who was charged with the task of keeping and learning about this strange opening. Without realizing it at the time, I became a student of the between.

The dream has effectively placed me in the thrall of Mystery. It introduced me to a space between, and at the same time made acquaintance with that mysterious space my business. Since that time, I have been constantly on the lookout for anything resembling a passageway, a portal between the worlds. More germane to this discussion, I have also been fascinated with the space between. I can only barely begin to give words to this fascination. Something existed on the borderline, the interface, the meeting place, where one thing became another.

The more I looked into this, in rites of passage, initiations, collective rituals, and theories of human development, the more I got the sense that what exists there was obscured, could not be seen and described. What seemed to exist in the between was not nothing, but it was like nothing that could be seen or known. I had a sense that what I was trying to capture was like "dark matter," a theoretical substance that astrophysicists have been speculating about and trying to prove despite it being undetectable to their instruments. I had a sense that something was there but had no way of talking about it. It was, and is, a kind of mystery.

The reason I am telling this story of myself, revealing this fascination, is that my engagement with this mystery has shaped my perception, resulting in the awareness that has informed this book. While I was looking into the Mystery that resided at the middle of the between, Mystery was looking into me and affecting me, changing my awareness. And so I have been brought to this moment, where I am compelled to acknowledge the place of mystery in this work.

The Between

A psychology of interdependence teeters on an amorphous foundation. Reverence for the unknown lies at the heart of this work. In some ways this is the most solid and enduring foundation and, of course, it is also the most indefensible. It is solid because the unknown will always be with us. It is indefensible because it is in the realm of the implicit, never to be adequately described. It is a vulnerable psychology, solid and emphasizing integrity, and at the same time relying upon uncertainty and a relationship with something large and inexplicable.

I didn't know it when I had the dream, but I had set out on a path that was going to keep me constantly in the proximity of the mystery of the between. I tended to think of the portal as a thing, a solid object. Not so. The portal, what really transports and transforms, is the inexplicable something that resides in the zone between here and there. What I have learned, been taught really, is that I want to stay as close to this place of uncertainty as I can bear. I want to convey my reasons why, and at the same time show how this place, which I call the between, is the core of the orientation I'm helping to bring forth.

I have pictured the power, the transformer, that lies at the heart of the between as a black hole. There is some kind of irresistible gravitational pull that sucks one in. But the black hole doesn't capture the pregnant, procreative, effulgent action of this mystery. It takes and it gives. It destroys and it creates anew. I am naturally ambivalent about being too close to what will surely swallow me as well as give me back to myself, re-made. Still, I have discovered that if I can bear these wrenching feelings I can gain access to a way of life that incorporates Mystery.

Why is this important, worth the discomfort, freeing? I can't tell you why this may matter for you, specifically, but I have found through my own experience four reasons for my wanting to stay close to the unknown, these are:

- not-knowing,
- learning,
- perspective,
- humility.

Not-Knowing

There are two aspects of not knowing that I want to convey: one that I cultivated and one that cultivated me. The one I cultivated was a result of my fascination with the between. The one that cultivated me occurred when Life thrust me into the maw of the between and I was taken beyond myself. Each shaped me, and each informed the realization that is expressed in this work.

I have stayed as close to Mystery, to the unknown, as I dared. I did this because I was more than curious; I had the intuition that the unknown was a kind of wellspring and that out of it could emerge the things I needed to know. At first this was only an intuition, but a French mathematician gave me a metaphor that helped convert this intuition into a way of life.

The French mathematicians of the 19th and early 20th centuries had a fascination with spheres. One of them, I forget who, envisioned knowledge as a kind of sphere. He pointed out that if all knowledge formed a sphere, then when knowledge grew, so grew the surface area of the sphere. What this meant was that as the sphere of knowledge grew its surface came into greater contact with the unknown. This simple model made clear to me what Albert Schweitzer had said, that "As we acquire more knowledge, things do not become more comprehensible, but more mysterious."

The more you know, the more you don't know. For me the reverse was also true. The more you submitted to, the more you showed interest in not-knowing, the more you got to know. Not-knowing led me deeper into the world. Subsequently, I have cultivated a reverence for the unknown, a kind of expectancy, a belief that if I kept myself open, close to not-knowing, I would be introduced to a world that existed beyond my normal perception.

I also came to know through the experience of being between. The first time I had a large dose of this was after my first marriage ended. For a long time, I didn't know who I was. My marriage had ended; the man I had been was no more, and I didn't have the replacement part on stand-by. I was eager to be anybody. But for an unbearable time, I was nobody. I learned a great deal during that time about transitions, about exploring, about the rigors of no identity. And when I began to become somebody, I was surprised by the fear and anxiety that I then had. I was afraid (and it turned out rightly) that I was becoming somebody too soon, that there was another somebody I could be.

All in all, this journey of not-knowing had been thrust upon me. I was delivered to a period of creativity, learning, and possibility. I wasn't mature enough to handle the anxiety of being that uncertain of myself

I learned about anxiety much later, and I think that is why I rushed into the next possible self. I did, however, notice when I discovered I was afraid I was becoming somebody, that I also liked being indeterminate, free to explore. This was my first experience of the power of possibility that accompanied not-knowing.

In graduate school and after, when I sat with a lot of people enduring transition, I got a lot better acquainted with the rigors and the possibilities that accompany the formless time. I cultivated not-knowing because I thought it was a good idea, but experience was teaching me that not-knowing was indispensable to transition. All of this prepared me as nothing else could have for the long stay in uncertainty that came with my stroke. For almost three years after my brain hemorrhage and surgery, I lived, if you could call it that, in the underworld.

The underworld is a limbo place, a place of endless uncertainty. It is a place where those, such as myself, who are near death, go. Everything is grey, lifeless and structureless. There is no sense of time, so everything is now. There is no such thing as planning, as tomorrow, as knowing, to the terminal. Journeying there taught me a lot about uncertainty. I learned that I was not in charge, that this was not my life, and that there was nothing I could do, nothing I knew, no desire of mine, that could break this spell. It lifted when, and if, it lifted.

I came back to life, thankfully! And I learned some invaluable things. These things are too numerous to describe here, but the learning about not-knowing is amongst the most profound. When I came back to life I had been transformed. Not through any choice of my own, I had taken a deep draught of uncertainty. Possessing nothing I could hold, I came into possession of the miraculous. Unburdened of what I thought I knew, and knowing nothing, I was introduced to what I could not know. I can't say what I was introduced to, nor can I say I know anything.

But I do have a deep regard for not-knowing now. I imagine my life in the following way: I live as close as I can to a roaring Mystery that keeps me alert, awake, ever expectant, and grateful. There is something about knowing that I know nothing that lets me dare everything, which keeps me open. In the end, all I can say is that not-knowing is an intrinsic part of the between. Journeying between, by choice, or by the actions of Life, is a process of being stripped of the known world, softened up, and prepared for the world you couldn't know otherwise.

I have come to believe that Life really resides between the worlds. Unknowing is a preparation and a condition of this middle realm. I don't think one comes to this level of unknowing through effort alone. But I do believe effort is required. Ultimately, Life has to pluck us, has to ripen us through the rigors of metamorphosis. This is not a choice that is up to us; Life takes us for its purposes, but not-knowing helps us be prepared when the time comes.

Learning

Science, information technology, and our great academies give the impression that all is known or will be known shortly. Learning then seems to be a matter of taking the time to be exposed to science, search engines, and great thinkers. This is true, but sadly, because this learning is promoted as the most valuable learning, it is only partially true.

Life is the miracle that keeps us awake at night and teaches us the most valuable lessons. But to learn these lessons often means being stripped of what one thinks is known in favor of the not-knowing that allows a new knowing to take place.

This is one of the painful losses that often accompanies metamorphosis. New knowledge replaces the old, bringing with it a new sense, but not before there is a period of not-knowing, of doubt and uncertainty. This period of confusion and loss of certainty precedes learning.

What lives in the heart of the between seems to be a kind of knowing that is infused with not-knowing. It is the presence of the unknown that is so shocking and yet so edifying. Because this is so, I have learned that keeping some kind of not-knowing, some regard for mystery, some sense of wonder alive makes it easier for me to learn.

Here again I feel compelled to refer to Nature's paradox: the known emerges from the unknown. The fire of metamorphosis burns away past knowledge before it releases new life. This is how renewal takes place. With enough doses of the between, I have discovered this is also how experiential learning takes place. Since Life seems to reorganize us, our brains, our lives, through putting us through hardships that promote new learning, it only seems sensible to cultivate the attitude of openness that invites learning. This attitude of openness does not immunize one from hardship but it does promote learning, the leading edge of development.

Perspective

The renewal that is metamorphosis, the journey between, seems to stretch perspective out in two different directions. The most common assumption about perspective is that it involves seeing more dimensionality in the world. This is true. The change of consciousness that comes with the journey through the unknowing realm between introduces a world that suddenly has new dimensions of stimulus and meaning. There is more complexity, greater nuance and more depth. The world is broader, it seems bigger and deeper; there are more levels to attend to.

It is especially the depth that we are not used to. Now truth has many layers and is a much more complicated thing. No decision or action seems complete until it accounts for the full range of complexity that is now perceivable. At the earliest levels of development, when perspective is expanding but still not that great, this is less troublesome. There is always something new outside to identify with and to feel good about.

But at later levels of development, new perspectives open up inside, and create a sense that the floor is giving way, of knowing becoming unknowing. This kind of indeterminacy adds depth, but it doesn't just show up in the world. The question "Who am I?" gets harder to answer and becomes more important. This new vision sees that the world is more multidimensional, layer upon layer, and so is the self, making new choices possible if one can stand the new layers of anxiety that come with choosing.

The journey between reintroduces us to the world and to ourselves. By and large this introduction is welcome, new freedom comes with it, but so too comes new responsibility. New perspective brings with new options and a new chooser. This is a complicated maneuver, however, that takes some getting used to. There are also new dangers, so expanding one's consciousness is not a child's sport. Nature sees to it: we play, but we determine how.

Transitions are not new. Life has always been knocking at the door. Indigenous people noticed this. They had initiation rites, rituals that were designed to help make these necessary transitions. We have largely lost that wisdom today. But that loss, which is a significant part of our cultural lack of support for development, hasn't stopped the knocking. Anthropologists such as Van Gennep and Victor Turner observed some of these indigenous cultures and noticed a predictable structure to their rites of passage. This structure, described in three phases, works just as well today to depict these chrysalis periods. The three phases they observed were named: separation, threshold (the between), and incorporation.

Separation

When Life comes knocking, the unimaginable takes place. It is like we are being abducted from our lives. Suddenly we find that the world we once knew and relied upon doesn't function like it used to. Usually there is an unwanted discrepancy between the world we relied upon and the place we now occupy. Sometimes we recognize this ourselves. But sometimes our dogged persistence is so great that someone else has to point this out to us. Inevitably we come to the realization that we are not in Kansas anymore.

This sense of displacement, of separation, is a hallmark of the transition process. Frequently, it is accompanied by a sense of confusion. What used to work, doesn't any more. This could be a personal practice, such as a way of organizing and identifying oneself; or it could be a relationship practice, such as a way of interacting with others. Because Nature is also wild, it could be waking up in a body that looks like yours but now behaves differently. In any case, you are wrested away from your familiar world.

In indigenous cultures elders took one away. Today it still happens; that is, one is taken away, but without the reassuring knowledge that someone who has been there and made the transition is overseeing the process. We no longer have such elders, or we no longer empower them to serve this function. We lack these valuable cultural supports, but this doesn't prevent Evolution from pushing us out of the nest.

All of the dynamics that separate us from the world we knew, discrepancies between the world we favor and the real world, internal contradictions, illness, loss of a job, death of a loved one, or relationship gridlock are ways that Life unseats us and pushes us out onto the precipice. The way back is no longer a painless inconsequential option. But the way forward is not yet clear. You know you aren't where you were, but you aren't sure where you are headed. Welcome to the Threshold: the between.

The Threshold (The Between)

The between is where all the magic happens. This place between the Worlds, the threshold, is where Life has its greatest chance to shape us. The threshold is Life's invention. It is Life's way of initiating our development.

The process is hair raising. Not just because cultural supports for this growth experience are missing, but because the process, like all real death/rebirth experiences, contains initiatory ordeals. These ordeals come in many forms, but invariably they come in forms that are customized to provoke the kind of awareness that leads into a new world.

In the literature of initiation, the anthropological field studies, this middle period or the threshold has been labeled liminal. Anthropologists such as Victor Turner have selected the word liminality, rooted in the Latin word limen, meaning the threshold between two spaces, to refer to the difficult conditions that prevail in this space between. Liminality describes the dream-like world between the worlds.

It is a world that is invisible, unrecognizable to those who live in the ordinary world, who have "sealed up" and belong somewhere. This means that one of the typical ordeals that accompanies this period is that you are invisible. Others do not see the part of you that is between the worlds. There is a pervasive feeling of being alone, of being unrecognized, unseen. It is true, you do not exist as you had. You may look the same, but your body is now occupied—by someone else.

Another ordeal is that, like the caterpillar in the chrysalis, you lose your shape. You become unrecognizable to yourself. This usually provokes a lot of anxiety. As a misshapen being you go through the motions of your life, knowing there is little life there and looking for some relief. This is often mistaken for depression and treated as such, obscuring the movement of Life and pathologizing the doorway to your potential. This is a typical, modern day ordeal that often accompanies the journey from one world to another, from one form of humanity to another.

In some traditional cultures they refer to the person between the worlds as "the un-born and the un-dead." This is an aspect of the ordeal. A person making this transitional journey can be like a zombie, more dead than alive at one moment and, like a fetus throbbing with life and potential, yet so vulnerable in the next. This gives a taste of just how paradoxical this world between the worlds can be. As David Schnarch has pointed out, it is the zone of "inherent paradox." No paradoxical interventions are needed. The natural systems of Life have delivered us through the looking glass, to a place where our own usual efforts produce opposite results, and we have to go in the opposite direction to get anywhere.

All of this softens us up, makes us malleable, and allows Life to shape us anew. Here in the between, we become the proto-human, like the undifferentiated stem cell. We can become what is needed. Like the undifferentiated cell, we take our cues from the surround, and we become what fits best. Unlike the cell, however, we have to go through this metamorphosis several times to become all that we could be, to manifest all of the complexity that is our potential. We have to be willing to undergo the rigors of relationship, to experience interdependence with all of its loss of control and necessary longing to make this journey because, ultimately, it is a collaborative process.

Integration

Eventually, because of our efforts and because of our willingness to surrender, Life washes us up on a shore. Then it is our task to occupy this new world. Again, we look around for cues. Depending on the world we come to, we take our cues accordingly. In the early worlds guidance is found in others. In the later worlds guidance comes from within. In either case, fully occupying the new world means stretching out and becoming oneself as fully as one can.

Sometimes this involves a reintroduction to loved ones, to friends and colleagues. As Robert Kegan has pointed out, in our modern world we too easily mistake changing relationship contexts for making the developmental journey. This undermines community and forestalls social growth. It also means that often we have no one who knows us and can see the real change that has taken place. The journey is incomplete if it is only for the self, Life wants us to merge with our relationship contexts and grow them too. We ourselves are agents of Evolution, thus the way we occupy the world we find ourselves within is also an important part of transition. Nature uses us as efficiently to promote evolution as She learned to use sunlight to promote growth.

The journey is the permanent feature. Not the world one is occupying. Seal up, enjoy the predictability of this New World and occupy it as best one can, but be prepared, Life has other stops in mind. The journey of separation is going to re-occur. We live long enough now to be sure that this experience will arise more than once. And, each step of the way we become more of what a human can be, more of what Life asks us to be.

Pain, Anxiety, Depression & Natural Therapy

Transformation often hurts. Losing one's shape, being in between and confused for a while, manifesting potential, acquiring a reformed shape: all of this hurts an organism as conscious and complex as we are. That is how we know that initiation is real. We don't need the ritual wounds and scars of traditional people to know something real has happened. We have survived what seems brutal to us, but is no more brutal than all births. The pain tells us it is true, we have been transformed, altered, and we are entering a new world.

We often know going in that we are going to be running the gauntlet and that a painful labor is going to be required, and choose instead to resist Life. This choice assures a different lifeless, listless, meaningless kind of pain, the pain of emptiness, of having no purpose. This is why differentiation therapists like David Schnarch and Edwin Freidman point out that maturation requires a willingness to undergo pain for growth's sake. Like it or not, to answer Life's call we have to live on Life's terms instead of our own.

This isn't what most of us desire. In the era of painkillers, pain is an option, isn't it? Well, no. Pain is one of the by-products of Life. It is emotional pain, the suffering that accompanies the complexity of Life that lets us know that we are making ourselves available to Life. Paradoxically, joy also depends, upon our being available to experience suffering. Joy and pain are like sunshine and rain; we need both.

As the conscious animal we are, we know that we are about to suffer. We feel anxious, afraid that Life is asking more of us than we can deliver. Or we get depressed because we cannot understand what is happening to our well-ordered lives. Sometimes depression follows years of out-running Life's call, but there is an inevitability to it. No matter what prescription drugs we are given, no matter how well adjusted therapy has rendered us or our significant relationships, the rug is going to be pulled out from underneath us. This isn't a failure of medication, therapy, or a personal or relationship shortcoming—it is the way of Life.

Natural therapy is at work. Life puts some organisms, like the butterfly, through a multi-stage life cycle. I believe humans as complex organisms with such enormous potential, take multiple stages to manifest all of our capabilities. So, it is easy for me to see that Life unfolds the human mind through multiple stages that include chrysalis periods, periods when natural therapy seems to assault us with Life's exacting nature. At those times we lose our shape and we suffer. These are the rare moments in life where we have the opportunity to grasp that life really is a gift, given to each of us, not just for our sakes, but because Life has an evolutionary agenda of its own. We become malleable to the shaping influence of Life, like it or not, through natural therapy, at Life's behest not our own.

Humility

Being subject to metamorphosis, to having Life take over the steering wheel, is a humbling experience. Western culture may teach us that we are supposed to be in charge of our lives, and it may provide us a host of medications and products to convey the sense we are, but it fails us when it comes to recognizing the obvious. Life is going to have its way with us. This difficult truth, which gets denied every day and causes so much unnecessary suffering, can free us. But it is a humble freedom, sobering by virtue of the realization that Life does not belong to us.

I didn't take to the idea of giving up my ideas about what was happening, and being humble, that easily. Maybe I'm just stubborn. I was intent upon being a good citizen, a wise user of life, someone who created opportunities and capitalized on them, a good American. But Life had other plans for me, and it painfully altered my awareness and intent. There is much I have had to learn before I could see my way to acknowledging the role Life was playing in what I called "my life."

Life is teaching me humility. My second marriage unraveled because we were both over our heads. What that means is that staying married took more development than either one of us had. In my case, the lack of development related to my refusal to really see my partner as other, to let her be somewhat of a mystery to me. Although I knew that I was a better, happier person when I was learning, I was so attached to my version of my wife that I could not, would not, see her. I treated her like I knew what motivated her when in truth I should have been paying attention. I have now come to realize the truth of e.e cummings' poem:

love's function is to fabricate unknownness
. . . how lucky lovers are (whose selves abide
under whatever shall discovered be)

I only became Lucky later, and by then I could see my arrogance and the cost I inflicted upon everyone involved. Now I know that "love's function is to fabricate unknowness."

Humility arrives because Life delivers awareness of the partiality of all of one's assumptions. This is a good thing, and it is usually painful enough to promote an attitude of humility and openness, a readiness to meet what is instead of what you have prepared for. Staying humble is staying close to the moment, aware of the presence of the between, of Mystery.

Relationship

Life, the miracle, plays havoc in our long-term relationships too. Near the center of every relationship lies a mystery spot, a metamorphosis place. This is usually such an anxiety-provoking set of feelings and circumstances that most relationships put this place out of bounds, in the de-militarized zone. It is simply a "no go" space that the couple may perceive but generally know little about. Frequently, underneath what is perceived to be a communications issue, lies a metamorphosis spot, the passageway between the worlds.

As David Schnarch points out, the living system that is a long-term relationship is a "people growing" phenomenon that is guaranteed to deliver a couple to this place. Couples don't usually go willingly, preferring to believe (as our culture does) that something is wrong. It is easier (in cultural terms) to suspect one's partner, oneself, or the relationship, than to accept the fact that Evolution has come knocking. Prepared or not, a couple will find itself confronted by an elegantly designed and often painful dilemma that challenges each to reach deep inside and find the ingredients of a new-found sense of integrity.

This phenomenon is widespread. It is exactly what makes long-term relationships with friends, family and co-workers, so valuable and so difficult. This potential for greater integrity gets lost in our consumer culture, where relationships are viewed as commodities that can be disposed of in favor of another model, presumably having different features. The illusion of change that comes with changing partners, doesn't really change anything. The new relationship, just like the old, holds a metamorphosis spot too. Transport from one world to another is always available.

For most of us the relationship landscape is literally strewn with such conveyances, doorways to a new way of being, but they are rarely welcome. In part they are unwelcome because we lack cultural supports for these kinds of opportunities, and because they ask so much of us.

In the early stages of development, when one tends to be seeking some form of "reflected sense of self," relationship dynamics are valued for the image they convey, not the growth potential they hold. In later stages, when there is more desire to become oneself, it is hard to find the way to cut across the cultural grain and discover what a dilemma really holds. Again there is an absence of cultural support. Add to that the fact that couples therapists, who haven't yet been through what Schnarch calls the "crucible" and I call metamorphosis, are rarely helpful.

We live in a low synergy culture. Isolated and lacking community, we labor with relationships without knowing their real value. This kind of unknowing is just sad. It contrasts sharply with the kind of unknowing that love "fabricates." Synergistic, truly collaborative relationships are organized around expectancy. They are all about emergence. These kinds of relationships are part of our social potential, and they are available to us. But to actualize this potential we need more cultural supports, more willingness to step into the between, and to cultivate the unknowingness that gives us access to a new world.

Conclusion

Life asks much of us. It put us through metamorphoses, though chrysalis periods, when we are thrust in between the worlds. These are painful times when life as we have known it is being dismembered. The between exists as a kind of death. It is inscrutable, all encompassing, and unpredictable. It is brutal, wild, and sometimes seems savage. No one looks forward to it, but it comes nevertheless. These changes, as rough on us as they are, are a part of the miracle of life, a necessary part, a part that gives Life just as surely as it alters it. To be viable, to be useful in any meaningful way, a psychology of interdependence has to recognize, and come to terms with humanity's dependence upon the renewing power of Life.

Cultural change also hinges upon our availability to Life. Evolution is an inexorable process. No political entity, ideology, or market stratagem is going to survive that isn't responsive to the tides of change. This much we know. But are we prepared to go to places between the worlds collectively? Are we ready to turn over our way of life, our sense of freedom, ourselves, to the seeming chaos of the between? Nation-states, corporations, cities, neighborhoods, families and marriages are all subject to the mercy of Life. The green helix is moving; as individuals, as social organisms, and as a species we need to move along with it. We are moving, knowingly and unknowingly, but are we going into an evolutionary cul de sac, or are we aligning with Life?

Metamorphosis is important to our survival. The viability of our species rests upon our willingness to journey between the worlds. This is true at an individual level, where the need for meaning, right livelihood, growth and good relationships are most important. It is also true at social levels, where getting along, community, collective meaning and the cultural and ecological health, are important. Despite this, cultural supports are missing, Life labors to cross our cultural grain, increasing the stigma, trauma and confusion that accompanies these important moments.

"Love's function is to fabricate unknownness." Nature seems to do that just fine. Life strips us down to an unknowing, quivering mass, and then it renews us. We need to cultivate some similar form of loving, some ways to revere the mystery that is Life. There is a lot at stake for us as individuals and as a species. We can do it, because this form of adaptability is built into us, and Evolution has got our backs. Life will keep insisting. Let's find a better way to answer the incessant knocking.

Ultimately, this is about connection. Life has seen to it that we are connected. We are coupled with our living environment, each other, and our social milieu. This is the good news. The more troublesome news is that with these connections come challenges, new responsibilities and new choices. Living fully with this awareness is a complex affair. So much of the how lies before us in the provinces of the unknown.

SECTION IV
Sociotherapy

SECTION IV

❧

Sociotherapy

Your health cannot be disengaged from the society's, and the society's health cannot be disengaged from the planet's. Until we accept these facts nobody can say that they are truly healthy. Not without cutting themselves off in a very unhealthy manner from level upon level of reality. To be physically astute and psychologically tended yet morally insulated and conceptually blind is to be crazy, not healthy.

—MICHAEL VENTURA, 1993

Introduction

In this section I want to convey how some of the ways that seeing things as a psychology of interdependence does, changes what I do as a psychologist. As a disabled person, I am probably slow in integrating into my approach all of the ways my outlook has been changed. Awareness of the pervasiveness of connection is changing my life and challenging all the assumptions on which I was professionally brought up. My integration of this new perception is no doubt incomplete. Since I don't know if I will live very long, and I have reason to believe I may not, I offer only this partial take. It seems appropriate for this psychological orientation to depend on others to render it more useful and nearer completion.

I have found that perception of wholeness and connection has altered how I function in two significant ways. My work as a psychotherapist has predictably changed, given what has been described earlier. Certainly, the rigors and joys associated with being a human holon, constantly in an unstable relationship with my world, have reformed my estimation of the importance of relationship to human development. I have also had to create a new modality to address the level of human potential that was previously unrecognizable.

Psychotherapy

One of the things you discover when you begin to integrate the developmental perspective is that behaviors may look and be the same, but something qualitatively different is going on. For instance, if you were a fly on the wall in my office, you might notice that I appear to be meeting, greeting, and conversing with my clients in much the same manner that talk therapists have been doing for years. There, however, the similarity would end.

Remember that this orientation is non-pathological, strength-based, systemic, relational, and developmental. This means conversation will focus upon challenges instead of problems, the now instead of the past, values instead of deficits, capabilities instead of weaknesses, the challenges associated with connection instead of disconnection, and the natural anxieties that accompany a shifting level of development rather than something being wrong. Periodically the conversation will be about the rigors of metamorphosis. And always the conversation will focus upon action, upon responding to the challenges of the moment.

The hardest part of my psychotherapy work, be it with individuals, couples, or families, is convincing them that what brought them in is not a problem, some indication they are defective or deficient, but a challenge that they can grow through. You would be amazed at how stubbornly some people cling to the traditional idea that psychological challenges mean illness or maladjustment. Stepping out from the cloud of deficiency, which seems like it ought to be desirable, means accepting personal responsibility for responding now. When people take responsibility for themselves they become a lot easier to work with.

Therapy then moves to the nature and meaning of the challenge that confronts one. This challenge, which is invariably customized by the work of natural, living systems to be as idiosyncratic and specific as possible, reflects the choices and integrity of the person or persons I'm sitting with. Realizing how accurately the dilemma fits the one(s) being challenged promotes new, unexpected growth. Now it becomes possible to see that one never escapes from the net one inadvertently weaves.

Through being impacted by our choices, Life responds with a dilemma that brings home the consequences of those choices. Some people cannot face themselves and take responsibility for the world they have crafted, but surprisingly some people do. Both choices are poignant and consequential. Both deserve compassion, reflecting as they do the complexity of the human situation. But the choice to face and take responsibility, which happens more often than not, is what gives me hope. I work on this level because I get to see the everyday heroism of the human heart in these folks, and it encourages me to keep going, personally and professionally.

From early on in my practice I experienced an ethical dilemma. This dilemma has led me to a whole new dimension of psychological work. I call this work "sociotherapy." In order to understand how I came to practice in this new way, and what it means, you have to understand something of the ethical dilemma I was facing.

I came to realize that many of the people I was working with were suffering from feeling isolated, alone, and disconnected. I soon came to the conclusion that the consulting room, as a construct of our individualistic culture with its emphasis on privacy and confidentiality, exacerbated the problem. There seemed to be an aura of shame and unwholesomeness surrounding psychological inquiry. This constellation of circumstances seemed to deepen the isolation of those who dared to look for help, and at the same time, further alienated others. Standing by and letting people believe something was wrong with them because they felt the absence of community in their lives was, to me, contributing to suffering rather than trying to rectify it.

I was already sensitive to the healing and wholing power of community, as described in this book's introduction. It seemed I had to find a way to introduce my clients to community. I also wanted to develop a way of addressing the ongoing impacts of social isolation in my town. This led to my first attempts at providing a community context for people to do psychological inquiry. Naturally, what I discovered was that community depended upon relationships, and that when relationships became strained people relied on prevailing assumptions about what was going on. These assumptions didn't help. Observing how tenuous community was, and how current practices didn't really help, sent me on a quest, which eventually changed how I worked as a psychotherapist, and later led to my work as a sociotherapist.

Sociotherapy

Sociotherapy is a term coined by British psychoanalyst and large group worker, Patrick de Mare. It was his way of describing psychological work that addressed internal beliefs and external cultural assumptions. He saw large group therapy using a method he called dialogue as a means for transforming individuals and culture. Thus, he called this work, with its two-level focus (including society), sociotherapy.

Staying close to de Mare's original meaning, I use the term sociotherapy to describe the multifaceted form of psychological inquiry that happens when a group begins to focus on the between. I had come to the realization that multi-systemic approaches were needed to make palpable the connection between the levels for people to see, and address, the pattern of connection that links personal choices with relationship, community, and even cultural and environmental challenges. So, for me, sociotherapy became an adjunct to psychotherapy, a practice that was designed to provide a psychology of interdependence, a way to be a psychology of the many, not just one or two. It addressed alienation and isolation by placing them in context and by providing a shared means of addressing an ailment that is cultural and not just individual.

What you will see in the following chapters is how this work took form. In chapter 10, "Getting Along Together," you will be exposed to the results of my original research that clued me into a dimension of social connection that was described as "true community" by psychiatrist M. Scott Peck. This pattern of connection is rarely achieved socially, although it could be. It also reveals itself in an even rarer order, or stage, of consciousness. Exposure to this seemingly rare phenomenon set me upon the path that led to a psychology of interdependence and to sociotherapy.

Chapter 11, "Our Story," reveals another way-station in my growth of awareness. It reveals how learning in a community context alerted me to not only the power of collective learning, but also to recognizing the importance of dealing with the underlying causes of what truly undermines us. This experience forms the seed that ultimately led me to learning community as my preferred way of promoting personal and social awareness. It also describes the beginning of an ongoing awakening to the link between psychology, sociology, and ecology.

Chapter 12, "The Social Koan," describes an application of large group work, a learning community, to stimulate development. This was before I learned about the instruments that measured development, but after the development of a group method that utilized learning in a community to create a way to see the linkages that exist and couple us to each other and our surroundings. This chapter describes one form of sociotherapy at work.

Conclusion

These chapters elaborate upon the realization that hidden social potential can be liberated with practices that are designed to reveal the pattern of connection that underlies our social reality. This potential lies dormant and unaddressed by traditional forms of psychotherapy that look primarily within at the intersubjective life of the dyad. Sociotherapy is an attempt to bring to life a psychology of the many by focusing on the between, creating an experience of the pattern that connects. Sociotherapy is a work in progress, awaiting more creative practices that illuminate even more of human social potential.

It stands to reason that a psychology of interdependence based upon a perception of wholeness and connection, would co-evolve with a new form of psychological inquiry. Sociotherapy is in its infancy, as is the realization of how connected we really are. Newer, more efficient methods of bio-psycho-social inquiry will certainly follow as more people experience the joys and rigors that accompany a life of connection. This is an important development, coming as it does with the change in our climate. We are linked inextricably with our living environment. How we treat it, as the Dalai Lama says, is how we treat each other and ourselves.

CHAPTER 10

ᴡ

Getting Along Together:
The Challenge of Communitas

A midst the mayhem and destruction of the Los Angeles riots in 1992, Rodney King expressed what may be a core question for our time: "People, can't we all just get along?" His plea gives voice to the urgent need that we have to cooperate, as well as to the uncertainty we feel about our capacity to do so. We now live with extraordinary cultural and ethnic complexities that arouse fear and mistrust. Never before has humanity faced the challenge of creating a sense of community that includes such great diversity. The life of the planet and of future generations may depend upon how we respond to King's question.

Can we all get along? It is clear that we don't. One does not have to look solely at racial, ethnic, and religious hostilities to confirm this perception. The national rates of divorce and domestic violence dramatically convey the tensions that abide at the heart of our daily interactions. An honest appraisal of the distance and distrust that separates us from neighbors and co-workers reflects this perception as well. This is a grievous truth of life in America.

The tension that exists within American culture can also be seen operating globally. In 1993 The Carter Center monitored 124 wars worldwide. The preponderance were civil wars, occurring between neighboring and often related peoples manifested atrocities such as those associated with Bosnia, Somalia and Rwanda. Another disturbing facet of how we behave in relationship with other forms of life is revealed by our abuse of the planetary environment. Much of the concern about the sustainability of human culture and our endangered biosystem revolves around our inability to get along with otherness, be it human or non-human.

How have we come to be here? Despite the best intentions of the pilgrims who pledged at Plymouth Rock to live "as members of the same body." the American way emphasizes the rights and privileges of the individual. This great nation was born by freeing individuals to pursue their own forms of happiness and self-expression. Now it is threatened by its own success. By sacrificing a sense of the common good, America provides fertile ground for narcissism, alienation, isolationism, and fear of anyone who is significantly different.

This continuing emphasis upon individualism conflicts with our critical need for connection and commitment to one another. Our inability to get along leads to cultural and political gridlock. Modern ecological and geopolitical issues are complex and involve large systems that require sustained collective attention, yet our mistrust of otherness retards our ability to respond collectively. The dilemmas we now face ask us to care for the good of the whole as we care for the good of ourselves.

How do we achieve this development? When we turn toward traditional concepts of community for guidance we see that community has been associated with long-standing relationships that occur among people who share a geographical location and a common worldview. These communities are distinguished by the common values they hold, by the norms they create to implement those values, and by the shared means they employ to survive and thrive. In the language of sociology, these communities would be referred to as "communities of affinity."

Organized around shared values, they demonstrate cooperation and the power of unifying principles. At the same time, however, these communities of affinity contain seeds of the very dilemma that now threatens our cultural and biological survival. In our multiethnic and multicultural society, we are overwhelmed with a diversity and complexity that traditional communities have never had to embrace. If we adhere to traditional approaches, we are quickly stymied by the inevitable question: Whose values are the "right" values? Whose principles will determine the organization of society? This question, laden with the struggle for cultural identity and ideological supremacy, fuels much of the conflict now ravaging the planet.

An answer to King's question does not lie in communities based upon similarities. A new basis for community is needed: one that values diversity and confirms the integrity of multiple co-existing realities and is based upon a palpable experience of how profoundly connected we all are. This form of community could be described as a shared experience of interconnection, as social communion or as a collective state of consciousness.

Over the last several years my research has identified large group processes that appear to generate such experiences of a unitive state of consciousness. I have labeled this state of consciousness communitas, a term borrowed from cultural anthropologist Victor Turner. Fascinated by the collective rituals of indigenous peoples, Turner noted that these rites generated a form of social communion. He called this communitas, and his observations provided the vision that informed my research.

Turner observed that these communal processes created a "ritual space" that existed outside of the normal cultural context. He employed the term "liminality," derived from the Latin word limen, meaning threshold, to describe this central aspect of the ritual process. He defined liminality as "anti-structural," meaning that in ritual space cultural structures dissolved and all forms of identity conferred by cultural status also dissipated. In this space betwixt and between the usual social structures, ritual participants met one another as whole and equal beings to examine their relationships and culture.

Turner also described the "liminal zone" as an empty space. Communitas emerges as equal individuals collectively submit to the ordeal associated with having no status, no role, and no mitigating or mediating structure to temper their encounter with the human dilemma. Communitas was sacred and holy and suffused with a renewing and generative power. These perceptions led Turner to assert that cultural transformation could be attributed to the impact of communitas upon collectives.

Turner's descriptions of ritual liminality provided useful criteria for identifying contemporary group intensives that might generate experiences of communitas. One such group intensive is the Community Building Workshop developed by M. Scott Peck and The Foundation for Community Encouragement. The workshop is a large group intensive that often involves fifty or more participants. It usually occurs over three full days and is totally experiential. The sole task of the participants is to create an experience of community: toward this end they sit in a large circle and interact.

Two trained leaders facilitate the experience, providing simple guidelines that include: listen deeply, speak when you feel moved to speak, use "l-messages," practice inclusivity, observe how you maintain separation, and share responsibility for the outcome of the workshop. Facilitation also includes the use of silence, teaching stories, re-emphasizing the guidelines, and brief feedback to the group as a whole.

According to Peck, the workshop proceeds through four phases: pseudo-community, chaos, emptiness, and community. The initial stage of the process, pseudo-community, is marked by congenial, comfortable and polite interactions. These interactions avoid conflict and preserve a superficial sense of harmony.

Chaos emerges when differences come into the open and attempts are made to establish what is appropriate behavior in the group. As different opinions emerge, group members attempt to ignore or change each other's positions, a process that leads to tension and distrust. This chaotic phase reveals a struggle for power in the group, the same dynamic that occurs in our larger culture, resulting in fear, hatred and withdrawal. The chaos phase constellates on a small scale the cultural crisis that is being played out in the streets of our cities and within the halls of our government. In the workshop, participants are confronted with the stark realization that despite their intentions, they themselves are sources of this terrible dilemma.

In Peck's model there are two ways out of the chaotic phase. Both work, but only one leads to community. The group can organize its way out of chaos (and its chance for community) by choosing a task to focus on, a member to "heal," or a subgroup to scapegoat. Or it can "empty" itself of the expectations, preconceptions, and prejudices that prevent community from emerging.

Emptiness calls for a form of dying. Group members create a space for community by voluntarily sacrificing their needs to be right, to be in control, and to remain invulnerable. The members surrender their methods for protecting themselves from personal and existential vulnerability. Community emerges as vulnerability increases and as group members surrender their expectations and enter the unknown together.

My research involved surveying and analyzing the reported experiences of over 200 participants in a number of these workshops. Using a statistical method known as factor analysis, the results revealed three primary factors that describe the participant's experience. These factors were labeled: "a sense of community," "the experience of otherness," and "the sense of the human existential dilemma." The "sense of community" factor reveals that many participants shared what they described as an important and profound experience. This experience included a shift of consciousness to an enlarged sense of self accompanied by strong feelings of peace and tranquility. Those who scored high on this factor reported a strong sense of connection and feelings of compassion and kindness for each other. It included transpersonal features such as a sense of unity, feelings of sacredness, an ineffable quality, and a sense of timelessness. In essence, participants reported experiencing a collective shift into a unitive state of consciousness.

Remarkably, this shift in consciousness occurred despite a high degree of awareness of the differences or experience of "otherness" that the group included. The experience was reported to be painful and disturbing; it included feelings of annoyance, resentment, alienation, distrust, and conflict with others in the workshop. These same participants also reported awareness that they were judging others and that their beliefs about these others, or themselves, created distance. This factor highlights the difficulties associated with the encounter with differences, personal and cultural.

The third factor, "the sense of the human existential dilemma," shows that the workshop resolves these difficult feelings and preserves the diversity of the group by providing a mutual experience of humankind's underlying existential vulnerability. Those scoring high on this factor indicated recognition of the degree of human uncertainty, of how limited humans are, and of how vulnerable others are. Participants also recognized the desire to avoid feeling the pain and uncertainty that is part of human life. They reported that awareness of this level of shared vulnerability engendered compassionate feelings and an emotional sense of connection. (See Chapter Notes for details of this study.)

The findings of this study show that large groups can integrate diversity and survive the difficult tensions that accompany the presence of otherness, and that this becomes possible when the group shares an experience of human vulnerability. This catalyzes the emergence of a collective state of consciousness. The results demonstrate that large groups can generate experiences that make palpable a recognition of our interrelatedness. They provide confirmation of our underlying social and ecological interdependence. The study also reveals that transpersonal experiences of an enlarged sense of self can occur at system levels beyond the individual.

These findings have important implications for psychology and for the practice of psychotherapy. By establishing that large groups can address the tensions that create and sustain cultural issues, the way is paved for a new form of psychology; a psychology of interdependence. This psychology is founded upon direct experience of the underlying interconnectedness of life and recognizes that individuals suffer in a culture that denies this interrelatedness. Such suffering bears important feedback about cultural processes that need to be transformed.

Understanding that large groups represent a microcosm of the culture at large, this emerging psychology attends to the suffering associated with cultural tensions. It explores and examines the psychological and the cultural dynamics that create racism, ethnic distrust, homelessness, and our abusive relationship with the environment. As a transpersonal psychology, it assists collectives through developmental steps while educating individuals about how they contribute to this transition. Thus, this psychology treats individuals and the culture simultaneously.

This new psychological perspective is emerging from many sources. A number of independent practitioners are pioneering the development of new models, techniques, and practices that address our ability to get along together. British psychiatrist Patrick de Mare refers to the beneficial effects these processes generate as "sociotherapy." De Mare reports that groups uncover the underlying dynamics that generate cultural structures by employing "dialogue," a form of collective free association. In so doing, it brings to awareness the basic assumptions that shape a group's interactions. It makes explicit the ideological basis for the sub-groups and cultural structures that separate, divide, and create conflict.

Physicist David Bohm, renowned for his theory of a holographic universe, developed the practice of group dialogue over more than two decades. Viewing dialogue as culturally transformative, he described it as a method for achieving "group mindfulness." With practice, groups achieve a sense of impersonal fellowship and group consciousness. In this state it is possible to examine cultural assumptions and to witness the effects that such collective thoughts produce. Bohm and De Mare both insist that the individual and the society can be simultaneously humanized by the use of group dialogue.

Arnold Mindell, founder of the Global Process Institute, has developed a process-oriented form of psychotherapy that he applies to working with groups sometimes numbering in the hundreds. He addresses cultural conflicts such as racial and ethnic tension through processes designed to make a group's collective unconscious more conscious. To Mindell, every group generates a "field" of information, which impacts upon the behavior of the group, and every group participates in cultural fields. By rendering the contents of these fields conscious and working with the conflicts inherent in them, his work models "deep democracy," a more inclusive form of participation in our underlying interrelatedness.

Businesses are being increasingly viewed as "learning communities," where collective processes can be practiced that benefit the development of the participating individuals, the organization, and the larger culture. The rapidly changing business climate has made it imperative that organizations adapt quickly and efficiently. The need for such flexibility and responsiveness has led to innovative methods for working with collective processes. Management and organization development experts, such as MIT professor Peter Senge, are experimenting with techniques that emphasize systems thinking, dialogue, shared vision, and total participation.

These new practices, employing a larger context to focus upon cultural dynamics, offer a timely response to the concerns of those who have been critical of psychotherapy's effectiveness as an agent for social change. These concerns focus on the one-to-one emphasis in therapeutic practice and its limitations in addressing mass disorders such as addiction, environmental illness, and domestic violence. Healing in the therapeutic context is seen as an "inner experience." By emphasizing the subjective experience of the client, it reinforces individualism and isolation, leading to cultural passivity rather than political and social action. James Hillman suggests that self should be redefined so that it becomes more inclusive, that self should be seen as an "interiorization of community." Critics concerned with the environment are arguing for a therapeutic perspective that views the person and the planet as part of a single continuum. To them, successful treatment must incorporate the needs of Life as a whole. Believing that the pain of the ecosystem is being expressed through our private emotional and spiritual anguish, they are concerned that this travail cannot be effectively understood by a psychology that reduces this sensitivity to an individual pathology.

Underlying these concerns, we hear the essential recognition that communal models for healing are needed now. This returns us to the question of whether or not we can "get along." We now live with the uncertainty and urgency embodied in this question. Our best response lies in leaning bravely into this question until, as the poet Rilke points out, we can "live the answer."

The question invites us to struggle together for insight into the psychological dynamics that create the cultural tensions and conflict that threaten us. Engaging with this question can lead to new psycho-spiritual insight and functional capabilities. My research has shown that these abilities can be awakened through an experience of communitas. Subsequent developments have shown that participation in a large group employing a learning community approach provides a social context where these capabilities can be further developed.

When individuals realize that their well-being is linked inextricably with the well-being of the whole, and they can see a way to develop the skills that provide them with a functional capacity for interdependence they will very often begin to practice community building as a form of psycho-spiritual discipline.

Turner described the social bond that arose from communitas as a "strong sentiment of human kindness." Practicing community means cultivating the conditions that can make an experience of human kindness real. When we practice community, we invest our lives and our hope in a mutual effort to ensure that we, and the generations to come, will know that we can all get along.

CHAPTER 11

"Our" Story:
Awakening in Community

As a psychotherapist I occupy a unique position in our culture. Daily I sit with ordinary people who are struggling to
make their lives meaningful and healthy. I experience the heroism
of everyday people working hard to be whole, to make a place for
themselves in life. They tell me their stories and show me their pain
and self-doubt. As I listen, hour by hour, I have come to realize I am
not just hearing isolated, individual stories but our story—a story of
humanity's shared suffering. This realization hit hard. I was trained
to believe that my clients' problem were theirs alone. My job was to
help them change themselves so that they could participate in the
"good life" that our culture offers. For many years I was content to
believe that the sad, painful and often tragic stories I heard were the
result of broken families, disastrous relationships, careless parent-
ing and addictive substances. Today, I know differently. Now I know
that much of the pain and unhappiness I hear is a direct result of the
kind of society we have become.

To illustrate how my understanding changed I offer you "The
Parable of the Downstreamers." This story describes the way I once
saw things, a way that kept me from hearing the larger story that
my clients were telling.

*It was many years ago that villagers of Downstream recall spotting the
first body in the river. Some old-timers remember how spartan were the
facilities and procedures for managing that sort of thing. Sometimes, they
say, it would take hours to pull ten people from the river, and even then,
only a few would recover.*

Though the number of victims in the river has increased greatly in recent years, the folks of Downstream have responded admirably to the challenge. Their rescue system is clearly second to none: most people discovered in the swirling waters are reached within twenty minutes—many less than ten. Only a small number drown each day before help arrives—a big improvement from the way it used to be. Talk to the people of Downstream and they'll speak with pride about the new hospital by the edge of the waters, the flotilla of rescue boats ready for service at a moment's notice, the comprehensive health plans for coordinating all the manpower involved, and the large numbers of highly trained and dedicated swimmers all ready to risk their lives to save victims from the raging currents. Sure, it costs a lot but, say the Downstreamers, what else can decent people do except to provide whatever is necessary when human lives are at stake.

Oh, a few people in Downstream have raised the question now and again—"What's going on Upstream? Why are these bodies in the river at all?" But most folks show little interest in what's happening Upstream. It seems there's so much to do to help those in the river that nobody's got time to check how all those bodies are getting there in the first place. That's the way things are sometimes.[1]

That's the way things were for me too. Like most other helping professionals, I had been trained to be a good downstreamer. I worked hard to salvage peoples' lives. I was proud; after all, I was helping people turn their lives around. I did so without really questioning what was going on upstream—without really wondering if there were other causes for this suffering and pain.

It wasn't until I began to sit with circles of people, that I began realizing that there was something going on upstream that I should pay attention to. About ten years ago I started acting on a lifelong interest in community. I sought out people who were interested in a shared sense of belonging. We began to meet on a regular basis to get to know each other, explore our differences and seek for common ground upon which we could create a sense of connection. In the process we told each other our stories—the stories of our pasts and the stories we were currently living.

---

1 "The Parable of the Downstreamers" is by Donald Ardell from *High Level Wellness: An Alternative Doctors, Drugs and Disease.*

As we began to trust each other, we started sharing the places where our stories made no sense to us, where we didn't know what to do, where we were feeling hopeless and lost. We recognized how we had isolated ourselves by hiding these aspects of our experience. And we recognized how close we felt to each other when we began to let these parts of our lives become known. We literally stumbled onto common ground when we saw that our personal uncertainties reflected the vulnerability of human existence. Our great discovery was that when we shared this vulnerability we felt a sense of communion—not only more connected to each other, but also more connected with ourselves and with the world we lived in.

It was at this point that I began to experience a change in my outlook. My new awareness—that what my clients and I suffered was utterly human—had a profound impact upon me. I began to look more deeply at what was going on in my office. What I discovered was troubling. I began to see how much I was operating like a Downstreamer. I saw that much of my clients' suffering was caused by social isolation, the pretense of wholeness, and the secrecy of self-doubt and uncertainty.

I saw that a lot of suffering was generated Upstream, by the cultural values we hold and the social conditions within which we abide. I realized that the way I practiced had a tendency to reinforce my clients' shame and isolation. I began to see how my Downstream approach was ineffective at relieving some forms of suffering. It perpetuated the very conditions that were causing that suffering. I knew I had to consider what was going on Upstream.

Looking at the way we as a species treat each other and our planet is not pleasant. In fact, it is intensely uncomfortable. I found that opening myself and really paying attention to what is going on around me—the homelessness, violence, crime, poverty, bigotry and unemployment is very frightening. Even more frightening is the degradation of our environment—the dumping of toxic chemicals, the pollution of our watersheds and the stripping of the forests. Viewing these facts of modern life is painful and overwhelming. When I tried to talk with others about what I perceived, I had the most frightening experience of all. No one wanted to talk about it. This evoked powerful feelings of loneliness, despair, and hopelessness. I knew I would collapse under the weight of this awareness if I did not find a new way of responding to what I saw.

I began to search for a response to what I saw going on upstream. To adequately respond I needed more information and I needed allies. Having learned so much in my community circle I turned toward this group and began by sharing with them this latest turn in my story. I shared what I was seeing, the feelings that were aroused and my anxiety about the future. I asked them how they thought and felt about what was going on. This began a process of opening up our hearts and minds to what was going on around us as well as what was going on within us. We extended our concerns to include the homeless, the dispossessed and those without voices, such as the animals, rivers, trees and future generations. Looking upstream together, our sense of community expanded.

And so did a new degree of painful self-awareness and responsibility. We saw that the stream was like the circle we sat in: we were not only Downstreamers, we were also those caught in the stream and we were the Upstreamers. We began to face the reality that our choices and actions were contributing to the social and environmental problems we saw. This realization brought on a new stage in the development of our community. We became activists. We began to look at how we could change our own behavior and how we could support the call for change that was coming from those who were environmentally ill, impoverished, and un-cared for. Knowing more and doing things differently led us to begin to feel more alive and hopeful. By becoming more responsive to the despair and outrage we felt as we looked Upstream, we discovered new parts of ourselves and our capacity to make a difference Downstream.

This experience changed the way I live and the way I work. Now when I sit with clients I ask them questions about their feelings about environmental degradation, their sensitivities to chemicals, their patterns of consumption, how they participate in the economy. I encourage them to look at how they feel about what is going on around them and how they are responding to what they perceive.

In addition to working with individuals, couples and families, I offer what I call learning communities. These are groups for people who want to learn how to create a sense of community. In these groups we share our sense of personal vulnerability and our concerns about what is going on in the world. We look at how to protect ourselves, and our families, from the cultural pressures that impact upon our lives. We also examine our lifestyle choices for ways to improve the quality of the impact we have upon others. We support each other in awakening to the dangers Upstream. We begin to discover our responsibilities as Upstreamers.

Learning together has had many advantages, which make the effort to create learning communities worth it. It is easy to get overwhelmed when you first begin to recognize the social and economic forces that are abusing our environment and driving us away from each other. This awareness arouses strong emotional responses. It is easier to bear this painful awareness when it is shared. It is easier to stay open to reality when you are not isolated by these disturbing truths. Upstream awareness also begs for a response: our hearts and minds cry out "something must be done!"

The forces operating upstream, however, are enormous. Just being a good Downstreamer isn't enough. To really make a difference we have to act in concert. We need each other to learn how to make a difference, to support each other as we act, to sustain an effort that will take time, to celebrate our successes, to console each other over our failures, to love each other for caring enough to continue trying.

Today, thanks to those who have shared their vulnerability, doubt, courage, love and wisdom with me, I am aware, as I listen to my clients' stories, that I am hearing our story unfold. It is the story of our participation as a species in the stream of life. It reveals our efforts to avoid feeling the vulnerability that is part of the natural fragility and interdependence of our existence. It reminds us how we have cut ourselves off from ourselves, each other and nature. It is a sometimes painful and tragic story that is still unfolding, that can change.

How can this change occur? I changed because I extended my circle of caring. I did this by sharing my story and listening deeply to the stories of others. By entering into community, I found a place where I could learn more about myself, humankind, and our relationship to this living, breathing planet. I found a place where I could share the struggle for a meaningful and hospitable future. And, perhaps most importantly, I found that with these others, I could make a difference.

You can have this same experience. Find or create a group of people who would like to feel a sense of community in their lives. Listen to their stories. Tell them yours. Share the unfinished, uncertain, lost and confused parts of your stories, as well as the happier parts. Show each other your vulnerability. Sit together and feel the preciousness and fragility of your time on this planet. Feel the delicacy of life itself. Tell each other about what matters to you, about your emotional responses to what is going on around you. Look at what you know and what you don't know. Pay attention to your impact upon the others in your community as well as your impact upon our environment. Make choices about how you live. Act on behalf of all Life. As you do, you will be transforming our story and giving our childrren's children a chance to tell their stories.

&

CHAPTER 12

🌿

The Social Koan:
Through Diversity to Interdependence

Introduction

At the Foundation for Interdependence, we focus upon developing the skills necessary for social interdependence. We see the need for creating community through diversity as a social koan, a paradoxical problem that cannot be resolved without the development of a new mode of consciousness. We focus attention upon the dynamic tensions that arise when members of a socially diverse group (or organization) interact. When the members of such a group begin to reflect deeply upon these tensions and their responses to them, a process begins that stimulates the emergence of a more complex and interdependent sense of self. In the following discussion we will describe how we use the social koan of diversity to facilitate self-development, cultural awareness and social interdependence.

A Psychology of Interdependence

The primary mission of our foundation is to develop a psychology of interdependence. Our underlying premise is that humans are embedded in a matrix of relationships that connect us with the larger processes of culture and Nature. To the extent that an individual is able to experience these connections directly, they are capable of acting in ways that ensure their own wellbeing and the health of the natural and social systems in which they participate.

Toward that end we refined the definition of interdependence, which has traditionally been defined as "needing and depending upon each other." This definition has placed too much emphasis upon dependence and is incomplete. An important new level of understanding emerges from examining the prefix inter, which refers to that which exists "between and among" discreet entities. Beyond depending upon each other, we depend upon what we create between and among us. Instead of stressing dependence (what we can get from our interactions), we emphasize focusing attention upon what we contribute to our interactions that enhances the quality of what exists between us.

A psychology of interdependence has two primary areas of emphasis. The first is facilitation of a direct experience of social and ecological interconnectedness. This inoculates the individual against the fragmenting and alienating effects of modern life and is a necessary precondition for the development of an interdependent sense of self. Secondly, emphasis is placed upon skillful interactions. This involves learning how to define and express one's perspective completely. It entails becoming permeable, and able to be influenced by another's perspective while remaining solid and holding onto one's sense of self. How does an individual become both open and solid?

The development of these social skills coincides with the development of a complex sense of self. This cannot be achieved in solitude. We have found that personal complexity evolves through immersion in a social setting that is itself complex and diverse. We have also found that when such a social setting places an emphasis upon community, the tensions inherent in community participation necessitate greater clarity about how one defines his or her sense of self.

Learning Community through Diversity

The heart of the work is an experiential educational process called "learning community." The term "learning community" gained prominence in the business world through the work of Peter Senge at MIT. He defines learning community as a collaborative learning process that occurs among the primary stakeholders in a "learning organization." In this context, such a group functions as a center of self-reflectivity within the organization. Practicing the disciplines of inquiry and reflection, the members of a learning community focus upon increasing the consciousness and coherence of its organizational culture.

We have adapted Senge's approach to address contemporary issues that influence personal and community development. A learning community is a group of people who meet together to learn how to function as a community, and to create a community in which particular kinds of learning can occur. The task is to create community and then use the collective intelligence of the group to learn new ways of thinking and behaving. As the members struggle to include all their perspectives, they begin to discover what impedes and what furthers their sense of connection. They also reflect upon their interactions and begin to discover more skillful ways of responding to each other.

For our purposes, a learning community is a large (16 or more members) ongoing group. The group's size provides a critical level of heterogeneity. It also makes the group larger than most people are comfortable with, making it difficult to develop personal relationships with every other member and insuring that the group remains a place where members interact with unpredictable "others." The ongoing nature of the groups—meeting weekly, bi-weekly, or monthly over a long span of time—increases the likelihood that the groups cannot rely on a superficial level of compatibility for a sense of connection, and also presents the challenge of how to create, relinquish, and recreate meaningful experiences together.

The large group also functions as a microcosm of our larger society. Thus, we employ it as a small-scale social laboratory where our cultural struggle with differences can be examined. By virtue of the group's need to cooperate for the sake of its own development, and the differences the membership embodies, the social koan is bound to arise. The group will be confronted by the necessity for creating community through its differences.

As the members begin to interact they soon discover that the way they relate to their differences presents an obstacle to their ability to learn together and collaborate. Learning community does not create a way around the tensions that are inherent in the social koan of diversity, but rather offers methods so that participants can develop themselves through these tensions. By steeping themselves in these tensions rather than rushing to eliminate or resolve them, the members of a learning community engage in a process of psychological and social transformation.

How does this transformation occur? As group members sustain contact with the differing realities of others, they are confronted by the relativity of their own ideas about human nature, relationship, connection, truth and so on. While the multiplicity of realities is something many people recognize intellectually, actual immersion in a struggle among multiple competing realities presents a very real dilemma. This is a process that arouses a deep sense of existential uncertainty—doubt about the solidity of the ground one's personal and cultural identity is built upon.

How we respond to this doubt determines the quality of inter-dependence we experience. When we defend ourselves against existential uncertainty by trying to control others, or by denying our relationship with them, we generate low synergy (a reduced sense of interrelatedness). This way leads to isolationism, scapegoating, imperialism, and other situations in which "otherness" is devalued and demeaned. On the other hand, we can generate high synergy (increased sense of interrelatedness) in situations when we tolerate the anxiety of uncertainty and develop the strength to occupy our own position while opening ourselves to new realms of complexity, contradiction, and diversity.

Carl Jung described a comparable transformation in his auto-biography, *Memories, Dreams and Reflections*: "The more uncertain I have felt about myself the more has grown up in me a feeling of kinship with all things." This special kind of uncertainty arises from an experiential recognition of the limitations and incom-pleteness of one's construct of reality. This realization provides an incentive for opening the self and allowing it to become more indeterminate and inclusive. In opening to this existential uncer-tainty, one actually becomes more secure and, in a sense, larger—interconnected with others and experiencing a greater sense of wholeness.

In a learning community the social koan of diversity presents itself as both an obstacle and an opportunity for personal and social development. In the large group the tensions arising from diversity frustrate and inform, impede and provide transport. They acquaint the participants with direct experience of a special kind of uncertainty as well as a way into a more fundamental ground of interrelatedness.

The Four-Fold Way: Practices for Transformational Learning

The overarching principles we employ with learning communities are found in the Four-Fold Way developed by cultural anthropologist Angeles Arrien. Studying patterns of psycho-spiritual practice across many different cultures, she identified four universal components:

- showing up and choosing to be present,
- paying attention,
- telling the truth, and
- surrendering attachment to an outcome.

The large group provides a social vehicle for change and its built-in diversity generates energy. The Four-Fold Way harnesses this energy and utilizes it to propel the members and the group as a whole into new realms of perception and behavior.

A learning community's process transports the group from one view of reality to another, from one form of social orientation to a larger, more encompassing social framework. This kind of learning does not proceed solely through informational training, or through the acquisition of skills, but through transformation—the "emptying out" of an established mind set and immersion in a different experience. As the group explores the tensions associated with community and diversity, it becomes evident that there are no ready formulaic solutions to these tensions. Participants may well despair about finding a way through these tensions. Inevitably, when they learn how to hang out with their limitations they come to the place where they become sensitized and discover genuinely new possibilities.

Showing Up and Choosing to be Present

The first element of the Four-Fold Way—showing up and choosing to be present—describes a minimum requirement for transformation. Nevertheless, it is an exacting practice, involving much more than simply being physically present. Showing up means making yourself known—taking a position, by communicating what matters to you about yourself and your experiences in the group and the world. In Arrien's words, showing up requires discipline in the sense of being "a disciple to the self."

Making oneself visible can be anxiety provoking. Many people assume that community means support and confirmation. This may be true in a community of affinity. In a large and diverse group, however, one learns very rapidly that whatever one expresses is likely to be met with a range of responses, including contradiction and conflict. There are no guarantees that others will understand, agree with, value or validate what is disclosed. Thus, showing up requires striving for self-definition, self-advocacy and self-expression in the face of disconfirming responses from those who see things differently. To continue to fully show up members must learn how to validate their own reality without withdrawing from interactions with those who differ. This learning takes time. Members must discover how to manage their anxiety about differing with others so that they can make the contributions to the group that are theirs to make by virtue of their unique perspective.

As the group matures, it becomes clear that something other than a capacity to take a position and assert a viewpoint is necessary for learning to occur. This is where choosing to be present becomes important. Presence means making oneself available to be touched and changed by others. It entails opening oneself to bear witness to others' perspectives, to listen attentively and respectfully, and to be shaped by the variety of contributions others make toward the development of the group. It also means experiencing what is painful, difficult, or incomplete in oneself and in the group.

Choosing to be present asks participants to stay engaged with a process that is beyond their singular control, to share responsibility for what occurs within the group. This challenges the tendency many have to wait for someone else to create an environment that "allows" them to reveal themselves. The goal is not to create special, "hothouse" environments that protect people from the anxieties and risks of taking their own unique positions. Instead, a learning community provides a social context where individuals learn to master themselves so that they can tolerate the possibility of conflict or discomfort in order to make their own unique contributions to the community's process.

Showing up and choosing to be present is an essential practice in creating community through diversity. It challenges members to bring themselves ever more completely into play and in the process, to reveal and sustain the experience of diversity in the group. As the members become more proficient at showing up and choosing to be present, they enter the realm of paradoxical tensions that can provide passage to a new way of being together.

Paying Attention

Paying attention is an essential practice without which transformative learning cannot occur. A distinguishing characteristic of a learning community is the quality of consciousness or attention that members bring to the task of being together. Increasing awareness sensitizes our perceptions and introduces increasingly subtle levels of reality, and this is what changes the participants.

In the formative stages of a learning community we encourage members to pay particular attention to tension—in oneself and in the group. Since the goal is to move toward inclusion and connection, the focus is particularly on the tensions that exist between inclusion and exclusion, and between connection and separation. Observing these tensions helps group members recognize their own struggles with differing and with responding to otherness.

The first tension—between inclusion and exclusion—has to do with who or what is encompassed within the group, and who or what is considered unacceptable or outside the boundaries of awareness. The fundamental questions underlying this tension are: "How much differing can be tolerated?" and "How can I (or others) tolerate the uncertainty aroused by differing realities?" Exclusion decreases diversity, thus diminishing anxiety, but also limits the scope of the group's potential for learning. On the other hand, inclusion increases anxiety in the group as new information challenges comfortable assumptions and demands the formulation of a more complex picture of reality.

When reality confronts a group (or individual) with more diversity than it can handle, the typical unconscious response is to try to reduce diversity—the encounter with otherness—through excluding part of reality: either one's own reality, another's reality, or the relationship between these realities. Excluding one's own reality occurs when participants devalue their own viewpoints, hide or silence aspects of themselves, forget what is important to them, are dishonest with themselves or the group, or wait for others to give them permission to make their own contributions (i.e., to be themselves).

Taking oneself out of the picture minimizes the possibility of differing or conflicting with someone else. It also undermines the feeling of belonging and gives the group an incomplete reality from which to operate. This attempt to minimize diversity tension feeds cultural dynamics such as the segregation and marginalization of those who lack social rank—ethnic minorities, the old and disabled, children, etc.

Excluding another's reality happens when group members try to impose their own perspective on others. This can occur through direct argument and denigration, but it can also happen through persuasion, teaching, healing, analyzing, converting, sympathizing, pitying, generalizing, and asserting rigid rules or "right ways" for participating in community. This attempt to minimize diversity tension feeds and reflects cultural dynamics such as political correctness, fundamentalism, ideological imperialism and ethnic cleansing.

Excluding the relationship means devaluing the significance of contact and denying the fact that every participant has something unique to contribute. In this case there is an attempt to minimize the impact of encounter by pretending that there is nothing held in common or no way of making a meaningful exchange. This form of exclusion may take the form of abrupt silent withdrawals from membership or a refusal to engage. Slogans such as "You do your thing, I'll do mine;" "We'll agree to disagree;" "My way or the highway," all reflect this pattern. On a cultural political level, this pattern is reflected in the self-marginalization of militia groups, cults and isolationistic national policies.

Each of these forms of exclusion is a way of reducing existential uncertainty by trying to maintain the illusion that there is only one reality, rather than multiple co-existing versions of reality. These responses to differences are toxic to the vitality of a learning community—as well as to social, political, global communities—because they limit the potential for the evolution of new awareness. Observing these tendencies increases awareness of the underlying roots of many painful cultural dynamics, such as racism, sexism, ethnic conflict, and environmental abuse. As awareness grows, members begin to perceive the parallels between personal choices and group dynamics. They experientially understand the origins of some of the worst symptoms of diversity intolerance. They also discover how their own choices contribute to either reinforcing or altering these dynamics.

Another focal point for attention to the social koan is the dynamic tension that exists between separation and connection. Here, paying attention means focusing upon how we maintain separation and cultivate connection, and observing what actually happens within oneself and in the group. "How do I maintain separation?" "When and how do I experience connection?" "When does there seem to be an atmosphere of connection in the group?" One of the common notions about connection is that it follows from safety. In a learning community, members discover that actions taken for self-protection usually obstruct contact and generate an atmosphere of distrust, both within the Individual and between the individual and the group. Members begin to observe how defensive behaviors are often offensive to others. With this awareness comes the realization that our attempts to preserve personal security frequently block us from the sense of connection with others, that maintaining safety—in the sense of invulnerability to others—perpetuates separation rather than connection.

Similarly, as participants pay attention to the actual experience of connection, they are often surprised to find that it arises precisely from situations that might be prejudged as "unsafe." For instance, conflict often feels threatening at first, as it highlights the diversity and autonomy of the members. However, as participants use conflict to deepen their positions and presence in the group, they find that they feel more connected and that the group becomes more inclusive. The deepest bonds often arise from the deepest differing.

Another significant awareness regarding separation and connection has to do with the notion that we connect with each other based upon expertise, accomplishment, status or strengths. In the learning community process, participants are asked to reflect on the ways in which role, rank and status affect group dynamics and the nature of connection. While accomplishment is valuable, it can also impede the deepest levels of connection based on shared humanity. One of the paradoxes of the social koan is that we must simultaneously bring all of who we are to the interactions, while temporarily suspending our roles and customary identities.

As a group works together over time, the practice of paying attention generates a form of group awareness, or mindfulness. Observing and reflecting upon the group's "thinking process," members begin noticing their own judgments and preconceptions. This is important because our assumptions are invisible lenses that filter our perceptions and separate us from direct experience. The practice of identifying, examining, and suspending assumptions arouses awareness of the relativity of our perceptions, reminding us that our preconceptions determine what we observe. This practice leads to the fundamental recognition that differing assumptions underlie our relationships and account for much of the confusion and conflict we experience with each other. Paying attention to the effects of our assumptions generates an open and observant form of attention that allows a fresh sense of discernment.

The growing mindfulness of the group reveals the subtle interconnections encompassing individual behavior, interpersonal relations, group processes, and cultural dynamics. The group's attention becomes more focused, creating awareness that is both more penetrating—revealing the nuances of a particular issue, and more encompassing—revealing the larger patterns of which the components are a part. Larger realms of meaning, ordinarily beyond the awareness of a single individual, become accessible. Cultivating this kind of awareness is hard and complicated work. The large group process, with its built-in social diversity, creates both the necessity for developing these attentional capacities and also the training ground where they can be fostered.

Telling the Truth

Transformational learning proceeds through the acquisition of a more accurate and comprehensive perception of reality. Telling the truth, like the other elements of the Four-Fold-Way, introduces us to unanticipated dimensions of reality.

In a learning community, as in life, the practice of telling the truth starts with discerning one's own position and viewpoint. Truth-telling is a way of making one's reality available to become part of the wisdom of the group. As members open up to each other, it becomes clear that truth is far more complicated than any individual's singular perspective. The emergence of a multifaceted sense of truth is disturbing and leads into the volatile heart of the diversity dilemma. It forces us to confront the realization that our reality is relative—one among many constructed perspectives. The experience of truth's complexity creates a kind of chaos, a cognitive dissonance that disassembles and disorients. Familiar reality is unraveled and we are thrust into an open space where what was once true is now seen as limited. One's reality is both deconstructed and reconstructed by exposure to unfamiliar truths.

Avoiding disturbing truths happens (psychologically and culturally) through two core patterns: denial and indulgence. We practice denial when we insist on the truth that has served us previously and refuse to see what currently is true, or when we deny the realities of others because we fear that we cannot handle the demands new truths will make upon us. We practice indulgence when we dramatize or sensationalize our particular sense of truth, insisting that it is *the* truth rather than *a* truth. In each case we want to avoid experiencing our truth's incompleteness because we fear losing the comfort, security and equilibrium we find in it. As these patterns occur in the large group, participants find themselves stretched between two desires: on the one hand, shielding themselves from the stress of opening to new realities, and on the other hand, optimizing their learning and connection in the group. Within this tension, transformation occurs as participants develop greater tolerance for complexity and paradox.

Sharing a multi-faceted experience of the moment makes significantly more of the wholeness of that moment accessible. As the diverse facets of the picture become known, these individual perceptions constitute an ever more realistic and integrated image of the whole, making new learning possible. The parts enrich the whole and the whole in turn gives deeper meaning to the parts. We discover an interconnecting coherence, a more fundamental reality that exists between singular perspectives but does not become evident until these discrete truths are brought into a dynamic relationship with each other.

Surrendering Attachment to an Outcome

Surrendering attachment to an outcome means emptying out our expectations in favor of opening up to what lies beyond them. This practice is built upon the premise that our attachments and visions of outcome reflect our knowledge and experience of the past; they perpetuate a world that is known and predictable and they protect us from a world that is not. These preconceptions reduce our capacity to respond to the call of the moment, to meet the truths of the present time: to learn. It is for this reason that detachment, the practice of non-attachment or emptiness, is emphasized as a universal spiritual discipline.

Practicing detachment is like voyaging into an unknown sea. Slipping one's moorings loose and setting sail for uncharted waters involves abandoning the safety of the familiar and sacrificing the comforts associated with old ways of knowing. When a learning community sets out together, it is a group of strangers with differing ideas about its destination and method for proceeding. These differing perspectives soon create tensions that manifest as chaos, alienation, and competition for the helm. The temptation for the group (and frequently for the society) is to throw some passengers overboard and elect others as leaders.

What actually threatens the group's journey, however, are the beliefs, prejudices, and preconceptions that have enabled the members of the group to come this far. The primary impediment the group faces is its own anxious desire to avoid relinquishing the safety of the known for the uncertainty of the unknown. The moment of real truth in a learning community comes when members begin to reveal the incompleteness and imperfection of their own knowledge. As they surrender their isolated realities constructed upon partial-truths, they begin to discover that despite their pretenses of certitude, they have all along been sailing upon a sea of uncertainty.

This is a terrible liberation. Members find themselves exposed as uncertain, imperfect and incomplete beings; they experience a vivid sense of openness and existential vulnerability. Difficult as this experience can be, it holds within it a great solace because this very vulnerability is the ground that humanity shares. Through practice, members build the strengths that allow them to be themselves and connect with others in the face of existential uncertainty. Standing upon this ground opens a new vista of self and world, profound interrelatedness, and a compassionate awareness of the challenges inherent in being human.

Conclusion

Humanity stands crowded together at an evolutionary threshold. We are increasingly aware of the otherness of those who surround us. At the same time, we are beginning to grasp how the political, cultural, and ecological problems that now threaten the survival of our species cannot be adequately addressed without collaboration with them. It seems that we face a dilemma: in order to get along with the business of human existence we must learn how to get along with each other. Can we do it? At the heart of this question lies a social koan. We face diversity, and we must discover our underlying commonality. We are presented with threats to our survival and must discover how to take our own positions without the righteous insistence about particular outcomes that inevitably threaten other's survival. Becoming responsible for a whole larger than ourselves, we must learn how to retain our own integrity without insisting that others forsake theirs.

Gathering together to address these paradoxical tensions in a face-to- face learning community, we utilize the complications presented by our differences to deliver us to the place where our limited ways of knowing become evident. This is the threshold of an entirely different way of knowing. If we can find the courage to empty ourselves of certainty and open to a world of greater uncertainty, we gain access to a new mode of consciousness and a correspondingly more inclusive and complex sense of self.

When this occurs, group members rediscover the world and a new sense of the commons emerges. Personal well-being and the well-being of the whole are seen to be profoundly interrelated, both depending upon the quality of what we create between us. Access to this new interdependent world is readily available to us. All we need do is turn toward each other and choose to learn what our differences have to teach us about the world we share in common.

SECTION V
LEARNING COMMUNITY

SECTION V

❦

Learning Community

....[A] truly "integral transformative practice" would give considerable weight to the importance of relationships, community, culture, and intersubjective factors in general, not merely as a realm of application of spiritual insight, but as a means of spiritual transformation.

—Ken Wilber, *An Integral Psychology*

Introduction

From the earliest moments of homo sapiens, we have been a social species. This is what gave us a leg up on all the other large mammals in our environment. We survived and evolved because of our inter-actions with each other. As we interacted, humankind became more sophisticated. We taught each other how to use tools, language, and eventually how to relate to the cosmos and the fact of our existence.

Out of small bands came all of the characteristics that we now think of as human. Even our unique (as far as we know) conscious-ness arose out of the interactions in small bands of our ancestors. I would even go so far as to say that community, the bond that con-nected our ancestors to each other (and the generations before and after), was the cradle, the natural social habitat of our kind. The com-plexities associated with social interaction, stimulated the evolution of a similar kind of consciousness. This, in turn, has set humankind upon an equally complex evolutionary course.

It is my estimation that we still need the complexities inher-ent in community—in being connected to each other and to all the permutations of what it means to be human—to keep evolving our consciousness. But the social depth that comes from being so connected does not occur very easily or very frequently today. So I have synthesized (from the work of others) a social learning approach that uses community to stimulate the growth of human beings. I call this approach learning community. There are problems associated with this name because it has been used for other reasons, but I've stuck with it because the power of this approach comes from combining learning with community.

What follows is a discussion of a socially complex phenomenon. The complexity of this approach reflects two important things. We now live in a world where social things aren't trusted like they used to be. People no longer know how to take care of themselves in social situations. The resilience that allows for social depth is not typically available. One of the reasons for learning community is to cultivate these things. And what used to come naturally, immersion in field of relationships, now comes suspiciously. The complexity of my description of learning community reflects how difficult it is to restore what used to be a natural part of human life.

Social Learning

We live in a culture that values learning. Sort of. We put a premium on early childhood education, school, and college. And we say we value life-long education and retraining for our workers, but when it comes to character, community, and personal growth and development, we are on our own. Maybe a few churches have programs where adults can examine the demands of Life, but few escape an ideological approach, and even fewer encourage the development of presence and real choice. We are not a society that easily tolerates being beginners, a prerequisite for learning, in any public way.

Social learning, discovering ourselves together, is a fringe activity. It is the stuff of social movements, such as consciousness-raising groups or non-violent trainings. Social learning is not something that we easily resort to. There is plenty of evidence that learning together is beneficial. Alcoholics Anonymous and its offspring, the myriads of 12-step groups, have shown the power of social learning for changing behavior and increasing wellbeing. Newer social learning modalities, such as "communities of practice," take advantage of the way relationships can convey important information and essential experience to folks that share a common interest. But social learning is a marginal activity that almost never addresses the real rigors of human life. Why is this?

A clue can be found in the psychological practice of confidentiality. There is still a great need in modern society for a place to try out feelings and behaviors that would just be too revealing. For that reason, we like anonymity. Confidentiality and anonymity generate a feeling of safety. Now, don't get me wrong; I think confidentiality is a necessity for psychological inquiry. I am also aware, however, that confidentiality and anonymity extract a social cost. As one of my clients put it, "I am comparing my insides with everyone else's outsides." We literally don't know each other and, as a result, we also don't know about what we hold in common—the struggle to be fully human and alive.

When we learn together, we give each other access to ourselves, to our partiality (our unknowingness), to the current state of our made-up reality. And that is the problem. For a moment we are exposed in all of our humanity; the bright light of attention shines on what is difficult or impossible to see, on what we may not want to see or have seen. This is an anxiety-producing experience. It often exceeds our tolerance for anxiety, rendering us self-conscious, defensive, and unable to learn. If we can stand the anxiety we gain access to our own self-discoveries, as well as those of others. The potential for learning, not only about a particular challenge but about being human, is greatly enhanced.

Social learning—the exposure of our limitations, unknowingness, partiality, our basic humanity—is an anxiety-producing activity. Becoming known is daunting. But there is no place else other than a social situation where one can discover the wherewithal to weather this anxiety. This is how one grows confident that one has learned how to take care of oneself. And it is this learning, that you can take care of yourself in the midst of others, rather than having to shut down, run away, or dominate the scene, that allows you to be free to be part of a larger social endeavor. Social learning promotes social selves. It provides the necessary social context for the development of the part of ourselves that can make a difference in the lives of others.

Community

What was once a regular part of human existence is now quite rare. Whereas our kind, human beings, once lived their entire lives in the cradle of a single set of relationships, we now settle for fragmentation. There is almost nobody, family included, who knows us, or whom we know, for an entire lifetime. This exacts a toll. Americans seem eager to escape the seemingly confining consistency of others' expectations. So, we pull a geographical. Or, to be economically viable, we move away. In either case, we lose one of the most valuable things money cannot buy—community, the experience of being known, and of knowing others. This loss is a standard feature of modern life and a costly one.

Rather than dwell on the disheartening loss of the social matrix that once served to humanize us, I would rather spell out the benefits that community still offers. My belief is that despite the absence of community in most people's lives, and the fact that there are those who have never experienced it, people actually know they are missing something that could help them feel more at home in their lives. This is the other side of their holonic nature yearning for expression, a larger place to belong.

Community has traditionally been the place where people gave themselves to each other. It has been the social ground where we publicly declared ourselves, where we also discovered ourselves. We get to be known, as Parker Palmer has said, "as we are knowing." This kind of public knowing of others, of ourselves, and by others, gave us the social connections that allowed us to know our own humanity. It is public intimacy that creates public bonds. Community also provides the invested others for us to push against to become ourselves.

Besides giving us an opportunity to discover ourselves, community provides us access to the world, access that is mediated by others, so we don't have to make it up by ourselves, so we don't have to recreate the wheel. So many people struggle alone to make sense of the world, and feel broken because they cannot, whereas community can make human limitations an opening to the world, instead of a sign of failure. We need each other to become fully human and to discover our own place in the world.

Community also comes with challenges. There is no free lunch. The more vital a connection, the more meaningful a relationship, the greater the challenge involved with being and becoming yourself. Most people react to this challenge by distancing themselves. But distance is not freedom. It is just a more subtle form of bondage. Real freedom, really being free to be yourself, is hard won. It occurs by running the gauntlet of those who are important to you and to whom you are important. Community provides the hardships, the grinding, irritating invested others who know you well enough to test your resolve and thus ensure that you become the uniqueness you can be.

Linguist Jeffrey Nunberg, of the Xerox Research Park and Stanford University, has captured the decline of community by recalling how the word "community" has been used. He says,

> Community is on its way to becoming one of those commodified American phrases like "heritage." You can buy it by the yard. There is something about the word "community" that ought to make us nervous. It's not just because of the rosy light it casts but because it's hard to see how there could be much meaning left in a word so elastic [here he is referring to the use of the word to describe any group that has something in common, such as the terrorist community, the Facebook community, or the vegetarian and vegan community] you can use it to wrap anything from an ethnic group to a bunch of people who like to exchange soup recipes online. Maybe it wouldn't be a bad thing if it was finally stretched so thin that it snapped.
>
> —*NPR, Fresh Air,* September 27, 2000

It is true, the use of the word as a public relations tool has reflected the diminished meaning of community in our lives. Interestingly, it also reflects the inchoate longing for connection that still exists. The commodification of the term has tarnished what community is, yet it shows how much connection is still desired and valued. What we need to do is restore the meaning of community by restoring the experience.

Learning Community

Learning Community, as I employ it, serves two purposes. One, it provides an opportunity to learn about and experience connection. And two, it uses connection to facilitate development. These are the characteristics that typify Learning Community. As it unfolds, it is:

- experiential,
- focuses on the between,
- socially complex,
- presents a microcosm of the macrocosm,
- offers a practice field,
- involves social disciplines,
- promotes development.

Learning Community is experientially rigorous because it involves the whole self. It is not for everyone because it is about taking action in the context of relationships, about being seen and known, about simultaneously knowing and about becoming fully human by discovering yourself in relation to something larger. Not everyone is willing to endure the spike of anxiety that participating in such a complex social experience can generate. This experience is designed for the intrepid learner, for the person who really wants to make a difference, who won't be satisfied until they have discovered their full potential, until they have known themselves as part of something larger.

Learning Community focuses attention upon the between; between aspects of the self, between self and other, between self and community, and between self and the overall surroundings (culture and Nature). By doing so the relationship between all the levels becomes visible. One can see the truth of the Dalai Lama's statement. We do treat others and our community, our environment, like we treat ourselves. There is, however, no substitute for actually experiencing how this is so.

Learning Community is a socially complex experience that breeds a more complex awareness. This in turn sets the stage for development. Here is what I mean. By virtue of the size, diversity, and depth of the group, most of the participants will be stretched. The group is larger than most people are comfortable with and is so large that the experience of otherness is always in the foreground.

Diversity ensures differing, which adds heat and promotes differentiation (growth). The presence of multiple experiences, perspectives, sensitivities, and realities, frustrates, impedes, and holds the door open for an enriched and expanded awareness to emerge.

Learning Community replicates the larger surrounding world. The large size of the group generates all of the dynamics that are usually excluded from a smaller group. In fact, one of the hardships presented by this approach is also one of its greatest virtues. Group members are often horrified to find out they themselves are doing all the things (like practicing exclusion such as racism, xenophobia or scapegoating) that generate the worst attributes of human social interaction. Discovering the perpetrators within, however, offers a real opportunity to change the social world. This approach makes those dynamics and their origin within palpable, and thus available for choice.

Learning Community provides a practice field. Humans need other humans to practice upon, to verify if one is doing something of consequence. Yes, this is also one of the hardships of this approach and another one of its virtues. Connecting is a contact sport. There are impacts, sometimes painful ones. These impacts, aroused by practices that are often conducted without reflection, generate awareness. This promotes two kinds of learning. People learn how to take care of themselves, and people learn how to generate impacts more like they intend. In either case, people awaken to their responsibility for themselves, and their responsibility to others, the mutual responsibility that makes community so desirable.

Learning Community, as I practice it, is invariably at first a structureless experience. This, too, is a hardship. The members are frequently disappointed with facilitation that lets bad social behavior, painful impacts, and negative cultural dynamics occur. This period is hard on participants and facilitators alike, yet while often chaotic and disheartening, offers some real benefits. First, the participants become aware of their collective limitations and they become amenable to practices that promote community, learning, and development. Also, these painful periods impress the group in retrospect; eventually it will help them realize how far they have come.

Learning Community offers practices that can be used to modify social behavior. Suffice it to say that the painful experiences of the group readies it for attentional, interactive, and reflective practices that enable the group and individual members to begin learning. These practices are transformational, being drawn as they have from the world's spiritual traditions. They are social disciplines, sets of practices such as shared reflection that, like any real spiritual or martial arts practice, deliver the practitioners to deeper and deeper levels of experience.

Learning Community is ultimately about development. This socially rich, complex, interactive experience is designed to facilitate connection, and then use that connection to promote new forms of awareness that then alter consciousness. It is very common to see participants in the early stages of development focusing upon what this experience will give them. Participants also can be seen who, at later stages of development, know that what they get out of the experience is proportional to what they put in. Occasionally, a participant who, arriving at the farther reaches of development, experiences community everywhere. All of them are aided and aid others through shared interactions that breed new awareness.

At the center of this seething cauldron of interactions is the experience of metamorphosis. It can happen in personal ways as individuals reach critical mass, learning something new about or the world they thought they occupied. It can also happen as a group phenomenon. The group can be put into a kind of chrysalis period by members bringing new awareness forward or by collective issues that require broader perspectives (see The Social Koan, Chapter 12). As individuals and the community-as-a-whole go through these transformations, there is a synergetic impact that increases the chances for these changes to gravitationally pull overall awareness ahead.

What Follows

The practice of Learning Community is both a sociotherapeutic endeavor and an experiment in social depth. It is an experiment that is evolving.

The chapters that follow reflect that evolution. I am presenting them in order (from 1993 to the present) to show how the work has grown, what it has taught me, and the direction this work is taking.

Chapter 14, "The Social Crucible" (2003), was the piece I was working on when I had the stroke. I have endeavored to complete it for this publication. It reveals how one of the existential threats we experience as a species is the threat we pose to ourselves. I try to show how Learning Community addresses this issue, views it as a paradoxical opportunity, and approaches it as an integral transformational practice.

Conclusion

Learning Community is not a workshop experience. The benefits described above are not a given. They emerge as the members of the group orient themselves to a world of connection. To orient toward connection, at first those connections have to show some endurance. Community is hard to find, even harder to maintain, because it takes time. Learning Community is no exception. What enables members to benefit from this experience, to know they have had more than a pseudo-experience, is the time it takes. I have a friend who says "sometimes you have to go slow to go fast."

Connecting, really knowing and being known, requires giving time to what takes time. The bonds that allow something meaningful, something transformative, to happen are composed of affection, respect, courage, wonder and love. These cannot be manufactured or coerced. The vitality of meaningful interaction is what produces the will to go through the rigors associated with going beyond oneself. Leadership takes time to emerge, just as it takes time to recognize maturity. Groups coalesce, but not deeply, until they have been through some things together.

Learning Community is an experiment in social depth. Depth is one of the things we sacrifice as we rush headlong, driven by too many concerns, financial considerations, and anxiety. Depth is all around and within us. Often, it terrifies us as it goes unrecognized or is mistaken for other things, but slowing down and connecting with others makes a lot more of that depth available to us and reveals just how depth holds us all.

❦

CHAPTER 13

*

The Disciplines of Learning Community

Introduction

We live at an interesting moment in human history. Life in this era is infused with poignant uncertainty. There is a growing sense that pivotal changes are underway which are determining the hospitality of our future. Under the burden of population growth, development, and the globalization of the economy our social and ecological systems appear to be breaking down. Our responsibility for these processes haunts us, arousing insecurity, fear and anxiety. This uncertainty, and the tension it generates, forms the psychological backdrop of our times. As a species we face an evolutionary challenge; our ongoing viability rests upon our capacity to grow ourselves up and learn to live on Life's terms rather than our own.

Ironically, our future depends upon the strengths that distinguish our species and provide us with the means to so thoroughly endanger ourselves—our consciousness and adaptability. Continuing our social evolution and restoring the health of our ecosystem require us to apply our consciousness to adapt and change the way we function. The history of our species suggests we have the innate capabilities to respond to our present-day circumstances. Can we transform the cultural surround we have created into something that will allow the human experiment to continue? Can we re-employ the strengths of our consciousness and adaptability for the sake of a more humane and hospitable future?

These questions define the evolutionary crossroads where we now find ourselves. They generate much of the tension and insecurity underlying our social interactions. Yet a strange and terrifying silence about these matters pervades our daily lives. Without open acknowledgement of the uncertainties that now face us, these questions cannot stir and engage our consciousness; they do not rouse us to respond in a timely fashion to the dangers we are creating.

A New Response: The Emergence of Learning Communities

Despite the silence and the lack of acknowledgement of our precarious situation, individuals are awakening. Overwhelmed by what they see and feel, they are nevertheless seeking a way to further sensitize themselves and to learn how to respond to what they perceive. These individuals are asking difficult questions and struggling to give voice to the uncertainties that underlie modern life. To sustain their capacity to hold the tensions generated by their awareness of what is at stake, they are turning toward each other for support and perspective. As they do, a new forum for personal and social development called learning community is emerging.

By turning toward each other and sharing their concerns, individuals are discovering a way to sustain themselves and to open to the larger levels of reality that our individually-oriented culture prefers to ignore. Together they are beginning to explore more fully their emotional response to the complexities of modern life. In the process they are discovering how sharing the uncertainty they experience in the world connects them with the larger processes of life. They are also finding that communalizing this uncertainty and making its sources conscious leads to a realization of interconnection, a deep sense of communion with Life as a whole.

The power of true community is enfolded into this experience of communion. It is this power that underlies the learning community experience. And it is this power that makes a learning community an effective way of responding to the evolutionary dilemma that now confronts us. For a learning community provides its participants with the possibility of extending their personal sense of self to include other life forms—human and non-human. This enlarged sense of self is capable of drawing upon a larger field of consciousness and energy than is accessible to the isolated individual. From this enlarged perspective new thinking and new behaviors become possible. Participation in a learning community also offers the prospect of collective action, enabling the individual to extend his or her influence into larger scale responses than previously possible.

When individuals meet to share their personal concerns, visions, sensitivities and desires for a better world, they begin a process that transforms awareness and empowers responses. These benefits, however, do not automatically occur. The transformative power of a learning community is hard won. Learning has to occur first, and in this case the difficult learning is about the self.

In the process of creating a social space that is congenial to learning the individual members will interact. As they do, they will begin to discover how their thinking and feelings define and drive their interactions. Intent upon learning, a group will make the rude discovery that their interactive dynamics replicate those of the larger culture. This discovery, that those present are enacting the very dynamics that pose such a threat to peace and our ecosystem, can evoke feelings of frustration and hopelessness. It is at this point, however, when the group realizes that it is a microcosm of the larger culture in which it is embedded, when the potential for personal and cultural transformation seems least likely, that, paradoxically, this potential is realizable.

For it is at this point that a learning community becomes a cultural laboratory where individuals can observe culture at work through the beliefs and actions of those present. This frustrating stage of learning increases awareness. If the group members are willing to take responsibility for their own actions, they can begin to observe how they participate in impeding learning and connection. By examining together the unconscious assumptions that underlie these actions, the group begins to construct an experimental "practice field," where new thinking and new behaviors can be tried. Testing these new practices results in direct experiences that lead to further increases in awareness, improved understanding and more effective actions. By practicing and learning together, the group as a whole discovers new social sensitivities, which are then available to be developed into new sensibilities. This development facilitates individual growth, the emergence of social communion, and underlies the dynamic capacities that promote learning.

As mentioned earlier, these transformations do not occur automatically when a group gathers together. The intention to learn bears fruit only as individuals acquire abilities which at first may not feel very comfortable or be deemed desirable (i.e., the ability to tolerate making mistakes in public, or to "not know" for the sake of learning). Achieving the openness that is optimal for learning often requires unlearning attitudes and interactive patterns that typify normal modes of social discourse. The unlearning that accompanies real learning creates confusion, uncertainty, and uneasiness. It has a tendency to arouse personal anxiety and self-doubt—calling into question the viability of "truths" once held as sacred.

Learning in such a community involves a "hatching out" of a world primarily organized around one's personal experience into a world of diverse otherness, which includes greater levels of complexity, ambiguity, and paradox. This type of learning is demanding. It involves developing an adult capacity to sustain tension and uncertainty while one gradually acquires the awareness and skills necessary to function in this new, more complex arena. Transformative learning of this type requires discipline. Not the kind of discipline that comes from without, but the kind that wells up with the desire to go beyond yourself. Angeles Arrien calls this kind of discipline "being a disciple to the self."

The Disciplines of Learning Community

I have found eight disciplines that drive and empower the learning community experience. What is great about these disciplines is that the practices associated with each one, can be practiced at multiple levels. These practices introduce one, as the practice proceeds, to subtleties and nuances that only become available through practice. These disciplines are:

- personal responsibility,
- skillful communication,
- inclusivity,
- focused attention,
- shared reflection,
- detachment,
- multi-dimensional thinking, and
- ecological awareness.

The practices that inform these disciplines come from Community-Building (CB) as practiced by The Foundation for Community Encouragement, or those of Dialogue (Dlg) as described by physicist David Bohm.

Discipline	Practices	Emergent Qualities
1 — Personal responsibility	• Full participation (CB) • Honoring time commitments (CB) • Sharing responsibility for the process (CB) • Suspension of roles (Dlg) • Respecting self and others (CB)	• Increases personal presence • Enhances the level of engagement • Facilitates differentiation and power of position, thus maintaining diversity • Promotes atmosphere of mutual respect and social equality

The discipline of personal responsibility is cultivated through an emphasis upon full participation, honoring time commitments, sharing responsibility for the process, suspending roles, and respecting self and other. This discipline cultivates personal presence and engagement. By emphasizing the power of fully occupying one's own position this discipline encourages differentiation and ensures that the group will benefit from the diversity it embodies. At the

Discipline	Practices	Emergent Qualities
2 — Skillful communication	• Full participation (CB) • Saying your name before you speak (CB) • Speaking only when you feel moved to speak (CB) • Employing "I Statements" (CB) • Speaking personally and specifically (CB) • Listening carefully and with respect for others (Dlg) • Avoiding crosstalk (Dlg) • Inquiring into and reflecting upon others' perspectives (Dlg)	• Reinforces assumption of personal responsibility • Increases awareness of otherness as differences are made explicit • Promotes respect for differences • Makes palpable the multi-faceted nature of truth • Supports the emergence of the chaos of multiple competing realities to occur in a socially responsible manner • Arouses consciousness of the complexities and rigors of social interdependence

furthest reaches of practice, one experientially grasps how integral he or she is to the group as a whole.

The discipline of skillful communication is essential but is not enough by itself. The emphasis placed upon saying your name, speaking when moved to speak, employing "I- statements," speaking personally and specifically, listening carefully and respectfully to others, avoiding cross talk, and reflecting upon others' perspectives, all help create a space that is congenial to full exposure, to an information-rich learning environment. This discipline promotes awareness of otherness and provides the means by which differences can be respected, made explicit, and used to increase learning and growth. Lastly, this discipline, when allowed to grow, makes palpable the multi-faceted nature of truth.

Inclusivity is essential for learning. It promotes the openness that makes learning possible. The emphasis upon observing and sharing tendencies toward exclusion of self and others, including observing

Discipline	Practices	Emergent Qualities
3 — *Inclusivity*	• Observing and sharing tendencies toward exclusion of self and others (CB) • Observing and sharing how separation is maintained. (CB) • Avoiding trying to fix, heal, or convert anyone (CB) • Inquiring into others' perspectives (Dlg) • Identifying, suspending, examining and sharing judgments	• Promotes awareness of patterns of denial and exclusiveness • Extends the awareness of the group toward its edges • Promotes engagement with the unconscious of the group • Creates maximum support for the emergence of minority positions •Promotes conditions that are optimal for learning.

how separation is maintained and noticing attempts to fix, heal, or convert, all contribute to creating an open field of ideas where learning can happen. Dialogue also contributes by bringing awareness to judgments and to inquiring into the perspectives of others. Thus, patterns of denial and exclusiveness are identified and the group can extend its awareness toward its edges; this promotes openness to what is contained in the unconscious of the group. So much of what promotes development, both personal and collective, is contained in what is on the edge of consciousness, what is known-but-unknown in the unconscious.

Discipline	Practices	Emergent Qualities

4 — *Focused attention*	• Identifying, suspending and examining: (Dlg)
	    judgments
	    assumptions
	    and agendas
	• Inquiring into the perspectives of others (Dlg)
	• Focusing upon context and meaning (Dlg)
		• Highlights forms of thinking, making palpable the underlying structure of beliefs that one or another may operate upon
		• Generates group awareness, thus creating a form of group mindfulness
		• Supports an emerging capacity to ask really important questions

The discipline of focused attention is cultivated to increase awareness. This discipline is particularly educative; it highlights the usefulness and limitations of mental models. Attachment to these models (ideas) impedes perception and separates one from a direct experience of current reality. This discipline supports the emergence of group consciousness by extending the range of individual members and by creating synergies. Emphasizing identifying, suspending and examining judgment, assumptions and agendas, inquiring into the perceptions of others, and focusing upon context and meaning, this discipline helps a kind of "group mindfulness" to arise.

Discipline	Practices	Emergent Qualities
5 — *Shared reflection*	• Identifying, suspending and examining: (Dlg) judgments assumptions and agendas	• Cultivates a capacity to hold coplex and multi-leveled perceptions • Allows patterns and inter-relationships to be made explicit • Supports the emergence of synergies that extend the group awareness • Renders more palpable and meaningful the interconnections of the group experience

By sharing inquiry into and examination of judgments, assumptions, perceptions and vulnerabilities, the discipline of shared reflection cultivates a capacity to hold a spectrum of complex and multi-leveled perceptions, allowing patterns and relationships to become visible. In doing so, new synergies emerge that extend the group's awareness and make even more visible and meaningful the connections that underlie group and individuals alike.

Discipline	Practices	Emergent Qualities
6 — *Detachment*	• Surrendering of: assumptions agendas (Dlg) • Emptying of: preconceptions judgments prejudices and ideological positions (CB)	• Makes explicit personal and existential vulnerability • Develops a capacity for "not-knowing" • Supports reflection and awareness • Promotes keeping all options open • Provides access to what Arrien calls "the human resource of wisdom" • Cultivates a capacity, as Arrien suggests, "to care deeply from an objective place"

Discipline	Practices	Emergent Qualities
7 — *Multi-dimensional thinking*	• Group inquiry into paradoxical and contradictory perspectives (Dlg) • Shared reflection upon complexities • Group examination of inter-relatedness of meanings made at the personal, comunity and cultural levels (Dlg)	• Discloses patterns such as the inter-relatedness of personal assumptions and larger cultural processes • Develops the capacity to think systemically and • To examine the effects of participation in larger systems • Provides access to the experience of the transpersonal nature of larger systems

Discipline	Practices	Emergent Qualities
8 — *Ecological awareness*	• Practicing inclusivity (CB) • Focusing attention upon how separation occurs and connections are maintained (CB) • Focused attention and shared reflection upon the patterns of interrelationship which extend through the personal and cultural to the environment (Dlg) • Focused attention and shared reflection upon the effects of assumptions and action on relationships, community and the world (Dlg)	• Sensitizes the group to the quality of connections • Supports emergent awareness of the implicit unity underlying the group's experience • Makes explicit that all behavior is social and ecological • Increases the likelihood of actions that are more socially and ecologically responsible

Detachment, or emptiness, is cultivated through the letting go of assumptions, agendas, preconceptions, judgments, prejudices, and ideological positions. This is a most rigorous discipline. The practice of detachment forms the core of most of the world's spiritual traditions. It allows all options to be kept open by developing a capacity to not- know. This openness provides access to wisdom and the ability to care without having to prevail.

The seven disciplines described above provide the foundation for the emergence of the seventh and eighth disciplines. By practicing these methods, groups develop synergies that will manifest larger perspectives that make new forms of learning possible. As the group gains these capacities, a larger perspective emerges and new meanings become possible.

The discipline of multi-dimensional (systemic) thinking serves an important role in enhancing the mindfulness of a group. The group's willingness to look into contradictory, or paradoxical, perspectives develops the capacity to hold greater complexity that disclose patterns and relationships that join personal positions, attitudes, and behaviors with larger cultural processes; this includes meanings made at both of these levels. The unity of all Life becomes visible when groups acquire this capacity, so it becomes possible to consider the role large systems play in defining reality and limiting the range of responses to culturally-defined reality.

These practices create the preconditions that support the emergence of ecological awareness. This discipline uses all the other disciplines to focus attention upon the ecological question: What is the effect on our neighbors and our place in the world, of our assumptions and actions on our neighbors and our place in the world?

With a mind toward the unity that underlies all experience, the group perceives the relationship that joins the personal, the cultural, and the environmental. All behavior is then revealed to be social and ecological.

Conclusion

The potential for generating personal and collective awareness in a learning community does not manifest without effort. It does not occur until members of the group are willing to face the complications inherent in differences of life experience, formal education, learning and communication styles, cultural background and social roles. These differences generate tensions and uncertainties that can be daunting.

Yet these tensions make explicit the level of challenge in a learning community. For a learning community is a microculture that encapsulates the cultural context within which it has developed. Thus, it constitutes a miniature culture where the social and psychological tensions that characterize our historical era can be experienced. Addressing these cultural stresses and uncertainties means opening up to the pain and denial that exists in our culture. It means coming into direct contact with what remains psychologically undeveloped in both our personal and national character. As the group observes and examines its interactions, it begins to experience the relationship between personal responses to these tensions and cultural dynamics.

The tensions in a learning community also present a significant opportunity. As a cultural laboratory, a learning community presents a context where the relationship between personal and cultural dynamics can be explored collaboratively. Sharing perceptions of how intrapsychic and interpersonal dynamics affect, and are affected by, cultural and global dynamics reduces the tendency inherent in our individualistic culture to view these emotional responses as personally pathological.

By inquiring together into the nature of the social uneasiness manifesting in the group, a context of mutual responsibility is created. When a group begins to share responsibility, this makes possible the apprehension of a new sense of the commons—a commons that reveals itself in the connections between individual experience, group dynamics, and global processes. This form of sharing unleashes potential for transformative learning that leads to an enhanced understanding of cultural dynamics and their relationship to personal well-being. Such awareness promotes healthier and more creative responses, empowering individuals and transforming culture.

Clearly the task of learning in such a complicated and emotionally charged environment is daunting. For many it may seem impossible. It is important to remember that the impossible has always been rendered possible through desire. The desire for change leads to the use of discipline. The preceding examination of the specific practices which support the creation of a learning community have shown that discipline can make learning and change possible. Application of these disciplines makes credible the assertion that transformative learning is possible for groups as well as for individuals. This offers hope that we can learn to get along together, and that we can support each other's learning to act in ways that are personally empowering, and socially and environmentally responsible.

CHAPTER 14

ꙮ

A Social Crucible

Introduction

Entering into the 21st century we find ourselves inhabiting a natural and social environment unlike any our ancestors have known. Through our own successes we have transformed our world. Once we occupied a world full of dangerous mysteries. The animal powers held sway and humankind huddled together in small bands. Now our numbers, restless energy, and creative curiosity have overcome the animal powers and unlocked many of Nature's secrets. Through our own success we now find ourselves crowded together on a rapidly shrinking planet, occupying a landscape that is increasingly man-made and thoroughly dominated by the activities of our own kind.

There are many uncertainties that attend this moment in our species' journey. We enter this century unsure of our future, not in the same way that our ancestors were insecure, because they felt so small in such a large and mysterious world. Instead, when we look out upon our world we are confronted by a distressingly familiar danger: we ourselves have become the most dangerous mystery we face.

Our journey has brought us to a point where we must confront our own kind. For it is evident that our technological virtuosity, having delivered us to an age of incredible possibilities, now threatens us (and the living systems we depend upon) because our social development, our ability to relate to our own kind, has not kept pace. This is the nature of our current evolutionary dilemma, to ensure a future worth living, we must find a way to embrace the complexity of our own humanity.

I believe our current evolutionary dilemma poses a kind of ingenuous developmental impasse, a paradoxical social koan that impedes our further development (on our terms) and stimulates new development (on Life's terms). In this chapter I want to describe how this social koan can, when we turn intentionally toward it, enable us to actualize our social potential and renew our confidence in ourselves as a species.

Finally, I hope to make clear how this new learning modality can become a social incubator for the new integral forms of consciousness that we as a species sorely need as we attempt to shape a more hospitable future.

A Social Koan

In order to understand the way that a learning community can serve as a social crucible, an incubator for new and more complex forms of consciousness, we must appreciate the deeper nature of our current situation. It is one fraught with danger; it is also one that is rich with potential. What is striking about this moment in our long journey is how elegantly designed our current dilemma is. Through some strange evolutionary alchemy, we have arrived at a place where before we can occupy a larger niche in the Cosmos, we must come to grips with the mystery of our own complexity; and before we can become a viable interplanetary species, we must learn how to preserve and protect the planet that Life has given us.

I believe that a critical dimension of our current evolutionary impasse resides in our social relations. How we interact with each other, interpersonally and cross-culturally, poses a dangerous problem for us as a species. We are thwarted, and our survival is threatened, by our inability to get along. At the same time that our development is impeded, I believe we are confronted with conditions that can propel us into a new stage in our evolution. This is why I refer to this impasse as a social koan. Why a koan? Because a koan presents a dilemma that has within it the ingredients that can catalyze a new, more complex form of awareness and thereby new social capabilities. That's the untapped potential that lurks within our current dilemma. Let's look at how this could be so.

What is it about how we human beings interact that could generate such a paradoxical problem? As a species we continue to exhibit a persistent intolerance for what we do not understand and cannot control. The social koan arises from the interhuman dimension of a continuum of intolerance that extends beyond human beings to the natural world in which we are embedded. This intolerance manifests as an unwillingness to tolerate contact with "otherness." As Parker Palmer puts it, when describing the interhuman dimension of this intolerance, we as a species "fear encounters in which the other is free to be itself, to speak its own truth, to tell us what we may not wish to hear. We want those encounters on our own terms so that we can control the outcomes, so that they will not threaten our view of [our] world and [our] self."

This description makes evident that intolerance of otherness is essentially an inability to tolerate existential uncertainty. When we encounter something that is unknown to us, the possibility arises that we might discover that our world, what we call reality, is more complex, wild and unknown than we imagine. Such a discovery can shift the ground beneath our feet and disturb the foundation upon which we have built our sense of self. When this happens, we are exposed to an awareness of how vulnerable and uncertain our lives really are. It is this disturbing experience that we are unwilling to tolerate.

But how does intolerance of this experience generate a paradox in our social relations? In essence, our attempts to avoid experiencing existential uncertainty (which arises when we come into contact with what is strange and new about others), generate greater existential uncertainty. How so? Our intolerance of otherness leads us to employ social practices designed to protect us from what is "other" in others; these same practices are inherently offensive to others, because they attempt to diminish (even obliterate) significant differences. The more intolerant we are of otherness, the more potent the means we employ to protect ourselves. The more offensive our social practices become and the more dangerous social reality gets, the more uncertain we are that we can survive together.

The persistence of our intolerance for otherness manifests very clearly in the way we interact with each other. It manifests in our personal (or cultural) refusal, or inability, to perceive other humans as beings embodying a different way of knowing and interacting with reality. We prefer to make sense of others on our own terms thus we are prone to assert the preeminence of our own worldview. This pattern manifests, interpersonally and cross-culturally, in forms of thinking and behaviors that diminish the other. The persistence of this tendency defines so many of our social practices.

Intolerance and the subsequent diminishment of otherness breed social mistrust. With this mistrust comes a hardening tendency to view ourselves, and those who are like us, as being the people, living correctly, while others are wrong, ignorant, immoral and dangerous. When this hardening takes hold, we end up inadvertently collaborating by erecting psychological and cultural structures of separateness, social practices that protect us from a living encounter with what is "alien" to us. The more cut off we are from the "otherness" of others, the easier it is to project the parts of ourselves that we fear and despise upon others. This pattern leads to the many forms of "isms" that now haunt our species' interactions, limiting our ability to collaborate and to act in concert to address the global issues that now threaten us.

This is the social dimension of our current dilemma: our intolerance of otherness (and of the greater reality that otherness introduces us to) separates us and makes us a threat to each other. It is easy to see how this characteristic impedes us socially and threatens our development, but how does it also serve as a potential passageway toward a new phase in humanity's development? In other words, how can it also serve as a koan?

At the most basic level, our intolerance for otherness reveals the degree to which we are unwilling to embrace reality as it is, unwilling to come to grips with the actual level of existential uncertainty that underlies human existence. In other words, this social koan reveals the disparity between our socially constructed reality and reality as it is, and points us toward a new possibility—one that could realign us with the cosmos and thereby with each other.

Here, then, is the possibility that lies at the heart of this social dilemma, the potential for transformation that makes this dilemma a social koan. Like all real koans, the solution to this dilemma lies in the dilemma itself.

> The solution to paradox involves going to a higher level of functioning. When the paradox results from embedded cultural values and beliefs, it is necessary to establish a viewpoint outside the culture from which the implicit cultural information can be viewed and examined. When paradox results from interlocking unresolved dynamics, the solution requires more than an increment in development; it requires

a paradigm shift in the way existing information and perceptions are understood. Resolution [then]...involves a shift and escalation to a higher order of perspective. It requires corresponding development of an observing ego, a tolerance for ambivalence and the simultaneous acceptance of multiple realities. Only by assuming the meta level can the individual (culture) tolerate ambivalence without conflict. [Schnarch, 1991, pg.477]

There is something uncanny and ingenious about the dilemma posed by this social koan. There seems to be some inexorable feature of the evolutionary process that makes this dilemma both inevitable and essential. It appears that we are inevitably subject to a form of ecological checks and balances, through which Life requires us to respect and embrace it on Life's terms, instead of our own. Embracing Life then requires us to extend our awareness, to grow our consciousness, and to develop our ability to relate to Life in its many forms. This is essential because our survival depends upon being able to develop a greater capacity to sustain contact with what we do not understand and cannot control. Without this capacity we will not adapt ourselves to conditions beyond our control.

From this vantage point we are threatened not so much by Life's terms as by our insistence upon our own terms. This insistence upon our own way has grown this problem into a vast dilemma that now threatens us on a global scale, making our world more dangerous than is really necessary. The social koan makes clear to us how destructive and dangerous our current course is. It also presents us with an opportunity by challenging each of us personally, and all of us collectively, to grow a more complex capacity to embrace Life. The stakes inherent in this challenge are high and so are the possibilities.

A Social Crucible

As long as humans have interacted we have had difficulty tolerating otherness. This difficulty can be found in the tensions that are common to marital and family life, as well as community and business interactions and on into international relations. Wherever we have differed, be it by age, gender, class, ethnicity, religion, culture, or race, we have come into contact with the possibility of something new and unpredictable—something which might undermine our certainty about the world we inhabit and about who we ourselves might be; something which, if we could tolerate contact with it, might also transform our consciousness.

The anxiety, frustrations and dangers associated with contact with otherness are familiar to all of us. We experience them on a local, personal and intimate basis every day as we interact. Intolerance, the inability or unwillingness to experience otherness, may prevent us from paying close attention to how we differ, or to being open to the difficult feelings that can come with differing. So we might deny ourselves awareness of this experience. Or intolerance may lead us to believe that we simply "prefer" those who are like ourselves; this can lead us to avoid interacting with others. As we do these things, in addition to denying others their distinctiveness, in each instance we are also denying ourselves access to a more complex experience of reality. By diminishing the distinctiveness of others and our own contact with reality, we diminish our chances for survival.

It is for this reason that we need to make a concerted effort to address the social koan. By doing so we can begin to defuse the threat to our children's futures. And because of the paradox inherent in this dilemma, we can acquire new awareness and a closer alignment with Life. Such a move enhances the prospects of future generations. How then can we employ this ubiquitous dilemma to transform our consciousness? This is the function of the social crucible.

What is a social crucible? To understand what a social crucible is we need to first have a clear picture of the function of a crucible. A crucible is a vessel that is designed to contain a catalytic process that generates metamorphosis. A crucible is used when we seek not simply to mix materials together, but to actually transform the mixture into something that is qualitatively different. A social crucible, then, is a social milieu where the paradoxical tensions that inherently arise when humans interact are employed to generate new consciousness. What distinguishes a social crucible from the day-to-day social contexts where intolerance of otherness exists, is that a concerted effort is made to hold the tensions associated with the experience of diversity instead of dissipating them. A social crucible amplifies these tensions while inquiring more deeply into them for the purpose of transformation.

A social crucible then has three major attributes:

1. A social crucible provides a social structure that serves as a container. The container has sufficient integrity so that it can hold the pressures that arise as the process it contains unfolds.
2. A social crucible contains a catalytic process. A catalytic agent (such as the social koan) then generates heat, pressure and tension. These elements lead to a transformative reaction.
3. A social crucible generates a qualitative shift in consciousness. It does this through a synergetic reaction that incorporates the awareness of each individual involved into a larger, more complex field of awareness. A meta-level shift in consciousness then emerges.

These attributes can arise spontaneously. Usually a social crucible only occurs in social contexts where there are long-term committed relationships, where a lot is at stake and where all parties will experience a significant loss if the tensions present aren't addressed in a constructive fashion. Such a situation, where the commitment of all the parties is great enough to create a container with sufficient integrity, is rare however.

Because this is generally so, I have found it necessary to create the specific form of social crucible that I call a learning community.

An Integral Practice

The social crucible of learning community is designed specifically to be transformative. It is designed to employ two social challenges: diversity and the size of the group (larger than most people are comfortable with) in order to alter the consciousness and social practices of those involved. When the social crucible arises, it is because integral practices are utilized, and it fosters an integral vision.

Why does this matter? Because we are entering a phase in human development where, if the human experiment is going to thrive, we as a species must become as complex in our awareness as the surrounding conditions we have created. In other words, the complex world we have created requires a multi-dimensional awareness of us, an integral vision. This requirement is existential, not optional. To remain viable, to maintain pace with Evolution, we need to access and integrate our potential. Developmental theorists have shown that we have within our potential the capacity to see the world as a whole, to know how interconnected reality is, to experience each other as parts of the same larger whole. These are all attributes of an integral vision. It takes integral practices to support the development of integral vision.

When it becomes a social crucible, learning community supports the emergence of a more complex awareness, a more integral vision. This development isn't automatic, however — it is an emergent phenomenon. Learning community is not a social technology. It is more unpredictable, more human, than that. The synergies generated by the practices described in earlier chapters only generate the necessary pre-conditions. Some strange alchemy unleashes a broader awareness. Described as serendipity, or as grace, this strange alchemy is actually a reflection of the vagaries of the human heart. A group can't just do the right things. It has to be willing to go beyond itself.

Conclusion

The special problems posed by otherness and the social koan are not new to us. What is new, however, are the conditions that our recent successes have generated. Population growth has made our planet smaller—we are crowded together now. We cannot avoid each other as we could before. Our technological success has extended the impact we can have upon each other: impacts such as mutually assured destruction, ethnic cleansing, and global warming have accompanied these advances. Where intolerance of otherness once meant only marital or family tension or perhaps, at worst, inter-tribal or inter-state tension, now it has consequences that threaten global survival.

To survive we need to grow our social capabilities. We need to reach for the farthest depths of human development (unity, non-dual states, and post-conventional awareness). Remarkable people work hard to become so aware. A similar type of commitment is required to produce a remarkable group. A social crucible emerges only when enough individuals begin to contribute themselves to an effort to learn and connect more deeply.

This is not a random event. A learning community can serve as an incubator, but the will of the members is required. Willingness is what ultimately provides the opening. If the fire of collective consciousness is going to break out, then some percentage of the group sets off the cascade. They do this by committing the modern version of apoptosis, that is, they metamorphize. Like cellular death for the wellbeing of the larger organism, human cells, members of the group, voluntarily go through the disassembling step that leads to a broader, more complex awareness. This step evokes new awareness in members and group alike. This step is aided by practices, disciplined efforts, but happens only because of love. Someone lays himself on the altar for the sake of the whole.

Strangely, this kind of sacrifice, which seems so rare in our culture (except in our military), is extraordinarily satisfying. This is deeply human. It is one part of our potential that is largely ignored by our individualistic social sciences. And because it is, we, our species, have tended to forget how much it means to us being part of something larger. We have tended to forget how giving self in this way opens the door for personal and collective growth. It is within us to do, and it offers us hope for a more hospitable future—one where the dignity of our differences is matched by the generosity of our hearts. Personal metamorphosis, when it happens in a group, sets off collective metamorphosis, integrating our lopsided emphasis upon individuality into a more complex, hospitable, and inclusive social reality.

SECTION VI

CONSIDERATIONS

SECTION VI

〜

Considerations

To be sane in a mad time
is bad for the brain,
worse for the heart.

The world is a holy vision,
had we clarity to see it–
a clarity
that we depend on each other
to make.
—WENDELL BERRY

Introduction

There is a movement happening. A shift is underway. An internal climate change is occurring, to match the external one. This isn't just a political, an economic, or a generational thing. There is a tectonic movement, a kind of re-balancing, taking place. We are moving from a story that was mainly about the individual, the survival of the fittest, to a more complex story, the individual in relationship, in context, the survival of fitting in.

There is no conclusion, in this context, to offer. The currents of flux are too great. So, what I will offer are some considerations for this moment. Even the past is changing, A new story is coming to pass. With it comes change—new possibilities, upset, discovery. This is a time for paying attention. Who we are, our potential, is being re-defined. We are waking up to a self that is torn open by the contradictory forces of communion and autonomy. These changes may be welcome in some circles, and less welcome in others, but in either case, they ask much of us.

The New Story

Almost 18 billion years ago, a huge energy event began. We call it the
Big Bang. From that dramatic moment, which we don't scientifically
understand, to the present, we have mapped a constantly expanding
Universe. We measure expansion in terms of time, rate and distance.
But it is just as accurate, perhaps more revealing, to consider expan-
sion in terms of increasing complexity, consciousness, and Life.

We are a product of the Universe's Evolution. From the Big Bang
we have arisen. Every species shares that same amazing parentage.
Yet we are the first (as far as we know) to actually know we are an
aspect of the expansion of the Universe. That knowledge has a dou-
ble-edge to it. The restless Universe is incessantly disturbing us,
changing everything. Like it or not, we are part of that growth.

We are an extension of something enormous, powerful, and
ongoing. The Universe, existence, Evolution is changing and complexifying us. The truth is, we really don't know what this is all
about. Philosophers have speculated about it, cultures have risen
and fallen with different answers, religions have been spawned with
the intention of putting this uncertainty to rest. Still the uncertainty
goes on and we find ourselves unseated, uncertain, and incessantly
unbalanced.

A remarkable aspect of our kind is that we are an expression of
all this ceaseless creativity. We are adaptable. And Evolution keeps
knocking on our door, changing us. Life keeps asking us to adapt!
Not just one time—we are asked over and over. We are a Life form,
and we are part of the process of Life, extending itself out, as part of
the expansion of the Universe.

We aren't just star dust; we are star dust evolving, being transformed, as part of the ongoing thrust of Creation. Being an extension of the Universe is no tea party. Evolving is not an easy task. It
is said that God sometimes asks much of those who are given a lot.
The Universe has endowed us with its powers, precisely because we
are operating as its living edge.

As part of that endowment, we are conscious. We haven't
decided completely if that is a blessing or a curse. With consciousness we are capable of anticipating the sunrise, marveling at the
birth of a child, or a star, sharing a joke, and looking into the night-
time sky and wondering at all we see. But so too we worry about the
possibilities we know, we miss what passes, and we suffer knowing

of our own limitations and death. It is this latter awareness we bear most ambivalently. For our consciousness participates in the strange alchemy I call metamorphosis. We knowingly feel and maintain awareness while we are being transformed.

We are adaptable. Evolution wants it and made us that way. We are also conscious. We participate in our own transformation. Our minds are made up for us, changed to suit the circumstances, and we are active in the process. We suffer confusion, heartache, loneliness, insight, movement, and elation. I call it a chrysalis experience, a metamorphosis that alters us, that re-structures our minds. We are awake during this radical operation, to participate in it. We become more of what the Universe wants for its own purposes. And because we participate, if we choose to, we aid that process by becoming ourselves, the bit of uniqueness that helps the Universe expand.

This isn't just a fanciful idea. Science, particularly the life sciences, have shown that it is "coupling" that has brought about Life and is so suitable for its environment. We are the product of millennia of relationships, interactions that brought Life into our world. The procession of Creation and the Evolution of our kind is one continuum of interactions. We are linked to all things, and it is the quality of those linkages, those relationships, those interactions, that perpetuates the becoming that is the Universe's expansion.

As the story tips beyond individuality, new light is shed upon what we thought we knew. Before our eyes something that seemed settled now is illumined and shown to be different. Things are in flux. The recent past has shown that Life has woven a net that is far more subtle and complex than our sciences have previously beheld. The linkages that are coming into view, with a more connected world, are all part of the shifting story, all part of what is changing us.

Natural Systems

Life is more inventive than we have given it credit for. Like an invisible ecosystem, it links us to the surroundings. We are a part of a culture, a community, a family, and a world. These things define us as we conform to them or struggle against them. In the old story distance meant separation, but in the New World no separation exists except through growth. Invisibly, Life has arranged natural systems of connection that couple us to one another and to our surroundings.

These links might feel like a kind of bondage, and they could be if we refuse to take responsibility for our responses to them, but they represent the real support and challenge Life holds for us.

The recent evolution of systems awareness has altered the landscape by bringing the role of relationship into the picture. Relationships are invisible. They have accoutrements that render their existence visible. You can see the signs, but they exist on another level, at a natural systems level. Human relationships, particularly family and long-term committed relationships, partake of these patterns of connection. Levels of relationship interweave us.

The old psychoanalytic view of two interiors colliding is slowly making room for a more complex and inclusive systems view. This perspective considers the interior as an important factor, but goes on to look at all of the connections that make up the relationship ecosystem in which individuals are embedded. It considers the relationship to the family, the community, and the cultural/ historical surround. Relationship is composed of all of these influences. Natural systems couple each of us. Excluding any level of connection rebounds badly upon the individual. To be human is to be connected.

This viewpoint, thanks mainly to the contributions of explorers like Murray Bowen, Rabbi Friedman, and David Schnarch, is changing the face of psychotherapy. Others, such as Ervin Lazlo, Ken Wilber, Joanna Macy, and Fritjof Capra, are rendering other dimensions of our natural inheritance more accessible by their attempts to map this emerging New World. It turns out that Nature, Life, has not abandoned us at the city gate or in our human-constructed abodes. We are persistently linked into a matrix composed of our relationships, human and more-than-human.

These kinds of linkages have existed from time immemorial. The Universe used linking (relationship) by combining protons with other elements to preserve them while creating newer more complex elements. Life, an extension of the Universe's expansion, used the same capabilities, to overcome the crisis brought on by the success of single-celled organisms (an oxygen-saturated atmosphere) and to inaugurate our ancestral line by combining into multi-celled beings.

Each successive living combination, an assemblage of formerly stand-alone organisms, formed a system, a living, natural system. And each is coupled to its environment. This is the world we move in, a realm defined by relational activity. As Ken Wilber is fond of saying, "It's turtles all the way up and down," referring to the fact that natural systems and the relational forces that bind them exist throughout the length of the chain of existence. This is a realization that has only come to us recently, but it is altering our world, changing what we see, transforming our notions of ourselves. Psychology has lagged behind, and that lag is endangering us.

A Psychological View

As my awareness changed, so did my psychological viewpoint. The biggest change came when I realized that human beings could be viewed as a holons. Perceiving the dual holonic nature of everyone started a cascade of realizations about the psychological project that continues to this day. This facet of "the pattern that connects," the twin urges, provided the missing link. Relationship was as fundamental to human life, as it was to Evolution.

At first I didn't recognize and value how fundamental relationship was. I was so enthralled with individualism that I simply could not see how connected we humans are. I hadn't yet achieved the development and growth that would let me see beyond consensus reality. I knew humans were social creatures; my community experiences had brought that home to me, but I lacked a way of seeing and articulating these interconnections. Then I made the linkages between Murray Bowen's assertions about the twin urges of protoplasm, our holonic nature, and Robert Kegan's model of oscillating human development. When I did, I began to see a pattern of relationship that was pervasive.

When I recognized relatedness as fundamental to human nature, I was forced to re-think everything I learned about the nature of the psyche, to re-imagine the psychological project, and to re-create my role as a therapist. I had miles to go; it took finding other explorers who had mapped portions of this emerging world to help me begin to formulate this synthesis.

Years passed. I wasn't what I had been led to believe. I needed to learn more to reach the critical mass that brought all the information together. I needed to grow myself up. I tried desperately to integrate all of these changes without getting too de-centered and uncomfortable. I wanted to shift my modus operandi, but I didn't want to lose control.

The stroke took care of that ambition and has colored my experience enough that I have determined that I must acknowledge its role in bringing me to this place. I will do that soon, before the end. Before I do, however, I want to underscore the changes that have come to me with the realization of our fundamentally social nature.

I realized two big things as I broadened my view to include the fact of connection. It was through this realization that we are all always connected—to each other and to the larger world we live in—that I came to understand some of the complexities already affecting us. Growing a self-defined self and dealing with the changes brought on by the larger forces of the world, made me understand that being connected wasn't simply good, or easy.

I could see that each of us was subject to forces that were large, pervasive, and readily misunderstood. As connected beings, the larger processes of Life, of Evolution, of the social systems we are embedded in, had an impact that we are often unaware of, and certainly unprepared for. Psychology dealt well with those forces within us, but not so well, and sometimes not at all, with those forces we are connected to. This is why I had to pick up on Robert Kegan's idea of "natural therapy."

Each of us is connected to larger processes that affect us. Sometimes this feels like support, the wind at our back; and sometimes this feels like a challenge, the wind in our faces. Always it is an opportunity. For most of us, however, because we are still subject to the prevailing story of isolated individualism, when these forces affect us it seems as if something is wrong within us. Natural Therapy would suggest, instead, that Life is asking us to adapt to the needs of something larger to which we are connected.

Adapting is a complex phenomenon. If the systems we are embedded within are healthy, then adapting is a good thing. If they are not, then it could be dangerous. The dangers of connection should not be underestimated. But the social potential of our species requires us to consider the benefits. First of all, what is asked of us, the change that pulls at us, may be good for the larger systems we are embedded within. This could be our environment, relationship, family, community, or culture. Secondly, changing may make us more complex, efficient, connected, and responsive. Invariably, we are asked to be more rather than less to grow ourselves.

This brings us to the second challenge of a connected life. Being always connected entails dealing with the hardships of growing a self–in-relationship. In essence this form of self-growth is much more complex and challenging than what is considered the norm by traditional psychology. Growing a self-in-relationship primarily places an emphasis upon integrity, not autonomy. Integrity is the ability to balance the twin urges of autonomy and communion for the sake of choice. Autonomy is still important but is seen more as a by-product of integrity—not a function of distance, but of growth.

As if these challenges are not enough, Evolution keeps upsetting us, demanding a re-balancing, a period of growth, and occasional metamorphosis in pursuit of the Universe's goals. We are upset by the ever-complexifying expansion of the Universe. It is as if we are constantly being retro-fitted, re-programmed, to make room for new capabilities. This is what is happening to us collectively. Being a complicated, tremendously adaptive species has its disadvantages, especially if we think we (or our culture) are supposed to be stable, in-control, unchanging beings. Life is asking more than that.

So, we are challenged in this connected Life to contend with growing a self-in-relationship, being subject to larger forces a la "natural therapy," and to having Evolution constantly developing and re-wiring us. All of these challenges seem to impede us. That, however, is the old way of seeing things. These are not obstacles to be overcome, problems to be solved; they are forms of initiation — supports that reveal how connected we are and that stimulate our immune systems, teaching us new responses that add to our repertoires and increase our comfort in a living, dynamic, connected world. We have been prepared, endowed with immune systems, by Life. We are challenged by Life to grow ourselves, to expand our immune responses so that we can be even more alive, more responsive to all that we are a part of.

The Vantage Point of Disability

I don't know what to say about my stroke; it is still happening, still altering me. The life I knew, the life I thought I had, changed completely as a result of the alterations that my brain is undergoing. I know that I was on the track of a psychology of interdependence before the stroke, but my brush with death and the prolonged chrysalis period that I have endured altered my awareness and resulted in this formulation.

I call myself Lucky sometimes. I do this to contrast my experience with what most people anticipate. I have been reduced by the stroke. I have experienced loss; I am disabled. I no longer freely walk the face of the Earth. All this is true. My medical condition profoundly disrupted the life I knew. But the story only starts there. I have also been enabled by the stroke, and this is what has taught me so much about connection, resilience, and our endowment.

In the first three years after my stroke, when the doctors didn't know why I was getting worse instead of better, I thought I was dying. Along with experiencing the gradual decline of my faculties, I had time to reflect upon this life. I could tell that everything, everybody, was passing so quickly. I felt the preciousness of everything, especially the people in my life. I had become sensitized by my losses. I knew my life, whatever it now was, was not mine anymore. I went from the driver's seat to the passenger seat. I was on a wild ride, and I didn't know if I was headed for oblivion or a new life.

The time I spent on the threshold of death taught me a lot. I had a lot of regrets—over my marriage, the home I had lost, how music, singing, dancing and the wilds had all gone beyond my grasp. I grieved a lot. There were days when I wasn't sure what I was grieving—the loss of my health or the life I had known. During this time, I became aware of two specific regrets. I envisioned them like big rooms in my inner house that had been closed up forever. They were my passion for community—practices and theory. I didn't relish the idea of taking this valuable part of my life and the hope they generated in me to my grave.

I came back to life after a three-year visit to the underworld. When I did, I knew I must write. This book is part of my return to life. It is the beginning of making sure that I deal with the two regrets I was haunted by. I have written this book despite my fear and anxiety about doing so, typing away with one hand, employing a lesser voice to speak what my spirit knows. It is the beginning of integrating the world that the stroke has introduced me to.

Recently I have seen books by other stroke survivors, most notably Jill Bolte Taylor's book, *My Stroke of Insight,* and Ram Dass' account of being "stroked by his guru" that appears in his book *Still Here,* and it is clear that the experience of a stroke, if it doesn't kill you, can transport one to a new form of awareness. Jill Taylor, who had a similar, more massive hemorrhagic stroke (in a different part of her brain) than I, reported that she had an experience of profound and disorienting connection to all things. Ram Dass, being a spiritual teacher, defined his shift as a spiritual experience.

I think we were each given access, via the forced growth that is the result of this kind of extreme experience, to a level of consciousness that reveals the world we live in differently than most folks perceive it. I don't think this is a miracle. I think that this awareness is part of the normal spectrum of consciousness that represents human potential. In this case, extreme circumstances, real hardship, brought this awareness into the foreground. This brings me to a significant lesson taught to me by this stroke.

Throughout this book I have tried to show that sometimes connection brings hardship. I have tried to avoid painting the connected life as a panacea. Sometimes Life asks so much of us, so much that we are barely recognizable as we answer. Any pregnant woman can attest to this. The larger processes of Life can totally wreak havoc in our lives (I know); but if we choose to respond, not as victims of Life but as co-creators, amazing gifts become available. Our immune systems are capable of delivering new capabilities. Sometimes what we need is hardship to challenge us, to discover how resilient, how connected we are.

I hasten to add that this is not a justification for poverty and starvation. What makes hardship transformative is our response. It must be voluntary. Structural forms of hardship are still systemic abuses that steal life and vitality from everyone. We need to keep working to improve the lives of those who are less fortunate, but we need to treat hardship with more sophistication. Sometimes hardship is Evolution's knock. We mustn't treat it like a disease or something wrong, lest we cut off our immune systems from the very challenges that help us discover new realms of vitality, creativity, and resilience.

The stroke disabled and stopped me. It took me beyond myself. It asked me to grow up even more than I had. And it delivered me to a world beyond my imaginings. I am Lucky. I now live the connected life, imperfectly to be sure, but aware that I am more than a guest. Life has had its way with me, worked me over good, nearly killed me, but in the end has given me this small ability to see and celebrate connection. For that, I am Lucky.

Some Considerations

Connected life, then, has its own challenges. These challenges are every bit as important and difficult as those presented by traditional ideas of the psychological project. The main difference is that you get a better balanced, connected individual, someone capable of seeing beyond himself, and acting on behalf of the whole. Connected life de-pathologizes a host of normal experiences and makes those experiences more useful.

Connected life makes living a form of giving, a generosity aimed at enhancing others. Connected life is not organized around the individual. Relationship is really what is important. What is created between people, between a community and its locale, between our species and the global environment, the quality of what we contribute to the between: that is what is important.

Connected life offers a constant reciprocity. Our lives are full of relationship. It is time we realized this on a large scale. Fortunately, this is not something we have to do—or even can do—alone. It is our nature. We are a part of everything that is happening. As the climate changes externally, so will we internally. This transition isn't one we will make happen, because it is already happening. We do have a choice to make, and that choice is about how we are going to respond.

Connected life is more than an antidote to the fragmenting effects of modern life. It is a form of immunity. There is a relief that comes with knowing that one cannot fall out of the pattern that connects, nor can one make a mistake capable of shattering wholeness. One may choose to respond to Life as if one is alone, but no amount of alienation will ever sever the tie that connects one to the Cosmos, nor will it ever separate one from the supports of Life.

Embracing Life

I've told the story before, but I've got to tell it again. After the stroke I worried, as a psychotherapist, a change agent, that I had been transformed by the stroke rather than by my own efforts. What business had I advocating for anyone to face their limitations and grow if I had not done so? I carried this anxiety, this doubt, as a kind of ethical dilemma until I realized that Life had changed me. When I realized that Life was feeding on me, making me more useful to Evolution, I settled down, and started appreciating Life. Now I believe Life is a partner, and I understand that my growth is not solely for my sake.

Life asks much. It sometimes challenges us severely. But it also provides the means to handle the challenging circumstances that we literally find ourselves within. We are grown, sometimes against our will, to further the Evolution of the Universe. We mistakenly think our lives are our own. This is a half-truth. We belong to Life. This is both the good and the bad news. Interdependence means that we have no control, but that we have more influence, through our ability to respond, than we ever thought imaginable.

We are in a time of change. A new story is emerging about never having been abandoned by Life. This story tells us we are desired, supported, and accompanied. Life has always embraced us. Now we must embrace Life.

〜

ADDENDUM

As I have been writing I've found myself thinking about two populations of people, both of whom have been traditionally marginalized by our culture. I think these folks could hold something for us. As I have thought more about them I have found that I want to work with them to help them cultivate the wisdom and development they contain. I think their voices could change our song.

I have found myself touched by the dilemmas of the many warriors returning from the wars, scarred by bodies and brains broken in battle. I keep thinking that these idealistic, battle-hardened men and women may be the best representatives of the resilience and freedom of the human spirit. If given the right kind of support—more than kudos, prosthetics, and disability pay—I think these veterans could continue to be the freedom fighters that show us all the possibilities that lie in hardship, the possibilities that are ours. I imagine a whole corps of broken men and women who demonstrate that we humans can be free in all kinds of circumstances.

I have also found myself thinking about elders, the most wasted generation of people—strangely, the ones potentially with the most development under their belts and certainly the most time, because of retirement, to devote to growth. There is a contribution this age cohort could be making that might increase the wisdom available to us all. Supporting this age group might, instead of being seen as the elderly, lead to them being seen, and looked to, as elders. I think we cannot afford to just write these folks off, that doing so is extremely costly to individuals and society alike.

I imagine that the quality of life for everybody would be improved if these age cohorts saw themselves and were seen as having a valuable, even crucial, contribution to make. I think their wisdom, life experience, and proximity to death would provide an important counterbalance to our culture's emphasis upon youth, material success, and surfaces. I would like to work with some committed seniors who would like to cultivate themselves to bring senior wisdom to our collective table.

There is much work to be done, more than I can do. I would love to have or make the opportunity to serve these populations. We need them in order to know our own capabilities.

Chapter Notes and Acknowledgements

Introduction Notes

Human beings have much in common and many differences. Thus, it is inaccurate to make generalizations about humanity. This work has a cultural skew towards the West, with its focus on psychological therapy and the welfare of the individual.

Many cultures do not participate in the individualistic ethos that is so pre-eminent here in the West. Traditional Asian cultures, African, and other indigenous cultures eschew the emphasis upon the individual in favor of an emphasis on the group. In many of these cultures there often is no language that describes or gives expression to the concept of "I," "me," or "mine" even as words exist for "we," "us," "us," and "ours."

It is not my intention to ignore these valuable parts of the human community and especially the contributions they have made towards the social evolution of our species. This work is intended to address the dangerous imbalances of the West where I've grown up, been educated, and have had the primacy of the individual inculcated into every aspect of my life. This is the culture that has impacted my thinking the most and that is shaping the modern world the most at the present time.

I tend to think that while the West suffers from "the fallacy of the individual," what is loosely known as the East also suffers from a tendency toward a "fallacy of the whole;" that is, placing a corresponding burden on human evolution by overemphasizing the collective. Both tendencies, it seems to me, would benefit by equalizing the emphasis on communion and autonomy that comes with the holonic viewpoint.

That being said, however, this work purposely speaks to the particular imbalances of the West. I believe that these imbalances imperil the experiment of life on our planet the most at this time.

Chapter 1 Notes

The best description of the universal powers at our disposal, and the way they manifest in individual psychology, are Brian Swimme's lectures on the subject. If you would like to learn more about this view of the cosmos, I recommend *The Powers of the Universe,* a two-disc DVD presentation of Brian Swimme's lectures at the California Institute of Integral Studies, San Francisco, CA.

For more on the sociability of the Universe and a sense of how much evolution relied upon "group selection" as well as "selection of the fittest," look to Howard Bloom's work, *Global Brain: The Evolution of Mass Mind from the Big Bang to the 21st Century.*

For more information regarding Zero Space Energy or Free Space Energy see the following web sites: www.steorn.net, www.alas.us, or www.magneticpower.com.

Chapter 2 Notes

I am indebted to Fritjof Capra and Elizabet Sahtouris for their descriptions of evolution through living systems. Each made the miracle of life more accessible. Elizabet also supplied me with the incredible description of how every human makes the journey, in utero, through the last billion years of evolution.

Professors Humberto Maturana and Francisco Varela did the seminal work that led to a greater appreciation of how every organism is "coupled" to its environment, including the other organisms within it. Their work revealed a variety of keys that systems scientists have used to unlock many of the mysteries of consciousness. I recommend their book, *The Tree of Knowledge: The Biological Roots of Human Understanding,* to all who seek a greater understanding of how Evolution naturally endows all living organisms with consciousness. I drew upon Dr. Deepak Chopra's succinct description of the lives of cells in the human body. He has made the dance of cooperation in the cellular community of the body look like the symphony it is.

I also drew on the work of Drs. Robert Augrus and George Stanciu to describe the collaborative and cooperative process that has been happening throughout the process of biological evolution. Their work alerted me to the story that was freshly emerging through what has become known as "new science."

Speaking of emergence, Steven Johnson's book of the same name reveals how ubiquitous this process is. Without his descriptions of the commonality of emergence, I might not have understood the gifts that await us if we can learn how to synergize our social efforts.

I also owe a debt to biologist Ma-Wan Ho who, along with Elizabet Sahtouris, made me realize the actual significance of the shift that is taking place in the life sciences—that is, the shift from the mechanism to the organism.

Dr. Robert Kegan, in his book *In Over Our Heads*, first introduced me to the idea of natural therapy. I've taken his original idea and expanded upon it in ways I hope he would approve of and agree with. He is one of the preeminent developmental psychologists practicing and teaching today and I will return to his work in my discussions of development (Chapter 6) and Natural Therapy (Chapter 8).

Daniel Goleman's book, *Social Intelligence*, validated much of what you will find herein. His work looks to neurobiology and the structures of the brain for their relationship with our social nature. His description of the research and of neurobiology is too detailed to include here, but for a better understanding of how coupled the human brain is to its social environment, I recommend his book.

Chapter 3 Notes
Complex systems scientist Peter Corning, Ph.D., has done more to awaken the scientific community to the role of synergy in evolution than anyone. I have drawn heavily upon his work. Thanks to his efforts, synergy might take its rightful place alongside competition as one of the primary characteristics of the evolutionary process.

I am also thankful that Abraham Maslow recognized and preserved Ruth Benedict's lectures on high and low synergy cultures. His notes on her lectures made it possible to view the beginning of a realization that social structures and beliefs can play a role in how the individual and the culture evolve.

Chapter 4 Notes
The story of the holon only became available because Arthur Koestler had the insight and the scientific acumen to recognize that if humanity were to progress, it would have to go beyond the polarization in thought it was stuck in. Koestler had the guts and the scientific prestige to press for a unification of the parts (the province of mainstream reductionists) with the whole (the emerging and yet

peripheral focus of the system sciences). He took both fields into unknown terrain. The consequences of that move are still coming to be felt in the social sciences. I recommend his later works, *Beyond Reductionism* and *Janus*, to all those who are interested in how the "pattern that connects" affects all social and environmental realms. I am indebted to his work for my own.

As stated in the text, no one has done more to bring about a truly integral vision of reality than Ken Wilber. He has worked diligently his whole career to create an integral approach to human cultural, scientific, spiritual and psychological evolution. In doing so, he made the effort to understand how the metaphor of the holon brought an awareness of how interrelated all things are. His tenets of holonic reality (which are listed below) brought greater illumination to Koestler's original work on the subject. Wilber, through his own attempts to make holonic reality more fully accessible, has ushered in the first real understanding of how Nature works to deliver its creations in as much diversity and unity as possible.

I have drawn on the following tenets regularly in my own efforts to make sense of the psychological reality of connection that permeates this work. The engaged reader will find these tenets described more fully in Wilber's book *Sex, Ecology and Spirit*.

1. Reality as a whole is not composed of things or processes, but of holons.
2. Holons display four fundamental capacities:
   c. self-preservation
   d. self-adaptation
   e. self-transcendence
   f. self-dissolution.
3. Holons emerge.
4. Holons emerge holarchically.
5. Each emergent holon transcends and includes its predecessor(s).
6. The lower sets the possibilities of the higher: the higher sets the probabilities of the lower.
7. The number of levels which a holarchy comprises determines its "depth," and the number of holons on any given level determine its "span."
8. Each successive level of evolution produces greater depth and less span.

Addition 1 – The greater the depth of a holon, the greater its degree of consciousness.

9. Destroy any type of holon, and you will destroy all the holons above it and none of the holons below it.

10. Holarchies co-evolve.

11. The micro is in relational exchange with the macro at all levels of its depth.

12. Evolution has directionality:
    a. increasing complexity,
    b. increasing differentiation/integration,
    c. increasing organization/structuration,
    d. increasing relative autonomy, increasing telos.

Addition 2 – Every holon issues an IOU to the Universe. IOU= Incomplete or uncertain agency or communion.

Addition 3 – All IOU's are redeemed in Emptiness.

(Emptiness is the reality of which all wholes and parts are simply manifestations.)

Wilber has spent a lot of his writing career making the integral vision of his four quadrants model available. You will find elements of his model in the other books listed in this bibliography. It is worth the reader's time to grasp how this approach unites inner with outer, and the I, We, and It. This understanding is essential if we are going to grasp reality completely.

Chapter 5 Notes

This chapter is all about maps. It is about the discovery of a New World, the explorers who have increased our knowledge of that terrain, and the maps they have made to show the way. It offers another way to see the "pattern that connects."

Someone had to go first. Who knows who may have already visited this world? There is evidence that several indigenous peoples knew of and occupied this landscape. The words "participation mystique," which were used by modern-day anthropologists to describe native sensibilities, may have described more about the limitations of the anthropologist's culture of origin than they described a people's reality. This is not a chapter about the history of an alternative way of seeing the world that may have pre-dated modern inquiry. I have made the assertion that this World has always existed, so I wouldn't be surprised to learn it was known a long time ago.

No, this is the story about how that world began to (re)emerge into view. Special attention is given to Murray Bowen here. Without his curiosity, commitment to his patients, and willingness to be taken on an odyssey, we might still not know where we really live. Dr. Bowen had to weather the most critical kind of scrutiny to bring us a totally new way of seeing, as well as a New World. This is an accomplishment that even today isn't widely understood. (Thus, one of the necessities of this book.) It has to be noted that it was Dr. Bowen's lead, ably assisted by Dr. Michael Kerr, which made it possible for others to explore this invisible landscape. To him goes the honor because he had to endure the rigors associated with bearing a new way of seeing amongst a blind populace. To say he had to deal with a skeptical world is too simple. No doubt it took all of the development Dr. Bowen could muster to maintain his sanity and patience. With all of that, he still managed to deliver a New World to human awareness—and a way to get there. The pattern that connects is more visible today because of his efforts.

This is also a story that addresses the strange failure of modern psychology. This failure becomes more obvious as the attributes of the New World begin to emerge. No psychology of the individual can account for the emergent properties of relationship. But that hasn't stopped it from trying. These efforts, well-meaning as they have been, have exacerbated suffering and inadvertently abetted climate change. That's all right. I'm not ignoring the pain and confusion. This is one way Evolution works; a crisis generates creativity; limitations become the place of possibilities.

It has been the awareness of limitations that necessitated the work of Dr. David Schnarch and Rabbi Edwin Friedman. Dr. Schnarch holds a special place in my heart. Besides having the courage and commitment to integrate marital and sex therapy, overcoming the limitations of a moribund field, he had the patience to oversee the development of an unseeing and arrogant young man—myself. He is a brilliant theoretician, a good teacher, and a truly compassionate practitioner. I would not have really grasped any of the significance of this newly emerging world without all of the contributions that David Schnarch has made. He especially has made the complexity of being human, and of human relations, accessible. Without his heart, his integrity, I would not have returned over and over to Crucible work; and it was my time in the fire that allowed me to see what I do.

Rabbi Friedman recognized early on the fact that Nature had endowed all of us with the capacity to live peerless lives if we could live as Nature intended. I was aware as I was re-reading his posthumously published work how much of my thinking had been shaped by his inscrutable vision. It was his clarity and wise insistence that evoked my vision, rendering new dimensions of the landscape visible, and helping me orient more usefully to what I was seeing. I am beholden to him for intrepidly going where he did, and for having the stamina and engagement to record something of the meaning of his 40+ years of exploring this exotic terrain.

All of these explorers, and probably others, preceded me and showed the way. The "pattern that connects" is not theirs, nor is it mine, but it is part of the endowment we all share in, because we are human, and because we are the embodiments of Nature. The maps are useful, not because they are completely accurate, but because they introduce us to a realm of connection and personal meaning that relieves suffering and offers new possibility. With them a new picture of the challenges, and resources, of being human arises.

Chapter 6 Notes

The evolutionary course of human development is something that has only recently (in the last 40 years) come into view, thanks to the work of developmental scientists. This chapter is a testimony to their scholarship. I am not a scholar, so I hope this work does justice to the blood, sweat, and tears that they have given to move our understanding forward. I hope here to give credit where it is due.

While a more complete picture is emerging, thanks to the efforts of those who are mentioned herein, it is likely that indigenous people who gave us their knowledge of rites of passage knew of more complex forms of consciousness. The anthropological record is full of accounts of our ancestors having vision quests, walkabouts, desert retreats, fasts and other forms of initiation. This may account for how Nature-based many of those old, so called "primitive" societies, really were.

Typically, a human life was much briefer for our ancestors. We don't know if that meant accelerated development or lower percentages of those who achieved the later stages of development. We do know that we have a much longer life expectancy. So much of what is said about more complex forms of consciousness and later emerging states is now more available to us. This is part of our untapped potential. These forms of development may be the province of mid-life and beyond. It may turn out that senior citizens may be our most essential resource in the future. Whatever our species' history may be, the linkage between human development and evolution seems to have been overlooked. Maybe it was just too obvious. All I know is that I've come to this stage in my life without anyone ever saying my development was any more than a product of my own desire. Development was a personal, private matter. It was also, like a college degree, optional. This, it turns out, is a very costly belief. So much suffering and so much squandered potential lies in this attitude. The cost is widespread, affecting us individually and collectively.

The scholarship and dedication of Dr. Robert Kegan, Dr. Jane Loevinger, and Dr. Clare Graves is awe-inspiring. Each of these individuals found a way to capture the restlessness of Evolution as it moved through the human mind. Without their passion for understanding human potential, the plasticity of consciousness, we would lack the overview necessary to catch a glimpse of the New World and its possibilities.

Dr. Robert Kegan made many contributions. It is perhaps too soon to say what his most valuable contribution might be. He formulated a stage theory of adult development. He recognized that Life played a role in development and coined the phrase "natural therapy." He also saw the lack of cultural supports, and pointed out how stressful modern life can be, when a culture demands more development than it supports, when it insists that we live "in over our heads." He also provides some perspective on the rigors of change, both for individuals and communities. He is wise enough to see that the challenges go both ways; it costs social organizations if they do, or don't, support individual development. Likewise, there is a cost that individuals pay if they rely too heavily upon pulling a geographical instead of changing in place. He makes clear that substantial change places strain upon individual and community alike, and that both benefit if they can withstand the force of change.

Chapter 7 Notes

It was my introduction to differentiation theory that made me aware of the possibility of a psychological approach that was non-pathological and systems-based. I owe a great debt to the work of such differentiation theorists as Murray Bowen, Dr. Michael Kerr, Rabbi Edwin Friedman, and David Schnarch. Without their leadership and scholarship, I would not have come up with a form of response to the pattern that connects that has any integrity.

As I have maintained throughout this text, systems thinking is a product of experience rather than education. By that I mean that through transformations of consciousness living systems become visible, not so much to the eyes, but to the mind. They become real, not just an abstraction. The linkages that always exist become palpable and are no longer theoretical. This hasn't stopped educational programs from trying to teach this valuable awareness, nor authors from describing its features, so I am providing a special bibliography here that refers the motivated reader to an in-depth description of systems thought. This is not a substitute for experience.

A Living Systems Bibliography

Buckley, Walter (editor) (1968), *Modern Systems Research for the Behavioral Scientist.* Aldine Publishing, Chicago

Capra, Fritjof (1996), *The Web of Life: A New Scientific Understanding of Living Systems.* Anchor Books, New York, NY

Ford, Donald H. & Lerner, Richard M. (1992), *Developmental Systems Theory: An Integrative Approach.* Sage Publications, Newberry Park, CA

Gray, William, Duhl, F., and Rizzo, N. (1969), *General Systems Theory and Psychiatry.* Little Brown & Co., Boston, MA

Hanson, Barbara Gail (1995), *General Systems Theory Beginning with Wholes.* Taylor and Francis, Philadelphia, PA

Laszlo, Ervin (1972), *The Sytsems View of the World.* George Braziller, New York, NY

Laszlo, Ervin (1973), *Introduction to a System's Philosophy: Toward a New Paradigm of Contemporary Thought.* Harpers Publishing, New York, NY

Macy, Joanna (1991), *Mutual Causality: The Dharma of Living Systems.* State University of New York Press, New York, NY.

Maturana, H. & Varela, F. (1998), *The Tree of Knowledge: The Biological Roots of Human Understanding.* Shambhala Publications, Boston, MA

Sahtouris, Elisabet (2000), *EarthDance: Living Systems in Evolution.* Published by iUniverse.com, San Jose, CA

Weinberg, Gerald, (1975), *Introduction to General Systems Thinking.* John Wiley & Sons, New York, NY.

What really distinguishes a Psychology of Interdependence from other mainstream psychologies is the integration of a developmental/evolutionary framework. I think this will be a hallmark of all truly integral approaches in the future. This integration owes a debt to the developmental theorists credited in Chapter 6, plus the integral vision of Ken Wilber. The contributions of all these people made possible a new formulation that took in the action of evolution's agent, Life.

When considering the transpersonal nature of this work a special debt is owed to the work of Arnold Mindell. We live in a culture that refuses to acknowledge the existence of a collective, co-constructed psychological realm. Dr. Mindell has steadfastly maintained that such a realm existed and has been a pioneer in studying the impact and content of the collective unconscious. I am glad to draw attention to his valuable contributions here.

Chapter 8 Notes

The inspiration for this chapter is the work of Dr. Robert Kegan. He has a chapter with the same name in his first book. He was, in my experience, the first to recognize the role that Life played in our lives. This chapter focuses upon the interventions of Life—the way, as Dr. Kegan pointed out, we are stymied in our best laid plans by a force that is completely natural. He focused upon the painfulness of our tendency to resist the actions of Life, while I, like differentiation theorists such as Rabbi Friedman, have focused more upon our overall response. I know I might not have picked up on the initiating role of Life if I had not become familiar with Dr. Kegan's realization.

I am also indebted to Dr. James Gordon, who has made relieving the suffering associated with depression his life's work. Thanks to his extensive research upon how depression is viewed medically, I have found a shorthand way to express my own less scientific perception that something much more mysterious and germane to Life is going on when depression strikes. His "journey" metaphor is consistent with the idea of initiation. He doesn't focus upon the utility of such a journey to the larger processes of evolution, but his chapter on spirituality shows that he grasps the larger benefits of such a journey. I am thankful that a medical doctor takes as seriously his Hippocratic Oath as he does.

Robert Kegan should also be credited with having conducted the first research that shows that depression can be developmental. Others such as Carl Jung had surmised as much; Jungian analysts such as Walter Odajnyk wrote about this as early as 1983. More research on depression as an indicator of developmental stresses needs to be done. There are significant metamorphoses that occur in the newly elongated human life; entering, being in, and exiting these transitions could well all have different flavors of depression and anxiety, which could benefit from different forms of treatment. Research such as this awaits a field that embraces and supports adult development.

The focus upon organismic response comes straight from differentiation theory. By emphasizing immune response in his posthumous book on leadership, Rabbi Friedman contributed to the realization that there was a link between the challenges of Life and the Evolution of our species. The immune response has been almost entirely ignored by traditional psychologies at the expense of individuals and social organisms alike.

Robert Kegan was also the first to point out the need for cultural supports for newer, more complex, forms of consciousness. He recognized that culture had a role to play in insuring that its members are provided what they need to participate in the emerging world. He also quickly recognized that this culture lacked a "curriculum" which would help people achieve these forms of awareness.

It was Philip Cushman who helped me realize that supports that exploited developmental vulnerabilities did exist, and that they had been consciously developed. His history of American psychotherapy (which should be required reading for all psychotherapists) includes the "therapy" that has been developed by American psychoanalysts and industry, an exploitive therapy designed to maintain a level of development that is economically useful.

Chapter 9 Notes

Tracing the advent of my interest in Mystery is not easy. I have identified three primary strains or threads for this interest. While each is important, having shaped my interest, I don't believe any of them accounts for the centrality of this phenomenon to my life.

I have been influenced by M. Scott Peck's perception of emptiness. He went so far as to name one of the most important stages of his community-building model, Emptiness. He was referring to the crucial stage that preceded the emergence of community, and that differed enormously from the corresponding stage in usual group development. A typical group would define the norms of the group members then organize its activities around these norms. Peck defined this typical pattern as forming, storming, norming and performing. In his community-building model the four stages were called; Pseudo- community, Chaos, Emptiness, and Community.

Peck realized that for a group to create a sense of community amongst themselves, they must go beyond themselves. "Emptying" is done by people who rid themselves of their preconceptions, prejudices, and anything else that they use to maintain separateness and ideological identity, and finally to reduce obstacles and evoke the shared spirit of community. Emptiness, for him, is a crucial practice that gives way to a shared state of recognition. I soon realized there existed a parallel between Peck's death-like practice of emptying and any adaptive system's attempts to reorganize itself near chaos. A time of structurelessness, or identitylessness, is necessary for reforming into a more desirable state.

This state of structurelessness is reinforced by two other similar but different sources of exposure. In her investigation of the practices of the world's spiritual traditions, Angeles Arrien, a cultural anthropologist who is interested in being a cross-cultural bridge, found similarities she calls "The Four-fold Way." The fourth of these worldwide spiritual practices is "surrendering attachment to outcome." Coincidentally, I found that Dr. David Schnarch has described one of the facets of a differentiation move as "letting go of a preferred, or expected, outcome." Both sources alerted me further to the attitude of openness that seems to be a prerequisite to meeting reality as it is, instead of as it is wanted to be.

So, the formal foundation of my interest in staying close to Mystery is my intuition that all three sources are talking about the same phenomenon. This all became much more real and less abstract when I went through my metamorphosis experiences. Then I knew that at the heart of these kind of transformational experiences is a period, which rites-of-passage people call liminal, but which I experience as paradoxically empty and full. This then has been the Mystery, a power of the Universe, which has been so captivating for me.

Chapter 10 Notes
This chapter synopsizes my doctoral research. I am particularly indebted to The Foundation for Community Encouragement (FCE). This organization, founded by psychiatrist M. Scott Peck, allowed me to question all of the folks in California who had attended one or more of their Community Building Workshops (CBW). At that time, Dent Davis, President of the foundation, took the extraordinarily risky step of letting someone outside the organization study a very complex experience that could be very controversial. I thought then, and I think now, that the choice to let me research the workshop and its aftermath was motivated by integrity. FCE wanted to know what served so well, and they wanted it to be in the world.

I am also particularly indebted to the work of cultural anthropologist Victor Turner. By providing first-hand observations of indigenous ritual processes Turner provided me with a way to begin making sense of what I had experienced in the CBW. He also provided me with the means to inquire into the experience of the participants in the workshop. Victor is now dead, but it is my hope that his observations, and particularly his three- dimensional model of community, will survive long into the future.

His assertion that community thrives best when it is periodically renewed through doses of communitas, through social rituals, is timeless.

Though I did not mention her specifically in this chapter, I also want to acknowledge Joanna Macy. In addition to being one of the leading scholars on systems theory, responsible for the first integration of systems thought and Buddhism, Joanna is a very powerful social and environmental activist. She has created her own workshops over the years that have used ritual, some would say experiential processes, to make palpable the links between the ecosystem, the interior life of the individual, and the effects of culture. Joanna let me use one of her workshops to act as my control group, to compare with the CBW. Her workshop also created a sense of community amongst her participants and showed me there were multiple ways of creating this bond.

Community is a very complex phenomenon. It turns out that people at different stages in adult development enjoy, or find difficult, different forms of community. Also, different experiences of community, can be had by emphasizing one side of our holonic nature. People may prefer a flavor of community that is no longer good for them. All of these complexities only came to my awareness because I was able to do the study that this chapter describes.

Chapter 11 Notes

A true picture of what is going on takes many perspectives. I was lucky enough to have found a community of hearty and brave souls who were willing to look upon the world as they looked within themselves. The connections, as painful and illuminating as they were, became visible. It was a very compassionate act, sharing so much complicity, truth, and longing for justice. I will always know what this community shared with me.

Chapter 12 Notes

Most of the influences that brought about this awareness and this form of response to that awareness are too numerous to mention. But I think it is important to acknowledge the contributions of Angeles Arrien, David Schnarch, Carl Jung, and Cynthia McReynolds.

Angeles Arrien is a cultural anthropologist. She grew up in two cultures and developed a desire to bridge the gaps that she experienced. The Four-Fold Way came about because Angeles had the wisdom to look at the world's spiritual traditions and try to synthesize their commonalities. What she found has been a gift that gives in many contexts. Groups often spend a lot of time looking for agreed-upon norms of behavior that can satisfy the sensitivities present in a group. Arrien's Four-Fold Way provides a short, succinct and powerful set of norms that have a transformative potential if practiced over the long run.

The synergetic emergence of something new like a transforming awareness requires the presence of two or more distinct beings.
David Schnarch provides the most cogent expression of this truth
in his work. He has focused primarily upon dyads. But his in-depth
understanding of the systemic dynamics that make a long-term
relationship such a powerful growth agent shed a great deal of light
upon the other system-levels. By correctly emphasizing the rigors of
growing a self-in-relationship, he has shown the role the differentiated self plays in vitalizing social interactions. His work provides
an essential component of what it takes to release the transformative
power of the social koan.

It took the words (found on the last page of his autobiography)
of one of the world's most important consciousness pioneers, Carl
Jung, to bring home the nature of the transformation of consciousness that emerges with choosing to be more uncertain. Without the
guidance of intrepid pioneers such as Dr. Jung, no one would take
such a paradoxical and counter-intuitive path. I certainly wouldn't
have. Indeterminacy isn't easy, nor is it socially rewarded; but it does
serve to introduce one to a world of connection.

No one truly travels alone. For a portion of the journey that
brought me to this place, I was accompanied. Cynthia McReynolds
was a partner who co-discovered stages of this journey. She introduced me to some facets of this work and, as a partner, frustrated me
enough that I had to grow myself into other aspects of it. Through
the rough and tumble of a long-term relationship, I learned to value
most the hard-won awareness that comes when one has reached
his limits. Cynthia did a lot to make this learning possible. She also
co-authored this chapter with me.

Chapter 13 Notes

I had already begun to feel there was a relationship between all
of the different group practices that I had identified. I didn't really
know how to describe how they were related until I encountered
Peter Senge's book, *The Fifth Discipline*. I very quickly realized that
each of the practices could be subsumed in a greater discipline, and
that the idea of a "discipline" helped to describe the multidimensional nature of these practices. Each practice promoted an unfolding awareness. With practice one began to see and experience new

things. The kind of awareness that unfolded was best described as a discipline, a set of practices that if practiced diligently led to a deepening realization. Senge provided me with the organizing principle. I did the rest.

Chapter 14 Notes

I am very much indebted to the work, one could say the passion, of Dr. David Schnarch. It was he who introduced me to the crucible. This introduction wasn't just theoretical. Although it was immersed in the context of a coherent theory, it became an experience that has had lasting effects. I have taken Dr. Schnarch's description of the crucible, a vessel that contains a transformative process, as a description of a highly functioning learning community. The crucible is also an alchemical vessel used by alchemists to transmute coarse materials into the finer, purer metals that they were pursuing. It is an appropriate metaphor for the quality of consciousness, development, and attention that is necessary to create a socially transformative event.

Dr. Schnarch also has had an important role as a pioneer in seeing the world of connection. He is a systems thinker par excellence. And as such he is responsible for helping me understand the "pattern that connects" and thereby seeing how living systems extend from inside us to the communities—human and more-than-human—within which we are embedded. The perspective contained in The Social Crucible is a by-product of a long-period of absorbing the work of Dr. Schnarch.

In addition to the many people listed in the above Chapter Notes, I am personally indebted to many for helping me cope with the devastating changes that confronted and transformed me. This wasn't a pretty or predictable process. I was aided over and over again by the men in my Men's Lodge. In so many ways, literally and figuratively, I was helped to move. Thanks to these men, no one can ever say in my presence that men lack the ability to nurture and sustain difficult relations. I know better. You helped me, held me, and believed in me. This book is a testament to the male heart.

There are others who supported this work and its author in a variety of ways. Perhaps the most important of these is my ex-wife Cynthia McReynolds. In the early years we struggled together to make sense of interdependence in our relationship, teaching, and community facilitation. She made many contributions to my thinking by inspiring, leading, and frustrating me. It was the crucible of our relationship that made this work experiential, vital, and essential. The world works in mysterious ways, and we have the scars and wisdom that failure brings to prove it.

There are those who are diligently working to bring our collective wisdom to light. This is an initiative we, as a species, sorely need in this time. I am ever so grateful to be associated with all those who are endeavoring to make palpable and available the deeper levels of our social potential. Thank you especially to Sherrel Erickson, the Omega Institute, and the many involved in the Collective Wisdom Initiative.

Alexandra Hart helped me come back to life. She befriended me and believed in me enough that I began to believe in myself again. No work that values relationship can happen without relations. I was blessed by her and came back from the underworld. In many ways her love made this work available. I lived because she saw beyond my disabilities.

I have been grown as a man, psychotherapist, human being, and author by the teachers who masqueraded as my students, clients, and the communities that worked with me. With them I was taken to the place where heartbreak meets open-heartedness and was taught how they are all one thing. This is a teaching that has been personal, persuasive, and precious. Without them giving voice to the world, I wouldn't have had the desire required to persevere. I hope what you taught me serves us all. Life has played the major role in what you find here. It called us (me) into being. And it placed the spark of itself in the center of my being. We aren't here just for our own sakes (I know I'm not). This book has tried to make this clear. We have been prepared. Now let us participate in the dance!

HELP

This book is my message in a bottle. You, Dear Reader, are the ocean. A New World is arriving. You can help.

Go the extra mile. Give life to what ensures Life. Send this word along to everyone you can think of who might find these ideas helpful, stimulating, change-inducing, and freeing, then be the change you want to see in our world. And feel the Universe supporting you.

This is a bottom-up approach to community. Community lives on the fringe. It isn't a mainstream activity. It can't be built with a slick promotional plan. It needs word from your mouth. It needs us to remain true to the connective tissue that holds us all together.

There is hope and renewed meaning in the connected life. If you feel similarly, then help this message touch the lives it needs to touch. This is a chance to make a difference. Not that a book can change anything, but if you feel moved to act, change can occur.

BIBLIOGRAPHY

Arrien, Angeles, Ph.D., *The Four-Fold Way: Walking the Paths of the Warrior, Teacher, Healer and Visionary.* New York, NY, Harper Collins, 1993.

Augrus, Robert, Ph. D. and George Stanciu, Ph. D., *The New Biology: Discovering the Wisdom of Nature.* Boston, MA: Shambhala Publications, 1987.

Bakan, David, Ph. D., *The Duality of Human Existence.* Chicago, IL: Rand McNally & Company, 1966

Barrow, John, D., Ph. D. and Frank Tipler, Ph. D. *The Anthropic Cosmological Principle.* Oxford, UK: Oxford University Press, 1986.

Beck, Don & Cowan, Christopher, *Spiral Dynamics: Mastering Values, Leadership, and Change.* Malden, MA, Blackwell Publishing, 1996.

Bellah, R., Madsen, R., Sullivan, W., Swidler, A., Tipler, S., *Habits of the Heart: Individualism and Commitment in American Life.* New York, NY: Harper & Row, 1985

Berry, Wendell, *Life Is a Miracle: An Essay Against Modern Superstition.* Washington D C: Counterpoint Press, 2000

Bloom, Howard, Ph.D., *Global Brain: The Evolution of Mass Mind from The Big Bang to the 21st Century.* New York, NY: John Wiley & Sons, 2000.

Bohm, David, Ph.D., *On Dialogue,* self-published by David Bohm Seminars, Inc. 1990.

Briskin, A., Erickson, S., Lederman, J., Ott, J., Potter, D., & Strutt, C., *Centered on the Edge: Mapping a Field of Collective Intelligence and Spiritual Wisdom.* Kalamazoo, MI: The John E. Fetzer Institute, 2001

Buckley, Walter (editor), *Modern Systems Research for the Behavioral Scientist.* Chicago: Aldine Publishing, 1968

Bynner, Witter, *The Way of Life: According To Lao-Tzu*. New York, NY: Capricorn Books, 1962.

Capra, Fritjof, Ph.D., *The Web of Life: A New Scientific Understanding of Living Systems*. New York, NY: Anchor Books, 1996.

Capra, Fritjof, Ph.D., *The Hidden Connection: Integrating the Biological, Cognitive, and Social Dimensions of Life Into a Science of Sustainability*. New York, NY: Doubleday, 2002.

Chopra, Deepak. M. D., *The Book of Secrets: Unlocking the Hidden Dimensions of Your Life*. New York, NY: Random House, 2004.

Colman, Arthur. D., M.D., *Up From Scapegoating, Awakening Consciousness in Groups*, Wilmette, IL: Chiron Publications, 1995.

Cook, Theodore Andrea, Ph.D., *The Curves of Life*. New York, NY: Dover Publications,1979.

Cook-Greuter, S., *Postautonomous Ego Deveopment: A Study of its Nature and Measurement*. Boston, MA: Harvard University, Unpublished doctoral dissertation, 1999.

Cook-Greuter, Susanne, Ph.D. & Miller, Melvin, Ph.D. *Transcendence and Mature Thought in Adulthood: The Furthest Reaches of Adult Development*. Lanham, MD: Rowan & Littlefield Publishing,1994.

Corning, Peter, Ph.D., *Nature's Magic: Synergy in Evolution and the Fate of Humankind*. New York, NY: Cambridge University Press, 2003.

Csikszentmihalyi, Mihaly, *The Evolving Self: A Psychology for the Third Millennium*. New York, NY: Harper-Collins, 1993.

Cushman, Philip, Ph.D., *Constructing the Self, Constructing America: A Cultural History of Psychotherapy*. New York, NY: Addison-Wesley Publishing Company, 1995.

Dass Ram, *Still Here: Embracing Aging, Changing and Dying* New York, NY: Riverhead Books, 2000.

deMare, Patrick B., M.R.C. Psych., Koinonia: *From Hate, Through Dialogue, to Culture in the Large Group.* London, UK: Karnac Books, 1991.

Flier, Len, "Demystifying Mysticism: Finding a Developmental Relationship between Different Ways of Knowing." *Journal of Transpersonal Psychology,* Vol 27, No. 2. 1995.

Friedman, Edwin, D.D., *A Failure of Nerve: Leadership in the Age of the Quick Fix.* An Edited Manuscript, published by the Edwin Friedman Foundation, 1999.

Friedman, Maurice, *The Confirmation of Otherness: In Family, Community and Society.* New York, NY: Pilgrim Press, 1983.

Ford, Donald H. & Lerner, Richard M., *Developmental Systems Theory: An Integrative Approach.* Newberry Park, CA: Sage Publications 1992.

Gerard, Glenna & Ellinor, Linda, *Dialogue: Rediscover The Transforming Power of Conversation.* New York, NY: John Wiley & Sons, 1998.

Goff, David, *Communitas: An Exploratory Study of the Existential and Transpersonal Dimensions of a Psychological Sense of Community as Found in the Community Building Workshop™,* unpublished dissertation. Palo Alto, CA: The Institute for Transpersonal Psychology, 1992.

Goleman, Daniel, Ph.D., *Social Intelligence: The New Science of Human Relationships.* New York, NY: Bantam Dell, 2006.

Gorden, James, M.D. *Unstuck: Your Guide to the Seven-Stage Journey Out of Depression.* New York, NY: Penguin Press, 2008.

Graves, Clare W., Ph.D., *The Never Ending Quest,* edited by Christopher Cowan and Natasha Todorovic. Santa Babara, CA: Eclet Publishing, 2005.

Gray, William, Duhl, F., and Rizzo, N., *General Systems Theory and Psychiatry.* Boston, MA: Little Brown & Co., 1969.

Hanson, Barbara Gail, *General Systems Theory Beginning With Wholes*. Philadelphia, PA: Taylor and Francis, 1995.

Hillman, James & Ventura, Michael, *We've Had a Hundred Years of Psychotherapy; And the World Is Getting Worse*. San Francisco, CA: Harper Collins, 1992.

Ho, Mae-Wan, Ph.D., *The Rainbow and the Worm: The Physics of Organisms*. Singapore: World Scientific, 1998.

Johnson, Steven, *Emergence: The Connected Lives of Ants, Brains, Cities, and Software*. New York, NY: Scribner, 2001.

Jung, Carl, M.D., *Memories, Dreams and Reflections*. New York, NY: Pantheon Books, 1963.

Kegan, Robert, Ph. D., *The Evolving Self: Problem and Process In Human Development*. Cambridge, MA: Harvard Press, 1982.

Kegan, Robert, Ph.D., *In Over Our Heads: The Mental Demands of Modern Life*. Cambridge, MA: Harvard University Press, 1994.

Kegan, Robert, Ph. D. & Lahey, Lisa Ph.D., *How the Way We Talk Can Change the Way We Work: Seven Languages of Transformation*. San Francisco, CA: Jossey-Bass, 2001.

Kerr, Michael. M.D. and Bowen, Murray. M.D., *Family Evaluation: An Approach Based on Bowen Theory*. New York, New York: W. W. Norton Co., 1988.

Koestler, Arthur, Ph. D., *Beyond Reductionism: New Perspectives in the Life Sciences*. New York, N Y: The Macmillan Company, 1969.

Koestler, Arthur, Ph. D., *Janus: A Summing Up*. New York, NY: Random House, 1978.

Kramer, Gregory, *Meditating Together, Speaking from Silence: The Practice of Insight Dialogue*. Portland, OR: The Metta Foundation, 1999.

Laing, R. D., M.D., *The Divided Self.* New York, NY: Pantheon Press, 1960.

Laszlo, Ervin, *The Systems View of the World.* New York, NY: George Braziller, 1972.

Laszlo, Ervin, *Introduction to a System's Philosophy: Toward a New Paradigm of Contemporary Thought.* New York, NY: Harpers Publishing, 1973.

Loevinger, Jane, Ph.D., *Technical Foundations for Measuring Ego Development: The Washington University Sentence Completion Test.* Mahwah, NJ: Lawrence Erlbaum & Assoc., 1998.

Macy, Joanna, Ph.D., *Mutual Causality in Buddhism and General Systems Theory: The Dharma of Natural Systems.* Albany, NY: State of New York University Press, 1991.

Macy, Joanna, Ph.D., *World as Lover, World as Self.* Berkeley, CA: Parralax Press, 1991.

Maslow, Abraham H., Ph.D. and John Honigman, Ph.D., "Synergy: Some Notes of Ruth Benedict." *American Anthropologist*, New Series, Vol. 72, No. 2, 1970. pp. 320-333.

Maturana, Humberto, Ph.D. and Francisco Varela, Ph.D., *The Tree of Knowledge: The Biological Roots of Human Understanding.* Boston, MA: Shambhala Publications, 1987.

Mindell, Arnold, Ph.D., *Sitting in the Fire: Large Group Transformation Using Conflict and Diversity.* Portland, OR: Lao-Tze Press, 1995.

Mindell, Arnold, Ph.D., *The Leader as a Martial Artist: Techniques and Strategies for Resolving Conflict and Creating Community.* San Francisco, CA: Harper Collins, 1992.

Murphy, Gardner, Ph.D., *Personality: A Biosocial Approach to Origins and Structure.* NewYork, NY: Harper & Brothers Publishers, 1947

Palmer, Parker, Ph.D., *The Courage to Teach: Exploring the Inner Landscape of a Teacher's Life.* San Francisco, CA: Jossey-Bass Publishing, 1998.

Palmer, Parker, Ph.D., *A Hidden Wholeness: The Journey Toward An Undivided Life.* San Francisco, CA: Jossey-Bass Publishing, 2004.

Peck, M. Scott, M. D., *The Different Drum: Community Making and Peace.* New York, NY., Simon & Schuster Inc., 1987.

Peck, M. Scott, M. D., *A World Waiting to be Born: Civility Rediscovered,* New York, N.Y: Bantam Books, 1993.

Roszak, Theodore, P h.D., *The Voice of the Earth.* New York, NY: Simon & Schuster, 1992.

Sahtouris, Elisabet. *EarthDance: Living Systems in Evolution.* San Jose, CA, iUniverse.com Inc., 2000.

Schnarch, David, Ph.D. *Constructing the Sexual Crucible,* New York, NY: W.W. Norton, 1991

Schnarch, David, Ph.D., *Passionate Marriage.* New York, NY: Henry Holt & Company, 1997.

Senge, Peter, Ph.D., *The Fifth Discipline: The Art and Practice of the Learning Organization.* New York, NY: Doubleday & Currency, 1990.

Swimme, Brian, Ph.D., *The Powers of the Universe,* a two-disc DVD presentation of Brian Swimme's lectures at the California Institute of Integral Studies, San Francisco, CA, 2001.

Tang, Yongming, Ph.D. and Joiner, Charles, Ph.D., *Synergic Inquiry: A Collaborative Action Methodology.* Thousand Oaks, CA: Sage Publications, 2006.

Taylor, Jill Bolte, Ph.D., *My Stroke of Insight: A Brain Scientist's Personal Journey:* New York, NY: Viking Press, 2008

Torbert, William, Rooke, D., Fisher, D., *Personal and Organizational Transformations: Through Action Inquiry*. Boston, MA: Edge/Work Press, 2001.

Ventura, Michael, *Letters at 3 A.M.: Reports on Endarkenment*. Dallas, TX: Spring Publications, 1993.

Weinberg, Gerald, *Introduction to General Systems Thinking*. New York, NY: John Wiley & Sons, 1975.

Wenger, Etienne, Ph. D., *Communities of Practice: Learning, Meaning and Identity*. Cambridge, MA: Cambridge University Press, 1998.

Wenger, Etienne, Ph. D., McDermott, Richard, PhD., Snyder, William, Ph.D., *Cultivating Communities of Practice*. Boston, MA: Harvard Business School Press, 2002.

Whitmeyer, Claude, ed., *In the Company of Others: Making Community in the Modern World, an anthology*. Los Angeles, CA: Jeremy Tarcher, 1993.

Wilber, Ken, *Sex, Ecology, Spirituality: The Spirit of Evolution. Volume 6 of The Collected Works of Ken Wilber*. Boston, MA: Shambhala Publications, 2000.

Wilber, Ken, *A Brief History of Everything*. Boston, MA: Shambhala Publications, 1996.

Wilber, Ken, *A Theory of Everything: An Integral Vision for Business, Politics, Science, and Spirituality*. Boston, MA: Shambhala Publications, 2000.

Wolff-Salin, Mary, *The Shadow Side of Community and the Growth of the Self*. New York, NY: CrossRoad Books, 1988.

Wright, Robert, *NonZero: The Logic of Human Destiny*. New York, NY: A Vintage Book, 2001.

Zohar, Danah, *The Quantum Self: Human Nature and Consciousness Defined by the New Physics*. New York, NY: William Morrow, 1990.

Zohar, Danah, *The Quantum Society: Mind, Physics and a New Social Vision*. New York, NY: William Morrow & Co., 1994.

About the Author

David "Lucky" Goff, Ph.D., M.F.T., served as adjunct faculty at the Institute of Transpersonal Psychology, where he employed large group processes to promote community and personal development. David also assists organizations, including therapeutic and spiritual communities, in their quests to create and sustain genuine community. His research into the "psychological sense of community" is the first to examine and describe the conditions that facilitate collective consciousness.

In 2003 David had a brain aneurism. As a result of his stroke and the onset of a rare brain syndrome, he nearly died and ended up permanently disabled. This experience had a transformational effect on David, which made him "Lucky" and cued him into how radically connected all things are. This broader awareness now informs his approach toward what it means to be human. He maintains a psychotherapy practice specializing in psycho-spiritual development. He also writes extensively about a psychology of interdependence, community, elders, and the conditions that lead to a social and ecological sense of connection. He can be reached at <dg1140@sonic.net>.

* 9 7 8 1 9 3 6 0 3 3 3 1 7 *